JUDICIAL REVIEW
OF LEGISLATION

IUS GENTIUM
COMPARATIVE PERSPECTIVES ON LAW AND JUSTICE

VOLUME 5

JUDICIAL REVIEW OF LEGISLATION

A COMPARATIVE STUDY OF THE UNITED KINGDOM, THE NETHERLANDS AND SOUTH AFRICA

By

GERHARD VAN DER SCHYFF

 Springer

Dr. Gerhard van der Schyff
School of Law
Tilburg University
PO Box 90153
5000 LE Tilburg
The Netherlands
G.vdrSchyff@uvt.nl

ISBN 978-90-481-9001-0   e-ISBN 978-90-481-9002-7
DOI 10.1007/978-90-481-9002-7
Springer Dordrecht Heidelberg London New York

Library of Congress Control Number: 2010927880

Printed on acid-free paper

Springer is part of Springer Science+Business Media (www.springer.com)

Foreword

Since Pericles and Ephialtes in 462 BC carried through the Athenian Assembly an act formally depriving the Areopagus – the ancient court of the Archons – of much of their jurisdiction and political influence, the relationship between the judiciary and the legislature has been near the heart of constitutional government in democracies. What are the proper limits on judicial power and how far may the judiciary call the legislature to account? This book with its study of the judicial review of legislation in three jurisdictions shines a light into that heart.

The three jurisdictions studied are well chosen. On the one hand, there is the United Kingdom with its sovereign Parliament that admits no challenge to its authority. So, in principle, in the UK there can be no judicial review of legislation (apart from subordinate legislation made under delegated powers). But there is also the Human Rights Act 1998 which does not allow the courts to quash legislation but does allow the court to scrutinise legislation for compliance with fundamental rights and to declare any incompatibility found leaving it to the elected authorities to remedy the position. There is also the possibility in the UK that the courts will take the bold step and assert a power to review legislation in appropriate circumstances. But this possibility, while supported by some scholars and the occasional *obiter dictum,* finds no echo from the elected representatives of the people. The attempted exercise of such a power would be very controversial and the political consequences impossible to predict.

On the other hand, lies South Africa. Following that country's political transformation it now has one of the most sophisticated and progressive constitutions in the world. Unsurprisingly it provides for wide ranging judicial scrutiny of legislation and the ability to test that legislation both against the Bill of Rights and against wider considerations. This is a marvellous constitutional achievement that compels admiration. But there remain tensions between the judiciary and the other branches of government in South Africa and the future resolutions of these must be awaited with interest.

And then finally there is the Kingdom of the Netherlands. In one sense the Netherlands lies close to the UK with its constitutional provision that provides that the constitutionality of acts of parliament shall not be reviewed by the courts. But in another sense the pre-eminence accorded to international law where international norms are hierarchically superior to national norms (including constitutional provisions) marks how different the Netherlands is to both the UK and South Africa. But this pre-eminence granted to international law creates the opportunity for judicial review of legislation being grounded in international norms, even if not in national norms. When the Supreme Court of the Netherlands was pressed to change this anomaly and assert a power to review national legislation on the ground that it infringed legal certainty it was understandably cautious. But the debate continues over this anomalous position where the predominance of international norms within the national constitutional order sits awkwardly with the constitutional restriction on judicial review. But it seems clear that reform will not come through judicial assertion of greater powers.

Into this rich tapestry of different constitutional approaches the judicial review of statutes the author brings his insights. And here lies the particular value of the book. As he remarks "parliamentary democracy cannot be treated as a synonym for constitutional governance". The elected representative does not have the final word in the age of fundamental rights. But howsoever this new "bi polar" constitutionalism develops it must do so in a way that is sensible to the constitutional traditions and forms. The insights in these three constitutional orders enriches the reader's understand of his or her own legal system. . .which is after all the best justification for comparative studies.

University of Cambridge, UK   Professor Christopher Forsyth
25 February 2010

Acknowledgement

I express my sincere gratitude to the Netherlands Organisation for Scientific Research for awarding me a VENI bursary which allowed me to write this book. An equally warm word of thanks must be extended to the Tilburg Law School, and in particular the Department of Constitutional and Administrative Law, whose appointment gave me the freedom to pursue this research. In this regard I would like to thank Professors Philip Eijlander (Rector of Tilburg University), Lex Michiels (Chairman of the Department) and Paul Zoontjens (Past-Chairman of the Department). The support of the following colleagues and friends, who are listed alphabetically, was also invaluable, Maurice Adams, Korine Bolt, Monica Claes, Dajo De Prins, Hans Gribnau, Kristin Henrard, Marc and Marie-Paule Huybrechts, Anamarija Kristic, Gert-Jan Leenknegt, Stefan Sottiaux, Hanneke van Schooten, Hans Peters, Rassie Malherbe, Karin Merkx, Jan Neels, Willem Witteveen, Ben Vermeulen, Frank Vlemminx and Jan Vranken. My Mother is also due a special word of gratitude.

I would like to thank Professor Christopher Forsyth who proposed me as Visitor to the Law Faculty of Cambridge University and who kindly wrote the Preface, as well as Professor David Feldman and Dr Mark Elliott for discussing my research with me during my stay there in 2008. I would also like to thank the British Institute of International and Comparative Law, in London, for welcoming me as Visiting Research Fellow in 2008, in particular Professor Robert McCorquodale (director) and Ms Ruth Eldon. I am also grateful to the Rt. Hon. Lord Bingham of Cornhill KG who generously granted me some of his time to answer my questions on the Human Rights Act.

I am also very happy that I was able to submit this work to Leiden University, in order to gain a second doctorate. In this regard I express my sincere gratitude to my supervisor, Professor Paul Cliteur and the remaining members of the commission, Professors Afshin Ellian and Wim Voermans, Tom Barkhuysen, Dr Hendrik Kaptein (all of Leiden University), Professor Tom Zwart (Utrecht University), Professor Wim Couwenberg (Erasmus University Rotteram) and Professor Maurice Adams (Tilburg University).

Lastly, I want to thank Neil Olivier, my publisher at Springer SBM, for his efficient and professional service and his capable assistant, Diana Nijenhuijzen and Poornima Purushothaman – as well as the peer reviewers for their helpful comments and Professor Mortimer Sellers (Baltimore University) for allowing my work to be published in his series *Ius Gentium: Comparative Perspectives on Law and Justice*. Dick Broeren (language editor at the Tilburg Law School) also deserves special mention for his careful editing of the manuscript. If I have neglected to thank someone, please accept my apology.

Tilburg University   Gerhard van der Schyff
10 May 2010

Contents

Chapter 1
Setting the Scene

1.1 Emerging Bipolar Constitutionalism

1 The problem of controlling the state is the central question in the strive for constitutionalism. This desire for control implies it is a worthwhile enterprise, as control can obviously not be an end in itself without serving a purpose. With constitutionalism, this purpose is usually found in the pursuit of freedom. It is the violation of freedom that convinces us of the need to control the state and teaches us through hard experience how this can be achieved.[1] Freedom though is multifaceted, often asking the state not only to avoid intruding on the personal sphere, but also to actively help people realise freedom in a socio-economic sense. In achieving this aim, society as the vehicle for all human activity may not be collapsed in the state's needs and aspirations, but must be dutifully governed in the cause of freedom.[2] This entails striking a balance between the state and society, as John Stuart Mill so eloquently put it:

> There is a limit to the legitimate interference of collective opinion with individual independence; and to find that limit, and maintain it against encroachment, is as indispensable to a good condition of human affairs as protection against political despotism. But though this proposition is not likely to be contested in general terms, the practical question where to place the limit – how to make the fitting adjustment between individual independence and social control – is a subject on which nearly everything remains to be done.[3]

---

[1] Cf. András Sajó, *Limiting Government: An Introduction to Constitutionalism* (Budapest: Central European University Press, 1999), at 12.

[2] Or as Lord Bingham of Cornhill put it: "For there is no task more central to the purpose of modern democracy, or more central to the judicial function, than that of seeking to protect, within the law, the basic human rights of the citizens, against invasion by other citizens or by the state itself", T.H. Bingham, "The European Convention on Human Rights: Time to Incorporate", 109 *L. Quart. Rev.* 390 (1993).

[3] John Stuart Mill, *On Liberty and the Subjection of Women* (New York: Henry Holt, 1879), at 15–16.

G. van der Schyff, *Judicial Review of Legislation*,
Ius Gentium: Comparative Perspectives on Law and Justice 5,
DOI 10.1007/978-90-481-9002-7_1, © Springer Science+Business Media B.V. 2010

As Mill also recognised, striking this balance has always been difficult, not less so in present times given the complex nature of modern society.

2 In rising to the occasion, the judicial review of legislation has become one of the prime hallmarks of constitutionalism today.[4] The United States of America, with its tradition of review dating back more than two centuries, is no longer the exception to the rule in allowing judiciaries to test legislation in the light of higher norms of law, whether such norms are to be found in constitutions or treaties. Nearly without fail since the Second World War, new democracies such as those emerging from the shadow of Communism choose some form of judicial review, while established democracies like Finland modify or discard their long-held reluctance in putting legislation to a judicial test.[5] After 1945, it was realised that the law could be as much a threat to liberty as its protector. This implied deflating the legislative process and its traditional safeguards in favour of a new appreciation of the judiciary's potential in controlling the law.

This faith in judicial power to control the legislative branch in its treatment of society forms part of the emergence of what may be termed *bipolar constitutionalism* – legislation is no longer simply subject to a legislative pole, but increasingly to a judicial pole as well.[6]

3 Although fast becoming the norm in constitutional democracies, the review of legislation is not without difficulty, as it hides two interrelated questions if not problems. Questions that keep stimulating debate and beg thought to ensure that the aim of controlling state power is continually met.[7] The first relates to whether such review is justified, can it be said that judicial review is desirable to the extent of being part and parcel of "good" constitutionalism? And, secondly, if the *principle* of review is acceptable, how may its *scope* be structured? The design of review and the factors that impact it may not be neglected, because although the principle of review

---

[4]Charting this evolution, C. Neal Tate and Torbjörn Vallinder (eds.), *The Global Expansion of Judicial Power* (New York: New York University Press, 1995).

[5]For overviews, *see* Edward McWhinney, *Supreme Courts and Judicial Law-Making: Constitutional Tribunals and Constitutional Review* (Dordrecht: Martinus Nijhoff Publishers, 1986), at 1–9; Tom Ginsburg, *Judicial Review in New Democracies: Constitutional Courts in Asian Cases* (Cambridge: Cambridge University Press, 2003); Wojciech Sadurski, *Rights Before Courts: A Study of Constitutional Courts in Postcommunist States of Central and Eastern Europe* (Dordrecht: Springer, 2005).

[6]Tim Koopmans, *Courts and Political Institutions: A Comparative View* (Cambridge: Cambridge University Press, 2003), at 247–251. Similarly, Ran Hirschl, *Towards Juristocracy: The Origins and Consequences of the New Constitutionalism* (Cambridge, MA: Harvard University Press, 2004), at 1, speaks of a transformation to "juristocracy".

[7]Proving, among others, the living nature of the debate, Jeremy Waldron, "The Core of the Case Against Judicial Review", 115 *Yale L. J.* 1346 (2006); Annabelle Lever, "Is Judicial Review Undemocratic?" *Pub. L.* 290 (2007); Richard H. Fallon, "The Core of an Uneasy Case for Judicial Review", 121 *Harv. L. Rev.* 1693 (2008).

may be accepted, it only becomes an added value to the constitutionalist project once its extent and character suits the needs and conditions of a particular system. Yet, the questions of judicial review's justification *and* its scope are seldom addressed in the same study, thereby making for an inconvenient divorce of these two related avenues of study. To narrow the divide, the object of this work is quite straightforward. Namely, is the idea of judicial review defensible, and what influences its design and scope?

1.2 Selecting Comparative Material

4 Due to the vast field these questions open up, they cannot be considered without a measure of context. Comparing the situation and experience of different legal systems is a very attractive method to study the justifiability of judicial review and the characterisation of its scope. Lorraine E. Weinrib has even come to observe that comparison is nowadays an integral part of the ideas necessary to understand a particular constitutional system.[8] Apart from the rise of the comparative method, recent years have also witnessed a focus on systems other than that of the United States of America in studying judicial review.[9] Although still important to understanding judicial review, the American experience can no longer be considered the one and only benchmark, as the experience of other systems has come to weigh heavy as well. In the words of Ran Hirschl, a "new constitutionalism" has dawned, whose context differs from when America was founded and which stimulates a "living laboratory of constitutional innovation".[10]

In view of the added value diversity brings to the topic of judicial review, three systems have been selected for this study, namely those of the United Kingdom, the Netherlands and South Africa. These systems provide fertile ground for comparison, as they present a spectrum of approaches to judicial review both in their history and present day situations.

5 The United Kingdom inhabits the one end of the spectrum, as it comes closest to full legislative supremacy over a law's ultimate fate. This is because although allowing courts to review acts of parliament in light of the Human Rights Act of 1998 (HRA), the Act does not allow the bench to nullify a law.[11] In other words, the HRA only allows for weak judicial review. Clearly, a very measured approach to bipolar constitutionalism.

---

[8]Lorraine E. Weinrib, "Constitutional Conceptions and Constitutional Comparativism", in Vicki C. Jackson and Mark Tushnet (eds.), *Defining the Field of Comparative Constitutional Law* 3 (Westport: Praeger, 2002), at 4.

[9]Ginsburg, *supra* note 5, at 15–17; Hirschl, *supra* note 6, at 222–223.

[10]Hirschl, *supra* note 6, at 223.

[11]Human Rights Act 1998 (c. 42).

South Africa inhabits the other end of the spectrum, as its emergent democracy, in contrast to the other two longstanding democracies, relies on
particularly strong judicial review in upholding the Constitution of 1996
in the face of any threatened violation. The Netherlands has been chosen for its interesting brand of judicial review, which places it between
the other two systems. On the one hand, Dutch courts may not apply
acts of parliament that contradict binding international law, on the other
hand they must apply acts of parliament regardless of whether they conflict
with national higher law such as the Constitution. Moreover, 2002 saw the
tabling of the Halsema Proposal, which aims to amend the Constitution by
allowing courts to refuse to apply acts of parliament which are inconsistent with the Constitution.[12] This development signals a possible shift in
Dutch constitutional thought away from a relatively dominant majoritarian
tradition to greater judicial activity in emulating treaty review.

6 What will not be included, apart from a few apt references, is European
Union law. The treaties governing the Union essentially created a new legal
order that deserves its own attention and as a consequence should be studied next to the selected systems of review. This is illustrated by the fact
that the provisions governing monism in the Dutch Constitution are not
interpreted as applying to EU law but only to other treaties such as the
European Convention on Human Rights.[13] Including EU law in the enquiry
might then confuse matters and hamper a clear exposition and study of
judicial review in the legal systems concerned.

7 On the basis of the discussion thus far, the function to be compared
has become clear, as well as the material selected for its study. Namely,
controlling the state's legislative power by means of judicial review in the
United Kingdom, the Netherlands and South Africa. What remains is to be
more exact about the extent to which the function of judicial review will
be investigated.[14] This is because references to "judicial review" are quite
common in literature and can mean a variety of things, thereby highlighting
the need for clarity. In this study, the focus is on national courts reviewing
legislation against higher law in the context of public law relationships. In
what follows, this qualified meaning of judicial review will be refined and
explained.

---

[12]*Parliamentary Proceedings II*, 2001–2002, 28, 331, no. 2; 2002–2003, 28, 331, no. 9.

[13]Cf. M.C. Burkens, H.R.B.M. Kummeling, B.P. Vermeulen and R.J.G.M. Widdershoven,
Beginselen van de democratische rechtsstaat (Alphen aan den Rijn: Kluwer, 6th ed.,
2006), at 342–346, on the European Union as a new legal order and its implications for
national legal orders.

[14]On the meaning of function, *see* K. Zweigert and H. Kötz, *An Introduction to
Comparative Law* (Oxford: Clarendon Press, 3rd ed., 1998), at 34–36.

1.3 Defining the Function of Judicial Review for Current Purposes

8 At its core, the act of judicial review entails measuring the congruency or compatibility of what may be termed common or ordinary legal norms with higher legal norms.[15] Legal norms cannot only be divided *horizontally* between various categories or topics, such as the law of contract or tort, but also *vertically* in various hierarchies such as between constitutional and non-constitutional norms. From a hierarchical point of view, higher norms are determinative for the validity of lower ordinary norms.

In other words, when it comes to judicial review, the focus is not simply on the judiciary *applying* ordinary norms once they have been posited, but also on *testing* their quality. The key question is whether a contested norm was properly constituted in the light of higher requirements – such an enquiry can obviously touch upon a norm's formal coming about or its substance. This entails that facts and norms cannot be treated as synonyms. To form part of a particular hierarchy, norms cannot simply be factual, but must conform to a higher norm dictating what such a lower norm should look like. All other matters ultimately relate to characterising the scope of such review, such as the judicial fora of review, the modalities of review, the content of review and the consequences of review.[16]

But first the focus of judicial review will be sharpened for current purposes. As it is through this lens that judicial review and the elements of its scope will be studied.

1.3.1 National Courts Applying Higher Law

9 There can obviously be no judicial review where courts lack the requisite power.[17] Turning to examples of the European Court of Human

---

[15]For definitions and discussions of the term "judicial review", *see* McWhinney, *supra* note 5, at XI–XVI; Martin Shapiro, "The European Court of Justice", in Paul Craig and Gráinne de Búrca (eds.), *The Evolution of EU Law* 321 (Oxford: Oxford University Press, 1999); Aalt Willem Heringa and Phillip Kiiver, *Constitutions Compared: An Introduction to Comparative Constitutional Law* (Antwerp: Intersentia, 2007), at 95.

[16]On these, *see* Chapters 4 (fora), 5 (modalities), 6 (content), and 7 (consequences), respectively.

[17]The power to conduct review can be expressly created for courts. E.g. s. 5 of the Namibian Constitution (1990) states that the Bill of Rights "shall be enforceable by the Courts". Alternatively, where such unequivocal powers are absent, the judiciary may imply them from the constitutional dispensation, bar evidence to the contrary. E.g. the well-known decision of *Marbury v. Madison*, 1 Cranch 137 (1803), where Marshall C.J. held that courts could strike down laws that were contrary to the demands of the United States Constitution. Similarly, the practice in Belgium of refusing application to laws

Rights and the European Court of Justice, it quickly becomes evident that competent courts do not have to be national courts. Even so, the focus here is on national courts, as they form a common denominator in the three systems to be studied, thereby heightening comparability. International benches, for instance, play a very different role in the legal systems of the United Kingdom and the Netherlands, than they do in South Africa. The domestic focus is also justified, because national courts are also closest to society, something which is important in allowing people to control the state. However, choosing national courts over international courts does not mean to say that international jurisprudence will not be looked at. Such an omission would be a mistake, as international jurisprudence influences the laws of each of the three systems chosen for comparison. One only has to think of the importance in the United Kingdom of the European Court of Human Rights' jurisprudence for making sense of the HRA.

Not only the importance of international jurisprudence in interpreting national norms of higher law, such as the HRA, should be recognised, but also the possibility of international norms themselves being applied by domestic courts. The Netherlands is a case in point, because in discharging their powers of review judges must apply binding international norms in judging whether legislation must be applied or not. A proper study of judicial review would therefore have to take into account that national courts can sometimes apply both national and international norms of higher law.

10   The source of higher norms reveals very little about their purpose though. Norms of higher law govern the legality as well as the legitimacy of lower norms. This means that higher law dictates not only the formal coming about of legal norms, the aspect of legality, but also whether the content of such norms is legitimate when measured against fundamental rights.[18] Both legality and legitimacy will be addressed in this enquiry, yet legality as it relates to the division of powers between various levels of government within a state will not be studied. The reason for this is that it makes little sense to compare the possibilities of federal judicial review in South Africa, to systems with a unitary character such as those of the United Kingdom and the Netherlands. Such a comparison would

---

that do not conform to directly enforceable international law came about by the Court of Cassation's judgment of 27 May 1971, *Pas.*, 1971, I, 886 (*Le Ski*).

[18]A right, as explained by Alan Gewirth, "Are There Any Absolute Rights?", in Jeremy Waldron (ed.), *Theories of Rights* 93 (Oxford: Oxford University Press, 1984) means that A has a claim to X against B by virtue of Y. A right is thus a construct based on a specific justification, which guarantees its bearer a claim with a particular content and extent, against parties expected to respect such a claim. In the case of *fundamental* rights, we speak of those rights that are deemed essential or basic in order to satisfy the purpose of law as an agent with which to ensure personal autonomy and freedom. Cf. Gerhard van der Schyff, *Limitation of Rights: A Study of the European Convention and the South African Bill of Rights* (Nijmegen: Wolf Legal Publishers, 2005), at 5.

only result in needless problems, as the division of power between levels of government in unitary systems is more often solved by administrative law means, than by constitutional adjudication as is the case in federal systems.[19] Adding administrative law matters to the equation would also shift the enquiry to the relation between constitutional and administrative law, and this might blur the focus on the justification and design of the judicial review of legislation.

1.3.2 Reviewing Legislation

11 Although bipolar constitutionalism essentially means judicial review of both the legislative and executive functions of government, this enquiry is fixed on legislation. Both these functions are best considered on their own. If only for the sake of investigating the justification for judicial review, as the electoral legitimacy bestowed on the legislative function is usually advanced as a primary argument in denying the judicial review of legislation.[20] An objection that is of little significance where review is confined to executive action without involving its legislative basis in any meaningful way.[21] Consequently, the judicial review of executive actions, as opposed to legislative norms, will only be considered to the extent that it aids the understanding of the justification and scope of reviewing legislation.

12 Legislation cannot be studied without paying at least some attention to its source. Within the separation of powers, legislation is usually the product of *both* legislative and executive organs. The executive then becomes a legislative agent, in addition to its responsibility of applying legislation. This is the case in the United Kingdom, where the Queen is traditionally considered to be "in" parliament when laws are made, and in the Netherlands section 81 of the Constitution defines the "legislature" as

---

[19]E.g. unlike in federal systems, there are no real constitutional safeguards for provincial powers in the Netherlands. Once parliament legislates in respect of the provinces, it is up to the courts to uphold the will of parliament. An administrative law doctrine, similar to the United Kingdom's *ultra vires*, then applies to ensure that national and provincial or local bodies do not act outside the powers assigned them by the relevant act of parliament. Cf. Burkens et al., *supra* note 13, at 286–291.

[20]Michel Troper, "The Logic of Justification of Judicial Review", 1 *Int. J. Const. L.* 99 (2003), at 109–121.

[21]E.g. in *R. (Q and Others) v. Secretary of State for the Home Department*, EWCA Civ 364, [2003], 3 WLR 365, it was held that although a statute was not incompatible with the HRA, the way in which it had been implemented in relation to the claimants was nonetheless incompatible with the HRA. For studies of judicial review and the executive, see Marc Hertogh and Simon Halliday (eds.), *Judicial Review and Bureaucratic Impact: International and Interdisciplinary Perspectives* (Cambridge: Cambridge University Press, 2004); J.R. de Ville, *Judicial Review of Administrative Action in South Africa* (Durban: LexisNexis Butterworths, 2005).

comprising both government and the two houses of parliament. And even
though the South African Constitution vests legislative power in parliament
apart from the president's required assent, executive dominance in initiating bills quickly lends perspective.[22] In this book therefore references to
the "legislature" or "parliament" are to be read as referring to the complete
legislative function, unless a different meaning appears from the context.

13 In studying the review of legislation, it may not be forgotten that the
United Kingdom and South Africa are both common law jurisdictions.[23]
However, because controlling the modern state is more a matter of the
courts reviewing legislation than developing the common law, this work's
preference for legislation is justified. Yet because similar techniques are
normally used in adjudicating both bodies of law reference to the common
law will be made where appropriate. Legislation and the common law are
also intertwined, which at times necessitates such a broader view.[24] One
only has to think of a legislature that fails to act in protecting fundamental
rights and the courts then developing the common law to fill the resultant
gap.[25] A blind focus on legislation would miss the fact that the courts in
such cases also keep the legislature's decisions in check, as the negative
effect created by legislative inaction is remedied by judicial action.

14 It still remains to explain more closely what is really meant by legislation and what it entails, especially where different jurisdictions are studied
together. In essence, legislation amounts to those rules formally enacted by
a body possessing the necessary powers to do so, as opposed to the common law that refers to rules based on custom that have been recognised
and developed by the courts.[26] On its part, legislation presents a varied picture and is often divided into primary and secondary (also called delegated

---

[22] I.M. Rautenbach and E.F.J. Malherbe, *Constitutional Law* (Durban: Butterworths, 5th
ed., 2009), at 120–121.

[23] For an interesting view on the relation between the common law and judicial review,
see W.J. Waluchow, *A Common Law Theory of Judicial Review: The Living Tree*
(Cambridge: Cambridge University Press, 2007).

[24] In *Pharmaceutical Manufacturers of SA; in re Ex parte Application of the President
of the RSA*, 2000 (3) BCLR 241 (CC), 2000 (1) SA 674 (CC), at par. 20, the Constitutional
Court of South Africa went so far as to hold that: "There is only one system of law. It is
shaped by the Constitution which is the supreme law, and all law, including the common
law, derives its force from the Constitution and is subject to constitutional control."

[25] E.g. in South Africa, the Supreme Court of Appeal developed the common law to allow
for same-sex marriages, *Fourie v. Minister of Home Affairs*, 2005 (3) BCLR 241 (SCA), at
paras. 38–49. On appeal the Constitutional Court was more cautious by giving parliament
the opportunity to address the matter itself, by suspending its own order developing the
common law in line with the Constitution for a year. *See Minister of Home Affairs v.
Fourie; Lesbian and Gay Equality Project v. Minister of Home Affairs*, 2006 (3) BCLR
355 (CC), 2006 (1) SA 524 (CC), at paras. 115–161.

[26] Rautenbach and Malherbe, *supra* note 22, at 4.

or subordinate) legislation.[27] Primary legislation, as the name suggests, provides the basis for any secondary legislation. Such as where an act of parliament delegates the power to legislate on a particular topic to the executive, or some other body lacking primary powers. However simple this may seem, this distinction can get quite complicated, especially in comparative law. This is because the distinction is tailor-made for a unitary form of state with only one primary legislature leaving all other bodies dependent on its grace to enact laws, hence their secondary nature.[28] This picture becomes less clear in federal systems, where the federal and state legislatures each enjoy primacy in their own fields as guaranteed by the constitution. In such a situation, there can be more than one primary legislature.

15 To steer clear of too much terminological confusion, this study will try to avoid the term *primary legislation* where possible. Instead, pieces of primary legislation will be characterised with reference to their source.[29] A law passed by a national legislature will be referred to as an act of parliament; while a law passed by a provincial legislature will be referred to as a provincial law, provided that such bodies enjoy primacy in relation to other legislatures of course. The term *delegated legislation*, which is preferred over secondary or subordinate laws, will be used to indicate legislation passed on the authority of another legislative body. In other words, the body that adopted a piece of legislation depends on a higher legislative body for its lawmaking powers. This will usually be taken to mean laws decided on by an executive body. Although it can also refer to an elected body, such as a local council, which passes bylaws by virtue of delegated authority.

1.3.3 Public Law Relationships

16 Lastly, judicial review can also pertain to the issue of public and private law relationships. May the judiciary only review what happens in public law relationships, namely those relationships where the state exercises its official power? Or may it review what happens in private

---

[27]E.g. Michael Zander, *The Law-Making Process* (Cambridge: Cambridge University Press, 6th ed., 2004), at 108–111, regarding the United Kingdom.

[28]The classic expression of this notion can be found in the English Bill of Rights of 1688: "That the pretended power of suspending laws or the execution of laws by regal authority without consent of Parliament is illegal; that the pretended power of dispensing with laws or the execution of laws by regal authority as it hath been assumed and exercised of late is illegal."

[29]This is also followed in the HRA. While, s. 3 expressly refers to "primary legislation", s. 20 elaborates on which forms of legislation are covered by the term.

law relationships as well?[30] These relationships are also referred to as vertical and horizontal, with vertical implying the exercise of state power and horizontal concerning private parties engaging each other.

It should come as no surprise that public law relationships are preferred over private law ones for present purposes.[31] This makes sense because the main line of enquiry falls on controlling the state, something which is a classic example of public law. Think for example of *S. v. Makwanyane*, a decision of the South African Constitutional Court in which the death penalty was declared unconstitutional, thereby making it impossible for the state to carry out such punishment.[32] Capital punishment had been a sensitive issue in South Africa, and while a political moratorium was announced on executions it fell to the judiciary to set definite limits to public power in this regard. Although the horizontal application of higher law could also mean that legislation must be changed in striking a proper balance in private relationships, it does not necessarily present the most obvious examples of constitutionalism and will therefore only be referred to in addition to and not instead of vertical relationships.

1.4 Outline of Study

17 In Chapter 2 the development and current position of the judicial review of legislation will be explored in the United Kingdom, the Netherlands and South Africa. Following the justification of judicial review will be considered in Chapter 3 with reference to theory and mindful of the experience of the three countries studied. Particular attention will be paid to objections against judicial review founded on the legitimacy of democratic decision-making. In addressing the second question raised above, namely the factors that influence the scope of review, Chapters 4–7 will each explain and compare an important aspect of this scope, these are the fora, modalities, content and consequences of review. Finally, in Chapter 8 the conclusions arrived at in Chapters 3–7 will be put in perspective.

---

[30] Incidentally, the state can be a participant in private law relationships too, but then wholly as a private party such as where it buys land without expropriating it.

[31] For the horizontal application of rights in the jurisdictions studied, *see* Neil Parpworth, *Constitutional & Administrative Law* (Oxford: Oxford University Press, 5th ed., 2008), at 424–426; L.F.M. Verhey, *Horizontale werking van grondrechten, in het bijzonder van het recht op privacy* (Zwolle: W.E.J. Tjeenk Willink, 1992); Iain Currie and Johan de Waal, *The Bill of Rights Handbook* (Lansdowne: Juta, 5th ed., 2005), at 50–55; and generally András Sajó and Renáta Uitz (eds.), *The Constitution in Private Relations: Expanding Constitutionalism* (Utrecht: Eleven International Publishing, 2005).

[32] *S. v. Makwanyane*, 1995 (6) BCLR 665 (CC), 1995 (3) SA 391 (CC).

Chapter 2
Three Systems of Judicial Review

2.1 Pursuing Constitutionalism

18 Judicial review as an instrument in pursuit of constitutionalism must be understood in relation to its particular constitutional system. One can only hope to understand the feature of review and its contours by grasping the context against which it came to develop and function. This chapter will chart the state of the judicial review of legislation in the United Kingdom, the Netherlands and South Africa, mindful of each country's background and legal system. The resulting overview will be used in later chapters to further study review as a means of controlling power.

2.2 United Kingdom

2.2.1 The Mother of Parliaments and the Rule of Law

19 An often repeated mantra of British constitutionalism is that the *rule of law* must be respected.[33] One of the aims of this standard precept is to avoid the arbitrary exercise of state power by providing that individuals may only be limited in or deprived of their liberty through the law as applied by the courts. While this is without controversy, the rule of law has traditionally been viewed in conjunction with the doctrine of parliamentary sovereignty.[34] This other cornerstone of Britain's unwritten constitution enables the "Mother of Parliaments" to make any law it wishes without legal limit, which traditionally leaves the courts to apply the law equally to everyone but unable to exercise judicial review over it.

---

[33]*See* generally, Lord Bingham, "The Rule of Law", 66 *Camb. L. J.* 67 (2007); Parpworth, *supra* note 31, at 36–38.

[34]For the classic exposition, *see* A.V. Dicey, *Introduction to the Study of the Law of the Constitution* (London: Macmillan, 10th ed., 1959), at 406–414.

G. van der Schyff, *Judicial Review of Legislation,*
Ius Gentium: Comparative Perspectives on Law and Justice 5,
DOI 10.1007/978-90-481-9002-7_2, © Springer Science+Business Media B.V. 2010

Yet, this understanding of the British constitution has seen a lot of debate and thought over the years and is increasingly coming under pressure. Especially as it is felt that this classic position entrusts too much responsibility to parliament over people's rights, leading to the need for more bipolarity by strengthening the courts' powers to review legislation. While some have called for this to be achieved by the adoption of a written and entrenched constitution to be controlled by the judiciary, it is also conceivable that the unwritten constitution can itself come to accept a new balance of power in controlling the legislative function.[35] In charting this debate, the focus below will rest on exploring the nature of the country's constitution against the background of parliamentary sovereignty and the traditional approach to fundamental rights protection. Attention will then turn to the HRA as a recent method of enhancing the judicial protection of rights while not intending to upset the accepted constitutional scheme of things.

20   The United Kingdom is nearly unique in modern constitutional law in that it has no formal or written Constitution.[36] The country's constitution is generally described as being unwritten, by which is meant that it is not embodied, either wholly or mainly, in any enactment, or even to be found in a formally related series of enactments.[37] Instead the "constitution" is to be understood as referring to the body of constitutional law itself and not to a definite constitutional text. A.V. Dicey expressed the standard position already in the nineteenth century:

> Constitutional law, as the term is used in England, appears to include all rules which directly or indirectly affect the distribution or the exercise of the sovereign power in the state.[38]

Dicey added that the use of "rules" instead of "laws" was intentional, as constitutional law was made up of two different sets of principles, each of a very different character. The one set refers to laws in the strict sense of the word. Namely, rules that are recognised and enforced by the courts as being law, be they written or unwritten, enacted by parliament or derived from the common law. The other set refers to "conventions, understandings, habits, or practices" which although they may regulate the exercise of the state's

---

[35]Parpworth, *supra* note 31, at 14–15.

[36]Israel and New Zealand are also usually referred to as countries with unwritten constitutions.

[37]David Feldman (ed.), *English Public Law* (Oxford: Oxford University Press, 2004), at 3–4, 6–8; O. Hood Phillips, Paul Jackson and Patricia Leopold, *Constitutional and Administrative Law* (London: Sweet & Maxwell, 8th ed., 2001), at 18. Since the Norman Conquest the country has only known customary constitutions, except between 1653 and 1660 when following the Civil War the Instrument of Government was drafted under Oliver Cromwell.

[38]Dicey, *supra* note 34, at 23.

power, are not enforced by the courts.[39] In other words, the one set refers to the *laws* of the constitution, while the other set means the *conventions* of the constitution. This orthodox distinction is still recognised today, bar a few qualifications.[40]

21 The fact that the British constitution cannot be traced to, or derived from a single entrenched document means that it is essentially a creature of tradition and therefore only as strong as the very tradition by which it is carried. This has as a consequence that the constitution is particularly flexible and easy to amend, as there are no special rules to change it, except the normal rules that brought it about.[41] Constitutional change is therefore less a matter of satisfying special legislative procedures, than it is a question of political will, the achievement of which can be more difficult in practice than appearance belies.[42]

22 Parliamentary sovereignty is a cardinal feature of the British constitution, so much so that it has been described as its *grundnorm* in a Kelsenian sense[43] and its "ultimate rule of recognition" in a Hartian sense.[44] Yet, to understand the doctrine properly, something of its development must be understood.

Since medieval times the conception was defended that governmental institutions were created by the common law, which also meant that such institutions saw their powers limited by that instrument.[45] However, the idea that parliament could not limit the common law, due to the fact that is was created by such law, was perceived as favouring royal power more than it did parliamentary power.[46] This was because the Royal Prerogative was itself a product of the common law, and therefore not to be limited by parliament. The growth of royal power under the Tudors though left the common lawyers feeling uneasy. This resulted in an alliance of sorts between parliamentarians and the common lawyers, who realised that if royal power were to be limited by law, that law would have to be parliamentary law, and not the common law. Consequently, the courts started to

---

[39] Ibid., at 24.

[40] *Madzimbamuto v. Lardner Burke*, [1969] 1 AC 645, PC, at 724; Feldman, *supra* note 37, at 16.

[41] Feldman, *supra* note 37, at 7–8.

[42] Ibid. Similarly, Dicey, *supra* note 34, at 145, warned that it would be "political madness to tamper gratuitously" with important acts of parliament, although doing so would be procedurally quite easy.

[43] George Winterton, "The British Grundnorm: Parliamentary Supremacy Re-examined", 92 *L. Quart. Rev.* 591 (1976).

[44] H.L.A. Hart, *The Concept of Law* (Oxford: Oxford University Press, 1961), at 145.

[45] *Bribery Commissioner v. Ranasinghe*, [1965] AC 172, PC, at 198.

[46] Winterton, *supra* note 43, at 594–595.

hold that the king could not simply change the general law of the land, but that such a change had to be made by parliament. For example, it became standard that offences could only be created by parliament and not by the king alone.

23 The Stuarts, who wanted to assert their divine right to rule even more than their Tudor predecessors, also met their match in parliament, as the monarchy was briefly abolished between 1649 and 1660 after the Civil War.[47] The Glorious Revolution of 1688 saw William of Orange accepting the crown, but only upon agreeing to expand the powers of parliament.[48] Parliament now adopted the Bill of Rights, in 1689, which limited the king's powers in a number of respects and made entitlement to the crown dependent on parliamentary authority.[49] The Bill was not so much a decla-ration of rights in the modern sense, as it was about subduing royal power to parliamentary power. Parliament became increasingly omnipotent, and developed from an institution that was limited by the common law, into an institution that itself limited that body of law.

There had been a gradual transition from sovereignty vesting in the king alone, to the king-in-parliament with the balance of power resting with the legislative houses. Leaving A.V. Dicey to write that:

> The principle of Parliamentary sovereignty means neither more nor less than this, namely, that Parliament [referring to the monarch, House of Lords and the House of Commons acting together] has, under the English constitution, the right to make or unmake any law whatsoever; and further that no person or body is recog-nised by the law of England as having a right to override or set aside the legislation of Parliament.[50]

Although many thinkers were glad to see royal power severely limited, they started to fear the parliamentary abuse of power. The king's powers might have been limited by parliament, but how were parliament's powers to be limited? The idea was not to simply replace one form of tyranny with another.

24 Importantly, the franchise helped to secure parliament's authority and allay fears of power abuse.[51] It was felt that as the people elected parlia-ment, its sovereignty in effect meant the sovereignty of the people.[52] The

---

[47] Ann Lyon, *Constitutional History of the United Kingdom* (London: Cavendish Publishing, 2003), at 221–227.

[48] Ibid., at 235–255.

[49] The Charter of Liberties of 1100 and the *Magna Carta* of 1215 can also be mentioned as early forerunners in seeking to limit the power of the king.

[50] Dicey, *supra* note 34, at 39–40. Footnotes omitted. Cf. Jeffrey Goldsworthy, *The Sovereignty of Parliament: History and Philosophy* (Oxford: Clarendon Press, 1999).

[51] Winterton, *supra* note 43, at 596; Koopmans, *supra* note 6, at 18.

[52] Michael Foley, *The Politics of the British Constitution* (Manchester: Manchester University Press, 1999), at 25.

strength of this theory was bolstered by the gradual expansion of the right to vote over the years. This was especially the case after the passing of the Reform Act of 1832, which created electoral constituencies in the large cities that sprung up after the Industrial Revolution, as well as increased the number of males eligible to vote. By the time universal suffrage for both men and women had arrived in the twentieth century, parliament had indeed become a more genuine reflection of the population, and therefore more legitimate than had previously been the case. "Virtual" or "presumed" representation, gave way to "actual" representation.[53] This democratisation of parliament over the years enforced the view held by many that parliament, and not so much declarations of rights, was the real protector of the people, thereby encouraging faith in the institution and its decisions.[54] Given this trust, parliamentary tyranny, although theoretically possible, was deemed a practical and political impossibility.[55]

But the pressing question is, should faith in a sovereign parliament still be boundless today, especially when it concerns the protection of fundamental rights, and what role should the judiciary have in this regard, if any?

2.2.2 Bringing Rights Home

25   The protection of fundamental rights in British law has been a duty resting in a large part with parliament because it is usually held that people enjoy all rights and freedoms imaginable subject to parliament's will.[56] In other words, one is free to do anything except that which is forbidden by the law. This is a theory of residual rights, as rights are any conduct or interests not limited or extinguished by an act of parliament.[57] Rights are therefore the product of the parliamentary process, and not so much normative starting points in setting a limit to what parliament can or cannot do with the liberty of its subjects.[58] The idea is that parliament's procedure and

[53] Ibid., at 20–21.

[54] E.g. Dicey, *supra* note 34, at 199, argued that: "The Habeas Corpus Acts declare no principle and define no rights, but they are for practical purposes worth a hundred constitutional articles guaranteeing individual liberty."

[55] Tony Wright, *Citizens and Subjects. An Essay on British Politics* (London: Routledge, 1994), at 16.

[56] Feldman, *supra* note 37, at 36–37.

[57] John Wadham, Helen Mountfield, Anna Edmundson and Caoilfhionn Gallagher, *Blackstone's Guide to the Human Rights Act* (Oxford, Oxford University Press, 4th ed., 2007), at 3.

[58] John Doyle and Belinda Wells, "How Far Can the Common Law Go Towards Protecting Rights?", in Philip Alston (ed.), *Promoting Human Rights Through Bills of Rights: Comparative Perspectives* 17 (Oxford: Oxford University Press, 1999).

its democratic base provide sufficient safeguards in allowing the institution such power in deciding people's rights.[59]

26 A separate conception or body of rights has also emerged over the years in the common law. These rights are not negative in the sense that they amount to everything which is not forbidden, but are positively formulated by identifying or laying claim to certain protection.[60] Such rights include the right to personal security and liberty, freedom of assembly and expression, as well as the rights to property and privacy.[61]

Rights so recognised have come to be referred to as "constitutional rights". The 1997 decision in *R. v. Lord Chancellor, Ex parte Witham* provides an illustration.[62] The applicant claimed that article 3 of the Supreme Court Fees Amendment Order of 1996 was not in accordance with section 130 of the Supreme Court Act of 1981. In other words, it was argued that the delegated legislation did not fit the act of parliament on which it was based and was therefore void. The amended Order meant that litigants who were on social benefits now also had to pay court fees, something which they were previously not required to do. The effect of the amendment was to deter impecunious people from starting or defending actions. In hearing the matter, Laws J. remarked:

> The common law does not generally speak in the language of constitutional rights, for the good reason that in the absence of a sovereign text, a written constitution which is logically and legally prior to the power of legislature, executive and judiciary alike (...) In the unwritten legal order of the British State, at a time when the common law continues to accord a legislative supremacy to Parliament, the notion of a constitutional right can in my judgment only inhere in this proposition, that the right in question cannot be abrogated by the State save by specific provision in an Act of Parliament, or by regulations whose *vires* in main legislation specifically confers the power to abrogate. General words will not suffice. Any such rights will be creatures of the common law, since their existence would not be the consequence of the democratic political process but would be logically prior to it.[63]

---

[59]Cf. Dicey, *supra* note 34, at 73 arguing that: "The electors can in the long run always enforce their will."

[60]Wadham et al., *supra* note 57, at 3; T.R.S Allan, *Law, Liberty, and Justice: The Legal Foundations of British Constitutionalism* (Oxford: Clarendon, 1993), at 135–143.

[61]E.g., in *Entick v. Carrington*, (1765) 19 Howell's State Trials 1029, at 1066, the C.J. of the Common Pleas identified what today would be called the right to property in the following terms: "The great end, for which men entered society, was to secure their property. That right is preserved sacred and incommunicable in all instances, where it has not been taken away or abridged by some public law for the good of the whole." Cf. Ian Loveland, *Constitutional Law, Administrative Law and Human Rights* (Oxford, Oxford University Press, 4th ed., 2006), at 59–61.

[62]*R. v. Lord Chancellor, Ex parte Witham*, [1997] 2 All ER 779.

[63]Ibid., at 783f–784a.

After reviewing the facts, the judge held that parliament had to make express provision for the limitation of the right of access, something which had not been done in the Supreme Court Act. The limitation of the right in the Order was not based on a very clear provision in the parent act, and therefore void.

27   Over the last 50 years another source of fundamental rights has grown in prominence, namely the European Convention on Human Rights. By ratifying the Convention in 1951 the United Kingdom became party to a body of supranational fundamental rights. However, the dualist nature of British law means that treaties once ratified still need to be incorporated into national law by an act of parliament before they can have any domestic effect.[64] This meant that inhabitants of the United Kingdom could not rely on their newly found rights before domestic courts, as the treaty had not been incorporated. Even so, the recognition in 1966 of the right to individual petition enabled individuals to lodge cases with the European Court of Human Rights in Strasbourg. The result was that the Court's decisions had an indirect effect on law in the United Kingdom, as parliament changed some of its acts on a number of occasions after the Court had found a violation of a Convention right.[65]

British courts also started to refer directly to the Convention and the interpretation given to it by the Strasbourg Court when they had to solve ambiguity in national legislation.[66] This was, and still is possible, as it is presumed that parliament does not intend to legislate contrary to international law, save by clear formulation.[67] The Convention was also put to use by the judiciary in developing the common law and to guide the exercise of judicial discretion.[68] Interestingly, the Convention was further used to inform domestic court decisions on European Union law. This is because the European Court of Justice itself refers to the Convention in matters where the protection of fundamental rights plays a role.[69]

---

[64]Loveland, *supra* note 61, at 691–692.

[65]The Court's judgments do not automatically change national law, it is up to the United Kingdom to effect any change. For example, the well-known decision in *Sunday Times v. The United Kingdom* of 26 April 1979, *Publ. Eur. Court of H.R.*, Series A, no. 30, led to changes in the law on contempt of court in 1981.

[66]*R. v. Secretary of State for the Home Department, Ex parte Brind*, [1991] UKHL 4, [1991] 1 AC 696.

[67]Wadham et al., *supra* note 57, at 4.

[68]*Derbyshire County Council v. Times Newspapers*, [1992] QB 770; *R. v. Khan*, [1996] 3 WLR 162.

[69]Cf. Wadham et al., *supra* note 57, at 101–109.

28 The arrival of the Convention evoked extensive debate about its ideal place in the legal order of the United Kingdom.[70] Traditional views feared that making the Convention enforceable law would needlessly jeopardise the doctrine of parliamentary sovereignty by allowing the bench too much say over acts of parliament. Such a redistribution of power, it was argued, was not necessary, as the common law and parliament itself provided sufficient protection for people's rights through the robust debate of bills and committee scrutiny. In essence, the United Kingdom's long history of freedom was put forward to argue that its sovereign parliament could be trusted with the nation's rights, unlike the political bodies of other countries.[71] Legislation such as the Race Relations Act of 1976 is often advanced as evidence of parliament being a guardian of liberty and not its enemy.

However, the changing face of modern society led some to call for the Convention's incorporation. They argued that rights were under-protected by traditional means.[72] Strong executive government meant that parliament was more likely to follow government than to question it, thereby putting the democratic argument in denying judicial review in doubt. As a consequence the judiciary was increasingly seen as a necessary counter-weight to control an ever-growing state.[73]

29 Incorporation, it supporters argued, would also mean that individuals could enforce their rights more swiftly at home, instead of having to rely so much on drawn-out and expensive cases brought before the Strasbourg Court.[74] In addition matters such as the *East African Asians* case did not serve to strengthen faith in the democratic process as the ultimate protector of rights.[75] In this case, the European Commission of Human Rights had found that Westminster was motivated by racism in not allowing British citizens of Asian descent in East Africa to flee to the United Kingdom – hardly a good example of parliament protecting rights. By 1990, Ronald Dworkin,

---

[70]E.g. Rabinder Singh, *The Future of Human Rights in the United Kingdom* (Oxford: Hart, 1997), at 17–37; Lord Steyn, "2000–2005: Laying the Foundations of Human Rights Law in the United Kingdom", 4 *Eur. Hum. Rights L. Rev.* 349 (2005), at 351.

[71]James Young, "The Politics of the Human Rights Act", 26 *J. L. Soc.* 27 (1999), at 29–30.

[72]Cf. Bingham, *supra* note 2, at 390; Singh, *supra* note 70, at 38–44.

[73]Steyn, *supra* note 70, at 349, opined that the traditional approach to protecting rights had become inadequate.

[74]The Government's White Paper, *Rights Brought Home: The Human Rights Bill*, Cm. 3782, October 1997, at par. 1.14.

[75]ECmHR, no. 4403/70 (joined with other applications), *East African Asians v. The United Kingdom* of 10 October 1970; 3 EHRR 1981, 76, at paras. 197–202, 207–209.

favouring incorporation and judicial review, stated the case thus under the heading "Liberty is ill in Britain":

> Great Britain was once a fortress for freedom. It claimed great philosophers of liberty, Milton and Locke and Paine and Mill. Its legal tradition is irradiated with liberal ideas: that people accused of crime are presumed innocent, that no one owns another's conscience, that a man's home is his castle. But now Britain offers less formal legal protection than most of its neighbours in Europe. I do not mean that it has become a police state, of course. Citizens are free openly to criticise the government, and the government does not kidnap or torture or kill its opponents. But liberty is nevertheless under threat by a notable decline in the *culture* of liberty – the community's shared sense that individual privacy and dignity and freedom of speech and conscience are crucially important and they are worth considerable sacrifices in official convenience or public expense to protect.[76]

The message was clear, freedom as protected by traditional means was no longer adequate, but had to be reinforced.

30   The political establishment eventually responded to such calls and arguments by adopting the Human Rights Act in 1998.[77] The achievement of the Act was to incorporate certain of the Convention's typically civil and political rights into domestic law, thereby "bringing rights home".[78] To further such rights, the courts and other public authorities were enjoined to act in a way that is compatible with any Convention right, to the extent that such an authority does not act contrary to any applicable legislation.[79] In this regard, section 3 of the HRA provides:

(1) So far as it is possible to do so, primary legislation and subordinate legislation must be read and given effect to in a way which is compatible with the Convention rights.
(2) This section-
  (a) applies to primary and subordinate legislation whenever enacted;
  (b) does not affect the validity of, continuing operation or enforcement of any incompatible primary legislation; and

---

[76]Ronald Dworkin, *A Bill of Rights for Britain* (London: Chatto & Windus, 1990), at 1. Justifying these assumptions, see K.D. Ewing and C.A. Gearty, *Freedom Under Thatcher: Civil Liberties in Modern Britain* (Oxford, Clarendon Press, 1990).

[77]Cf. Richard Gordon and Tim Ward, *Judicial Review and the Human Rights Act* (London: Cavendish Publishing, 2000); Feldman *supra* note 37, at 373–445.

[78]Cf. White Paper, *Rights Brought Home*, *supra* note 74, at paras. 1.18–1.19.

[79]S. 6(1)-(2) of the HRA. Cf. Wadham et al., *supra* note 57, at 72–76 on the meaning of the term "public authority".

(c) does   not   affect   the   validity,   continuing   operation   or
enforcement of any incompatible subordinate legislation if (disre-
garding any possibility of revocation) primary legislation prevents
removal of the incompatibility.

31 When reading the provision it becomes clear that the courts do not
possess the power to strike down offending legislation. Instead, the HRA
establishes rules of construction that must be followed unless they are contradicted by legislation. However, selected higher courts, if satisfied that
a piece of legislation is incompatible with any of the Convention rights
and that it cannot be interpreted otherwise, may make a declaration of
incompatibility.[80] Such a declaration is not binding on the parties before
the court, neither does if affect the operation of the provision in respect of
which it was given. Its purpose is to give a signal to the government and
parliament that they may want to reconsider specific legislation in the light
of the declaration, without them being obliged to do so. In the event that
the government were to choose to remove the incompatibility, the normal
course of action would be to remove it by an act of parliament. However,
where a minister considers that there are "compelling reasons", section
10 of the HRA empowers such a minister to remove the incompatibility by
using subordinate legislation to amend the offending act of parliament.[81] To
date, however, these powers have been used very sparingly by the courts.[82]

Not only judicial declarations of incompatibility are foreseen, but also
political statements of compatibility during the legislative process. Section
19 requires of a minister in charge of a bill to either make a statement that
the bill accords with the HRA, or that although such a statement cannot be
made the government still wishes parliament to proceed with the bill.[83]

32 Clearly, choosing a form of weak judicial review meant that a compromise was struck between retaining parliamentary sovereignty and opting
for judicial review at the same time.[84] This is typical of the incremental way in which constitutional law is reformed in the United Kingdom,

---

[80] S. 4 of the HRA.

[81] The so-called fast-track option, see § 303.

[82] By July 2006 15 declarations of incompatibility had been made, one of which was
remedied by a s. 10 remedial order. Cf. Department for Constitutional Affairs, *Review of
the Implementation of the Human Rights Act*, July 2006, at 17.

[83] Cf. Wadham et al., *supra* note 57, at 52–53.

[84] Cf. A.W. Bradley and K.D. Ewing, *Constitutional and Administrative Law* (Edinburgh,
Pearson, 13th ed., 2003), at 418–419; Wadham et al., *supra* note 57, at 7–8; Conor
Gearty, *Principles of Human Rights Adjudication* (Oxford: Oxford University Press,
2005), at 21–26.

revolutionary changes are shied away from in favour of evolution and compromise.[85] Litigants can now rely on the HRA and its incorporated rights to further their cases, while the courts must take note of such rights without depriving parliament of the last word. Nonetheless, the courts have held that the interpretive obligation under section 3 of the HRA is a strong one.[86] It applies even where there is no ambiguity about the meaning of legislation to be resolved by the judiciary.[87]

33 Moreover, in keeping with the flexible nature so characteristic of the United Kingdom's unwritten constitution, the HRA is not entrenched, but can be amended by an ordinary parliamentary majority. However, case law recognises the HRA as a "constitutional statute", meaning that it:

> [C]an only be repealed, or amended in a way which significantly affects its provisions towards fundamental rights or otherwise the relation between citizen and state, by unambiguous words on the face of the later statute.[88]

This status guards against later legislation repealing provisions in the Act by implication. In other words, seeing its important nature, the courts will only accept the express repeal of the HRA's provisions and not their implied repeal.

34 Evaluating the HRA, it can rightly be said that it has been the source of much controversy. Its supporters see it as a first step to introducing an entrenched bill of rights allowing acts of parliament to be struck down, or as something to be expanded to fill gaps in its current protection.[89] Its doubters on the other hand want it repealed or at least amended to allow tougher action against criminals, for example.[90] In contrast, a recent report by the government has come out in support of the HRA, but has also identified instances where the courts got the balance wrong in deciding

---

[85] J.W.F. Allison, *The English Historical Constitution: Continuity, Change and European Effects* (Cambridge: Cambridge University Press, 2007), at 175.

[86] *R. v. A.*, [2001] UKHL 25, [2001] 3 All ER 1, at par. 44 (*per* Lord Steyn). Cf. Aileen Kavanagh, *Constitutional Review Under the UK Human Rights Act* (Cambridge: Cambridge University Press, 2009), at 19–117, for an extensive treatment.

[87] In this, it goes further than the New Zealand Bill of Rights Act of 1990, but not as far as the Canadian Charter of Rights and Freedoms of 1982, *see* § 300.

[88] *Thoburn v. Sunderland City Council*, [2002] EWHC, 195, [2003] QB 151, at par. 63.

[89] E.g. the pressure group Charter 88. *See* http://www.unlockdemocracy.org.uk/, last accessed on 19 November 2009; Wadham et al., *supra* note 57, at 17–18, who highlight gaps in the HRA's protection.

[90] "Cameron to Fight Human Rights Act", *Daily Telegraph* (13 May 2006); Theo Rycroft, "The Rationality of the Conservative Party's Proposal for a British Bill of Rights", 1 *UCL Hum. Rights Rev.* 51 (2008).

cases.[91] Yet the fact remains that although the HRA's future may be somewhat uncertain it has left its mark on both civil and criminal law in the
United Kingdom and has come to be valued by senior judges.[92] Moreover,
although the nature and reach of the HRA might be debated, one thing
seems increasingly likely, namely that the courts will be very reluctant to
accept a sovereign parliament devoid of any constraint but its own judgment. As Baroness Hale, among other members of the House of Lords,
ventured in *Jackson v. Her Majesty's Attorney General*:

> The Courts will treat with particular suspicion (and might even reject) any attempt
> to subvert the rule of law by removing governmental action affecting the rights of
> the individual from all judicial powers.[93]

Therefore, just as the courts were willing to help establish parliamentary
sovereignty by recognising it in their judgments over centuries, they may
also be willing to help bring it to an end by insisting on a real bipolar balance
of powers in the unwritten constitution were parliament to negate judicial
review altogether.

2.3 The Netherlands

2.3.1 Consensus Democracy and an Internationalised Constitution

35 The constitutional dispensation of the Netherlands can be described
as that of a democratic *rechtsstaat*.[94] Democracy, although the primary
choice for national decision-making, is not left to its own devices but is
expected to operate within the recognised boundaries of the *rechtsstaat*.
Initially in the nineteenth century, this body of thought only required that
for state action to be valid, it had to respect the legality provisions laid down
in a written and rigid constitution.[95] Section 7 of the Dutch Constitution
reflects its old roots in this regard by indicating the appropriate body that
may limit different forms of expression, while not actually paying much

---

[91] Department for Constitutional Affairs, *Review of the Implementation of the Human Rights Act*, July 2006, 35.

[92] Wadham et al., *supra* note 57, at 18.

[93] *Jackson v. Her Majesty's Attorney General*, [2005] UKHL, 56, at par. 159. *See also* Mark Elliott, "United Kingdom: Parliamentary Sovereignty under Pressure", 2 *Int. J. Const. L.* 545 (2004), at 551.

[94] Burkens et al., *supra* note 13, at 11–37; Willem Witteveen, "Inhabiting Legality", in Sanne Taekema (ed.), *Understanding Dutch Law* 75 (The Hague: Boom Juridische Uitgevers, 2004).

[95] Cf. Ernst-Wolfgang Böckenförde, *State, Society, Liberty: Studies in Political Theory and Constitutional Law* (New York: Berg, 1991), at 53 et seq.

attention to how such a body must exercise its power.[96] On this approach, the real question centres on whether the democratically-elected legislature has to limit rights, something which is considered an added guarantee for the protection of people's liberty, or whether such power may be delegated to bodies with fewer or no democratic credentials.

36 However, with the passing of time thought has evolved into also stressing material constraints on the exercise of power in the *rechtsstaat* by exploring a new role for the judiciary in controlling the content of legislation.[97] Interestingly, this development has a decidedly international flavour in the Netherlands, as domestic courts turn to treaties in checking the justifiability of legislation before applying it, while still following the traditional approach in applying legislation irrespective of whether it violates national constitutional norms. Understandably, these contradictions, the one rooted in an attitude that welcomes international law and the other in an established tradition of trusting parliament's interpretation of the Constitution over that of the courts, invite debate. In discussing the issues raised here, the attention will turn to explaining the constitutional structure of the Netherlands at greater length, as well as to the possibility of change looming on the horizon in resolving such opposite approaches to judicial review in a single jurisdiction.

37 The constitutional fabric of the Netherlands can probably best be described as being a rich tapestry of documents and custom. In this regard, two national documents of particular constitutional worth are known, the Charter of the Kingdom of the Netherlands of 1954 and the Constitution of the Kingdom of the Netherlands, first adopted in 1815.[98] The latter has been extensively revised since 1818, most notably in the 1980s. The Charter is the higher of the two documents and states that the Kingdom consists of three equal partners, namely the Netherlands, the Netherlands Antilles and Aruba; whereas the Constitution is only applicable to the Netherlands and foresees a decentralised unitary state. In comparing the documents, it is striking that ideological statements are absent. The documents also do not state their ultimate source, for instance the will or sovereignty of the people. The closest to such a statement is the preamble to the Charter proclaiming that the Kingdom's three constituent parts voluntarily constitute a new legal order, after which the institutional structure is worked out. It is also noteworthy that the Charter does not contain a bill of rights, but only states that each part of the Kingdom has to implement fundamental

---

[96] S. 7 states that publishing thoughts or opinions may only be limited by an act of parliament, while the authority to limit radio and television broadcasts may be delegated. Commercial advertising is excluded from constitutional protection altogether.

[97] Cf. Böckenförde, *supra* note 95, at 60 et seq.

[98] Cf. Constantijn A.J.M. Kortmann and Paul P.T. Bovend'Eert, *Dutch Constitutional Law* (The Hague: Kluwer, 2000), at 28–34.

rights and ensure legal certainty and ensure a proper administration.[99] Nor in this regard does the Constitution contain any grand founding statement or declaration, it even lacks a preamble, although it does contain a bill of rights that ranges from civil and political to socio-economic rights.

38 Yet, although both are basic laws, the Constitution and Charter are not exhaustive documents. C.W. de Vries captured this quite succinctly with regard to the Constitution:

> The purpose of our constitutional law is not contained in the Constitution. The Constitution is only to provide an opportunity through which a system may develop.[100]

This is evidenced by the fact that the Constitution, which includes more substantive provisions than the Charter, leaves a great deal of power to parliament in steering the state and deciding on how power is to be channelled and exercised. For example, the development that limited the monarch's real powers in favour of parliament occurred without the Constitution being amended, and the procedure for the formation of a new cabinet is based on convention and not on constitutional provisions.[101] The Dutch constitutional order is therefore quite an open system with an emphasis on, and faith in parliamentary democracy above judicial wisdom.[102]

39 This aspect of the Constitution and Charter's character becomes more clear when the position of the judiciary is considered in respect of their enforcement. The judiciary, although recognised by both these instruments, is in general not empowered to enforce compliance with them in the face of the legislature's acts. In other words, the Charter and Constitution are not so much judicial documents, as they are political documents. Their implementation rests with political organs, more than it does with judicial organs. This can be traced to the bar that was included in the Constitution in 1848, which, in its current form as section 120 reads:

> The constitutionality of acts of parliament and treaties shall not be reviewed by the courts.[103]

---

[99] S. 43 of the Charter of the Kingdom of the Netherlands (1954).

[100] Foreword to J.R. Stellinga, *De Grondwet systematisch gerangschikt* (Zwolle: Tjeenk Willink, 1950). Author's translation of "De hoofdzaak van ons staatsrecht staat niet in de Grondwet. De Grondwet opene slechts de gelegenheid, dat zich een stelsel ontwikkele."

[101] Kortmann and Bovend'Eert, *supra* note 98, at 20. On the shortcomings of the Constitution, *see* also A.D. Belifante and J.L. de Reede, *Beginselen van het Nederlandse staatsrecht* (Deventer: Kluwer, 16th ed., 2009), at 24–25.

[102] Cf. G. Leeknegt, "The Protection of Fundamental Rights in a Digital Age", in E. Hondius and C. Joustra (eds.), *Netherlands Report to the Sixteenth International Congress of Comparative Law* 325 (Antwerp: Intersentia, 2002), at 327–328.

[103] "De rechter treedt niet in de beoordeling van de grondwettigheid van wetten en verdragen" in Dutch.

The effect of this provision is that acts of parliament (and treaties) may not be set aside for being unconstitutional, but legal norms of a lesser status may be refused application for being unconstitutional.[104] Similar thought also led to the Supreme Court, the *Hoge Raad*, refusing to review compliance with the Charter in the *Harmonisation Act* judgment, although the Charter itself is silent as to whether or not it may be enforced by the judiciary.[105] In the same judgment the Court further ruled that unwritten, yet, fundamental principles of law such as legal certainty could also not be used to set aside acts of parliament. No national higher law, be it written or unwritten, can thus serve to overrule an act of parliament.

40 In debating the future of the prohibition on review, some parliamentarians proposed the idea of weak review in the run up to revising the Constitution in the 1980s, yet their plans met with no success in amending the constitutional prohibition.[106] Nonetheless, the idea came to fruition when the Supreme Court observed in the *Harmonisation Act* judgment in 1989 that controversial legislation on higher education had violated the principle of legal certainty, a principle which was not only guaranteed in the Charter but also in unwritten law.[107] This the Court did although it was itself powerless to remedy the breach, given section 120 of the Constitution.[108] In other words, although courts may not set aside any act of parliament for violating national higher law, the bar on judicial review has come to be interpreted by the Supreme Court as allowing judicial pronouncements about whether an act violates such higher law or not. This means that section 120 might be understood to exclude the strong judicial review of acts of parliament, but not their weak review. One should be careful though not to draw too many parallels between the possibility of weak review in the Netherlands and courts' powers of review in the United Kingdom under the HRA. This is because although seemingly a distinct

---

[104]D.J. Elzinga, R. de Lange and H.G. Hoogers, *Handboek van het Nederlandse staatsrecht* (Deventer: Kluwer, 15th ed., 2006), at 205–206. *See* generally on judicial review in the Netherlands, Heringa and Kiiver, *supra* note 15, at 111–113; Belifante and de Reede, *supra* note 101, at 196; L.F.M. Besselink, "Constitutionele toetsing in internationaal perspectief", 52 *Ars Aequi* 89 (2003); Richard Happé and Hans Gribnau, "The Netherlands – National Report: Constitutional Limits to Taxation in a Democratic State: The Dutch Experience", 15 *Mich. State J. Int. L.* 417 (2007), at 420–423.

[105]Hoge Raad, 14 April 1989, *AB* 1989, 207 (*Harmonisation Act*), at par. 4.6. Cf. E.M.H. Hirsch Ballin, "De harmonisatiewet: Onschendbaarheid van de wet en van het rechtszekerheidsbeginsel", 38 *Ars Aequi* 578 (1989).

[106]*Parliamentary Proceedings II*, 1974–1975, at 2325, 2431.

[107]*Harmonisation Act* judgment, *supra* note 105, at par. 3.1; A.W. Heringa, "Constitutionele schijnbewegingen", in A.W. Heringa and N. Verheij (eds.), *Publiekrechtelijke bewegingen* 67 (Deventer: Kluwer, 1990), at 68–69; M.L.P. van Houten, *Meer zicht op wetgeving* (Zwolle: Tjeenk Willink, 1997), at 8–11.

[108]*Harmonisation Act* judgment, *supra* note 105, at par. 3.1.

possibility, weak review in the Netherlands is characterised more by its absence than its practise, as courts in the country still show great restraint in their dealings with national higher law. Nonetheless, weak review will be factored in as an option available to courts in the Netherlands in studying its system of judicial review.

41 Mindful of the discussion thus far, the two main constitutive documents of the Netherlands can be understood more as general maps and guidelines of power, than as documents that seek to actively limit state power by calling upon the judiciary for tangible enforcement. This explains the somewhat lacklustre and technical composition of the Constitution and Charter, as they are but elements of the constitutional order and not its supreme or deciding sources. This is particularly clear when it comes to the Constitution, which functions more as a codification of existing rules of constitutional convention and political practice than as the initiator of such rules.[109] The Constitution follows political practice and wisdom more than it dictates the course of events.

Such faith in the political process can probably be explained by reference to the Netherlands' relatively peaceful and democratic history noted for the absence of upheaval and revolution.[110] For example, the country participated in only one of the two World Wars, the composition of its population is in general quite homogenous and it had a stable tradition as a republic before becoming a constitutional monarchy. Much of the tinder in Dutch politics was also addressed by the Pacification of 1917, an accord which saw social harmony maintained by resolving longstanding disputes in society by appeasing the Socialists and Liberals with the introduction of universal suffrage, while the Confessionals had the funding of their schools guaranteed by the state.[111]

42 In the Netherlands these and other sources of potential conflict are traditionally resolved by democratic debate and agreement and not by violence and revolution. Much has been written about the peaceful and inclusive settlement of disputes and accommodation of differences in the Netherlands, a decision-making process that is usually referred to as the *poldermodel*.[112] Decision-makers pride themselves on seeking the input of

---

[109]Leenknegt, *supra* note 102, at 328.

[110]Cf. Gert-Jan Leenknegt, Raymond Kubben and Beatrix Jacobs, *Opstand en eenwording: Een institutionele geschiedenis van het Nederlandse openbaar bestuur* (Nijmegen: Wolf Legal Publishers, 2006); Sanne Taekema, "Introducing Dutch Law", in Sanne Taekema (ed.), *Understanding Dutch Law* 17 (The Hague: Boom Juridische Uitgevers, 2004), at 24–27.

[111]P.J. Oud and J. Bosmans, *Staatkundige vormgeving in Nederland 1840–1940*, vol. 1 (Assen: Van Gorcum, 10th ed., 1990), at 208–224.

[112]Th.L. Bellekom, A.W. Heringa, J. van der Velde and L.F.M. Verhey, *Compendium van het staatsrecht* (Deventer: Kluwer, 10th ed., 2007), at 280.

as many stakeholders as possible in the hope that consensus can be reached
on important matters, thereby ensuring the legitimacy of the decisions so
arrived at. The culture of consensus has very old routes in the Netherlands
and is no longer simply a question of elites appeasing each other but has
taken root at most levels of society, as Rudy B. Andeweg and Galen A. Irwin
explain:

> Newspapers routinely refer to *harmonie model*, *overleg economie* (deliberative
> economy), or *polder model*; citizens are more likely to recognize referrals to
> employers associations and trade unions as "the social partners" than as "pressure
> groups"; the word "compromise" has no negative connotation; and the untranslat-
> able *maatschappelijk draagvlak* (literally: societal weight-bearing surface) is a
> household term to connote the need for government policies to have widespread
> support from organized interests and citizens.[113]

Societal and political debate with a focus on inclusiveness has always been
one of the bedrocks of Dutch democracy, something which is reflected in
the electoral system that can correctly be described as one of the most proportional systems in the world.[114] Although the system leads to a great
variety of parties being represented in parliament this inclusiveness of
views is preferred to a system that produces hard and fast majorities, such
as in the United Kingdom for example.

Yet, this is not the full story, as international law is of great significance
to the constitutional dispensation of, and thought in the Netherlands.

43   The Netherlands is monist as far as the effect of treaties and the decisions of international organisations are concerned.[115] This means that rules
of international law do not require incorporation in order to be applicable
in the national legal system. In other words, no national order is needed to
convert international norms into national law. This principle is the product of national customary law, and has been recognised as such by the
courts.[116] This respect for international law stems from the wish to preserve the integrity of the international legal order by allowing its direct
operation in the national order.[117]

As a matter of fact, so important is international law to the Dutch
legal order, that international norms are hierarchically superior to national

---

[113]Rudy B. Andeweg and Galen A. Irwin, *Governance and Politics of the Netherlands*
(Basingstoke: Palgrave Macmillan, 2002), at 148.

[114]Gert-Jan Leenknegt and Gerhard van der Schyff, "Reforming the Electoral System
of the Dutch Lower House of Parliament: An Unsuccessful Story", 8 *German L. J.* 1133
(2007), at 1141–1142. To be found at http://www.germanlawjournal.com/ (last accessed
on 19 November 2009).

[115]Kortmann and Bovend'Eert, *supra* note 98, at 28.

[116]Hoge Raad 6 March 1959, *NJ* 1962, 2 (*Nyugat*).

[117]E.C.M. Jurgens, "Wetgever heeft laatste woord over uitleg van Grondwet", *Regelmaat*
68 (1995).

norms such as the Charter or Constitution.[118] Such international norms
can be considered "constitutional" laws that form part of the broader constitution, to the extent that they limit or extend the powers of Dutch organs
created by national constitutional law.[119] The European Convention on
Human Rights and the International Covenant on Civil and Political Rights
can be noted as two of the most important treaties in this regard.

44 Section 94 of the Constitution clarifies the operation of international
law by stating that:

> Legislative regulations in force within the Kingdom shall not be applicable if
> such application is in conflict with provisions of treaties or of resolutions by
> international institutions that that are binding on all persons.[120]

The effect of this provision is that treaty provisions and decisions by international organisations that bind all persons are to be applied by the courts;
while other international legal norms, such as the rules of international
customary law, are to be applied by the legislature and not to be enforced
by the judiciary.[121] The provision thus achieves a separation of powers.
The final word on implementing international rules that fall under section
94 rests with the courts, while the legislature has the final word on other
international rules.

45 Based on the above it can rightly be said that the constitutional dispensation of the Netherlands presents a mixed picture. Although national
constitutional norms, such as the Constitution and Charter are certainly
important, they are lower in the hierarchy than international constitutional
norms, such as the rights guaranteed by various international treaties.
The constitutional dispensation of the Dutch *rechtsstaat* is thus not exclusively or on balance composed of national elements, but has a very strong
international flavour as well.

Judicial review presents an even more diverse picture, as the courts
must exercise strong review over all national norms, in principle even
those contained in the Constitution and Charter, for their compatibility
with international norms provided that the requirements of section 94 of
the Constitution are met.[122] This leads to an interesting contrast in that

---

[118]Cf. Burkens et al., *supra* note 13, at 90.

[119]Kortmann and Bovend'Eert, *supra* note 98, at 28.

[120]In Dutch "Binnen het Koninkrijk geldende wettelijke voorschriften vinden geen
toepassing, indien deze toepassing niet verenigbaar is met een ieder verbindende
bepalingen van verdragen en van besluiten van volkenrechtelijke organisaties."

[121]A provision of international law is considered to bind all persons, if it is directed at
people and not only the state, requires no further legislative or executive clarification and
is based on a written instrument, *see* further Burkens et al., *supra* note 13, at 339–341.

[122]The precondition is that s. 91(3) of the Constitution provides that treaties which
detract from the Constitution must be adopted by the States General with a two-thirds

section 120 of the same document prohibits the judiciary from reviewing acts of parliament on their compatibility with the Constitution in a strong fashion. However, the role of constitutional review is under discussion at present, as the position of the judiciary regarding its enforcement is in the spotlight.

2.3.2 Revitalising the Constitution by Calling on the Judiciary?

46 The anomaly sketched above, namely the strong judicial application of international norms by the judiciary, as opposed to excluding such review when it comes to applying the Constitution to acts of parliament is the ever-green of constitutional law in the Netherlands.[123] For example, in 1966 the Constitutional Affairs Section of the Interior Ministry recommended that the bar on reviewing acts of parliament be lifted in respect of national civil and political rights.[124] Lifting the bar was seen as a way of increasing the protection of ordinary members of society, as international rights do not neatly overlap with the interests protected by national rights. The State Commission on the Constitution and the Electoral Act followed in 1969 by also proposing that the bar be lifted as far as civil and political rights were concerned.[125] The point being again that the position of the individual had to be strengthened against the state, and that judicially enforceable (national civil and political) rights provided an ideal vehicle for this to be achieved. Traditional arguments against allowing such review, such as insisting on a strict separation of powers to ensure that the democratically-elected legislature makes laws, while the judiciary is simply called upon to apply them were considered, but were found to be unconvincing on both occasions. Yet, nothing came of these proposals, as the grand revision of the Constitution in 1983 did not affect the bar in section 120.

---

majority, and not a simple majority as would otherwise be the case. Cf. D. Breillat, C.A.J.M. Kortmann and J.W.A. Fleuren, *Van de constitutie afwijkende verdragen* (Deventer: Kluwer, 2002).

[123]The debate is a long and extensive one in the Netherlands. No attempt will be made to restate the debate here, except for a number of important points in order to understand and evaluate it. Cf. Elzinga et al., *supra* note 104, at 204–205; Van Houten, *supra* note 107; Bellekom et al., *supra* note 112, at 322–337; L. Prakke, "Bedenkingen tegen het toetsingsrecht", 122 *Handelingen Nederlandse Juristen-Vereniging* 1 (1992); L. Prakke, *Toetsing in het publiekrecht* (Assen: Van Gorcum, 1972); J.M. Barendrecht, "Het constitutionele toetsingsrecht van de rechter", 122 *Handelingen Nederlandse Juristen-Vereniging* 85 (1992), for more extensive treatments.

[124]*Proeve van een nieuwe Grondwet* (The Hague: Government Publication, 1966).

[125]J.L.M.Th. Cals and A.M. Donner, *Tweede Rapport van de Staatscommissie van advies inzake de Grondwet en de Kieswet* (The Hague: Government Publication, 1969).

47 However, the debate flared up again in 1989 when the Supreme Court was called upon in the *Harmonisation Act* case to not to apply an act of parliament which limited state grants to students with retrospective effect. The applicants based their claim on international law, but failed on the facts, which meant that the enquiry turned to national law.[126] As explained above, it was averred that the act infringed legal certainty, which is recognised as a fundamental but unwritten principle of higher law and which the applicants argued was not covered by the bar in section 120, as that only extended to the Constitution and not to higher law not expressly contained in it.[127] The bench responded by holding that although the literal formulation of the bar was open to interpretation, the intent in drafting it was clearly to extend it to cover unwritten fundamental principles as well. The Court consequently refused the claim. It also refused to let the claim succeed based on the express guarantee of legal certainty in section 49 of the Charter, which is silent as to the role of the judiciary in reviewing compliance with it.[128] In this regard, the bench referred to the position under the Constitution, which it said reflected the "traditional position" occupied by the courts in the institutional structure of the Dutch state.[129]

48 The Supreme Court emphasised that the constitutional legislature had had the fullest opportunity to abolish the prohibition on judicial review in the Constitution during the comprehensive revision of 1983, but had chosen not to do so. The Court noted in this regard that although the need for civil society to be protected against the state had increased since 1983, it was not for the bench to exceed its powers in this respect.[130] In other words, positive law had to be upheld, which meant that the claims had to fail and that the contested act applied to the students. However, as explained above the Court was careful to point out that the acts did indeed violate the principle of legal certainty but that judicially nothing could be done about it.[131]

49 The *Harmonisation Act* judgment, far from ending the debate, kept the matter alive. As a matter of fact, the government went so far as to adopt a policy note in 1991 that argued that the question was not whether the bar had to be lifted, as in its opinion it could not be sustained; but that the debate had now moved to shaping judicial review once the bar had

---

[126]*Harmonisation Act* judgment, *supra* note 105, at par. 5.2.

[127]Ibid., at par. 3.1.

[128]S. 43(1): "Each of the Countries shall promote the realisation of fundamental human rights and freedoms, legal certainty and good governance." In Dutch: "Elk der landen draagt zorg voor de verwezenlijking van de fundamentele menselijke rechten en vrijheden, de rechtszekerheid en de deugdelijkheid van het bestuur."

[129]*Harmonisation Act* judgment, *supra* note 105, at par. 4.2

[130]Ibid., at par. 3.6.

[131]Ibid., at par. 3.1.

been lifted.[132] However, this intention to reform the bar in section 120 led to nothing as political reluctance again reared its head as had happened so many times in the past. Nonetheless, in 2002 a private member's bill, referred to as the Halsema Proposal after the member who introduced it, was tabled in parliament.[133] The bill proposes the strong judicial review of acts of parliament as far as a number of national rights are concerned. The precise reach of the bill will be explored later, the focus here is on the current state of the bill in the legislative process and the reasons for its coming about. Suffice it to say that the bill wants to add a subsection to section 120, which would qualify the bar by listing a number of rights to be exempted from the prohibition on judicial review. This would allow the courts to effectively enforce such rights in cases brought before them.[134]

50 In aiming to ease the ban in section 120, the Halsema Proposal is not alone. The National Convention also supports the general idea of diluting the force of section 120.[135] The Convention was an advisory body established in 2005 by the minister of administrative renewal, it was composed of fourteen members drawn from academia and other walks of life who had to report on how the divide between the public and government could be bridged. This question the Convention had to consider by contemplating the function and future of the Constitution in meeting the demands of the twenty-first century. Published in 2006, the Convention's Report argues, as does Halsema, that the strong judicial review of civil and political rights in the Constitution must be allowed, but differs from the Proposal on the issue of which courts are to be granted these powers, preferring a constitutional court to decentralised review.[136] The Convention's Report provides additional input to the debate, and although certainly valuable in its support of judicial review, it is the Halsema Proposal that currently dominates the debate given its tabling in parliament.

51 The Halsema Proposal builds on earlier arguments that seek to allow the courts to conduct constitutional review of acts of parliament, by stressing the need to increase the protection of ordinary people against

---

[132]*Nota inzake rechterlijke toetsing* (The Hague: Government Publication, 1991). The Supreme Court gave its support to the idea of lifting the bar on judicial review in s. 120 of the Constitution, but only in respect of a number of predominantly civil and political rights (published in 7 *NJCM-bulletin* 243 (1992)).

[133]*Parliamentary Proceedings II*, 2001–2002, 28, 331, no. 2; 2002–2003, 28, 331, no. 9.

[134]*Parliamentary Proceedings II*, 2002–2003, 28, 331, no. 9, at 20.

[135]R.J. Hoekstra, *Hart voor de publieke zaak: Aanbevelingen van de Nationale Conventie voor de 21e eeuw* (The Hague: National Convention, 2006).

[136]Ibid., at 9, 47. *See* also the working group's preparatory report which lists a few possibilities, Carla Zoethout, Jan Willem Sap, Roel Kuiper and Omar Ramadan, *Een grondwet voor de 21ste eeuw: Voorstudie van de werkgroep Grondwet van de Nationale Conventie* (The Hague: National Convention, 2006), at 34.

burgeoning state power. In this regard, support is sought in the fact that acts of parliament may already be reviewed against international norms, something which the Proposal lauds as having strengthened the position of the individual.[137] By extending the scope of judicial review, it is argued, the Constitution and its guarantees will be saved from becoming a dead letter. As W.J. Witteveen explains, the anomaly of allowing the (binding judicial) review of international norms, but not of national norms threatens to make an anomaly of the Constitution itself.[138] This is something which was evident in the parliamentary consideration of anti-terror legislation a few years ago, where attention was mostly devoted on establishing whether legislative proposals were in conformity with applicable international norms, while corresponding national norms were largely left by the wayside.[139]

52 The Halsema Proposal also criticises the view that legal certainty would be jeopardised by lifting the bar in section 120, as the review of international norms has not led to any great legal uncertainty.[140] Additionally it is argued that the role of the judiciary would be complimentary to that of the legislature in determining the constitutionality of acts of parliament, instead of simply sidelining legislative wisdom in evaluating such pieces of legislation.[141] The aim of the Proposal is thus to revitalise the Constitution by allowing the voice of the judiciary to be heard more than before, while not wanting to usurp the powers of the legislature.

The old-fashioned view of the separation of powers is also scuttled in the Proposal, as it finds that parliament has seen its role reduced over the years by the increase of delegated legislation.[142] This observation erodes the view that acts of parliament are examples of near pure democratic legitimacy, which an unelected judiciary may not refuse to follow. Modern reality has shifted the focus of the debate to ensuring the better protection of the individual, something which calls for a greater engagement of the judiciary, rather than simply relying on dusty old arguments.

53 But what are the Proposal's chances of success? In order to amend the Constitution, something which must happen in order to change section 120, a bill must pass two readings in parliament.[143] The first reading requires that each of the two houses of parliament adopts a bill with a

---

[137]*Parliamentary Proceedings II*, 2002–2003, 28, 331, no. 9, at 11.

[138]W.J. Witteveen, *Evenwicht der machten* (Zwolle: Tjeenk Willink, 1991), at 85–86.

[139]Cf. C.L.G.F.H. Albers and R.J.N. Schlössel, "Terrorismebestrijding: Het bestuursrecht aan zet, de rechtsstaat in gevaar?", *Nederlands Juristenblad* 2526 (2006).

[140]*Parliamentary Proceedings II*, 2002–2003, 28, 331, no. 9, at 15.

[141]Ibid., at 14.

[142]Ibid., at 12–15.

[143]S. 137 of the Constitution.

simple majority, after which a general election must take place before
the bill may be read for a second time. During its second reading a bill
becomes a constitutional amendment if it is passed by a two-thirds majority in both houses. At present, both legislative houses have adopted the
Halsema Proposal, although it met with quite some scepticism along the
way.[144] Especially the Senate has been very critical of the Proposal and it
passed its first reading by a single vote, a state of affairs that raises doubts
as to its ultimate success in the second reading.[145] The Senate's reluctance
is not so much rooted in the form that judicial review of the Constitution
has to take, but is more fundamentally aimed at the very question of even
allowing binding constitutional review by the judiciary. For instance, during the bill's first reading most political parties in the chamber expressed
doubts as to the implications of the bill for the traditional conception of
democracy and the separation of powers. The Socialist Party was particularly wary of allowing the bench to review rules of general application that
had come about on the basis of a democratic majority, as it felt this not
to be the duty of the courts – these only had to apply the rules to individual cases.[146] More generally though, the Halsema Proposal would have
to overcome something of an ingrained unwillingness in the Netherlands to
tamper with the country's constitutional arrangements, as reform proposals
usually have a low rate of success.[147] This reluctance is fuelled by the fact
that the Halsema Proposal was tabled by the opposition and failed to garner
the government's full support during its first reading in the Senate.

54   In summary, the Netherlands is faced with an interesting situation. It
probably has one of the most internationalised constitutions in the world in
allowing even the binding review of international norms by national judges.
At the same time it defends a nineteenth century conception of the separation of powers when it comes to barring the judiciary from reviewing acts
of parliament against the Constitution. This situation will be considered in
later chapters in comparing the country's constitutional dispensation with
that of the United Kingdom and South Africa.

---

[144]*Parliamentary Proceedings II*, 2003–2004, 28, 331, no. 11.

[145]*Parliamentary Proceedings I*, 2004–2005, 28, 331, B, C.

[146]Ibid., at B, 4–5. The party eventually voted in favour of the bill, which shows the
unpredictability of the debate.

[147]On the low rate of success of constitutional amendments, *see* Maurice Adams and
Gerhard van der Schyff, "Constitutional Review by the Judiciary in the Netherlands: A
Matter of Politics, Democracy or Compensating Strategy?", 66 *Zeitschrift für ausländisches öffentliches Recht und Völkerrecht* 399 (2006), at 405; M.M. Bense, "Aandacht voor
recente grondwetswijzigingen", *Regelmaat* 89 (2002).

2.4 South Africa

2.4.1 Parliamentary Sovereignty and Restricted Democracy

55 South Africa's tumultuous history is reflected in the fact that the country has had no fewer than five written constitutions since being forged out of British colonies and defeated Boer republics after the end of the Anglo-Boer War in 1902.[148] The country's place among the world's democracies is not something that came about gradually or peacefully, it is safe to say. Whereas recognition of the judiciary's role in reviewing legislation for compliance with fundamental rights is something that has developed gradually in the United Kingdom and the Netherlands, the same cannot be said of South Africa where radical change was not the result of a "natural" process of development, but rather that of an abrupt and decisive change regarding the place of the judiciary in the constitutional scheme of things.

56 The South African constitutional order has been characterised by two distinct phases in this respect. The first phase, which lasted from 1910 to 1994, saw the protection of fundamental rights left in the hands of the political process, while at the same time severely limiting the judiciary's constitutional role in controlling that process. The second phase on the other hand saw the social and legal order predicated on judicially enforced constitutional supremacy. This transformation of South African legal thought and practice from a colonial inheritance of the Westminster rule of law to a system that is best described as aspiring to the qualities of a democratic *rechtsstaat* deserves further attention.[149]

57 The origins of the decisive shift in the country's constitutional law must be traced to its first constitution, the South Africa Act of 1909 (the 1909 Constitution). This Constitution was largely the product of the all-white National Convention that was entrusted with charting a common destiny after the Anglo-Boer War for the two British Colonies – the Cape

---

[148]Cf. Rautenbach and Malherbe, *supra* note 22, at 15–22; Ziyad Motala and Cyril Ramaphosa, *Constitutional Law: Analysis and Cases* (Oxford: Oxford University Press, 2002), at 1–12; Iain Currie and Johan de Waal (eds.), *The New Constitutional and Administrative Law*, vol. I (Lansdowne: Juta, 2001), at 57–71.

[149]Francois Venter, "Aspects of the South African Constitution of 1996: An African Democratic and Social Federal *Rechtsstaat*", 57 *Zeitschrift für ausländisches öffentliches Recht und Völkerrecht* 51 (1997), emphasises the *rechtsstaat* paradigm. Martin Chanock, "A Post-Calvinist Catechism or a Post-Communist Manifesto? Intersecting Narratives in the South African Bill of Rights Debate", in Philip Alston (ed.), *Promoting Human Rights Through Bills of Rights: Comparative Perspectives* 392 (Oxford: Oxford University Press, 1999), at 397, speaks of a transition from the "rule of law" to a "bill of rights".

and Natal – and the two Boer Republics – the South African Republic and the Orange Free State. The 1909 Constitution created the Union of South Africa, with the four erstwhile territories each transformed into a province.[150] It was an overtly political document that focused almost exclusively on the creation of the state and its institutions to the exclusion of fundamental rights. A bill of rights was not included, nor were the courts entrusted with any explicit powers to review compliance with the Constitution – even though the majority of delegates to the National Convention were in favour of such powers being created.[151] The legislature created by the Constitution was a classic example of parliamentary sovereignty, bar the fact that it was subject to the authority of Westminster, as full independence was not achieved until 1931. People were considered to enjoy wide-ranging common law rights and freedoms, which were not committed to a bill of rights. These rights and freedoms could be exercised to the extent that they were not limited by parliament.[152]

This meant that the constitutional order was strongly based on the premise of democracy, people were free unless they were curtailed in their actions by the popular will as formalised and expressed by their elected representatives. In typical Diceyan fashion this was deemed acceptable as the electorate enjoyed the last word in calling their members of parliament to account for their conduct.[153] A heavy responsibility was indeed envisioned for the country's parliament and great faith placed in its democracy. However, the constitutional scheme faltered on one crucial point. The quality of the country's democracy was severely hampered by restrictions on the right to vote.

58 After the Anglo-Boer War, African communities expected the non-racial franchise, qualified in force in the Cape Colony, to be extended to all territories that were to become South Africa. This desire was especially fuelled in the light of the support and assistance given by many of them to the British during the conflict.[154] However, the 1909 Constitution proved to be a disappointment. Eligibility for election to the houses of parliament was restricted to whites only, while each new province retained its voting qualifications

---

[150]Leonard Monteath Thompson, *The Unification of South Africa: 1902–1910* (Oxford: Clarendon Press, 2nd ed., 1961); Martin Chanock, *Unconsummated Union: Britain, Rhodesia, and South Africa 1900–1945* (Manchester: Manchester University Press, 1977).

[151]Motala and Ramaphosa, *supra* note 148, at 2.

[152]E.g. Anthony S. Matthews, *Law, Order and Liberty in South Africa* (Berkeley: University of California Press, 1971), used the classic Westminster rule of paradigm to analyse South African public law.

[153]Dicey, *supra* note 34, at 73.

[154]Peter Warwick, *Black People and the South African War 1899–1902* (Cambridge: Cambridge University Press, 1983), at 181.

prior to its incorporation into the Union. This meant that the Cape Colony
retained its non-racial franchise which saw Africans and "coloureds" able
to be considered for the vote, whereas the other territories continued in
allowing only whites the right to vote. Importantly, this compromise saw
the non-racial voting qualifications in force in the Cape entrenched in section 35 of the Constitution. This was an interesting development, as the
Constitution in its entirety was not entrenched, apart from this provision
and section 137, which guaranteed the equal status of English and Dutch
as the two official languages. These provisions could only be amended by a
two-thirds majority in a joint sitting of both houses of parliament.

Entrenchment though was in effect little more than a political command,
as to all appearances the 1909 Constitution was an instrument that could
not be enforced by the judiciary. The legislature was left to decide how the
Constitution had to be implemented and respected.[155] In addition, even if
the document could be reviewed by the judiciary, it did not include fundamental rights, apart from perhaps the two provisions entrenching the right
to vote and the equal treatment of the official languages. The weak position
of the judiciary was, however, somewhat unexpectedly bolstered in relation
to the right to vote.

59   Moves were afoot to remove Africans in the Cape from the common
electoral roll, and a law to that effect was passed in 1936.[156] This piece
of legislation was adopted with the two-thirds majority required by the
Constitution.

As racial discrimination became more formalised in the form of
apartheid, an attempt was in the making to remove "coloured" voters from
the common electoral roll as well. Some legal opinion at the time supported
the view that the entrenched constitutional clauses no longer bore significance in the light of the Statute of Westminster of 1931.[157] The Statute,
being a product of the British parliament as its name suggests, provided
that colonial legislation could conflict with Imperial legislation, the 1909
Constitution being such a piece of Imperial legislation that could hence be
contradicted by the South African parliament.

Consequently, the bill foreseeing the indirect representation of
"coloured" voters was passed by ordinary means without paying attention to the special procedure dictated by entrenchment.[158] However, the
Appellate Division of the Supreme Court invalidated the act by finding that
the constitutionally prescribed procedure requiring a two-thirds majority

---

[155]Motala and Ramaphosa, *supra* note 148, at 2.

[156]Representation of Natives Act, no. 12 of 1939. Cf. John Dugard, *Human Rights and
the South African Legal Order* (New Jersey: Princeton University Press, 1978), at 29.

[157]Dugard, *supra* note 157, at 28–30.

[158]Separate Representation of Voters Act, no. 46 of 1951.

still had to be followed. A decision which exercised the leading legal minds of the day, such as dean Erwin Griswold of the Harvard Law School and Sir William Wade, as it seemed that the concept of parliamentary sovereignty might be redefined by exploring its limits.[159]

60 Far from allowing itself to be beaten, the National Party government reacted by creating the High Court of Parliament.[160] This body was composed of all members of parliament and had to decide the validity of legislation struck down by the courts. The act creating this body was also struck down by the Supreme Court however, by reason that the High Court of Parliament was merely parliament in disguise and that the entrenched constitutional provisions could not simply be brushed aside, as this would render them worthless.[161] The ruling party faced a dilemma, as it still did not possess the required two-thirds majority in order to pass its legislation in conformity with the Constitution.

Instead, it enlarged the Senate and the Appellate Division.[162] In doing so, the National Party handed itself the opportunity to increase the number of its supporters in both of these institutions, in effect packing these chambers. The result was that the South Africa Act Amendment Act was passed into law without hindrance.[163] The Act had "coloured" voters registered on a separate roll and the jurisdiction of the courts to review the constitutionality of acts of parliament was explicitly ousted.

61 Any doubt as to the nature of the 1909 Constitution was cleared up quite brutally in this way. The courts were not to dabble in constitutional issues, even if parliament decided to negate the Constitution. This state of affairs was carried through to the Constitution of the Republic Act of 1961, which replaced the 1909 Constitution and abolished the monarchy in favour of a republic. Section 59 of the 1961 Constitution provided unequivocally that:

(1) Parliament shall be the sovereign legislative authority in and over the Republic, and shall have full power to make laws for the peace, order and good government of the Republic.

(2) No court of law shall be competent to enquire into or to pronounce upon the validity of an Act passed by Parliament, other

---

[159]*Harris v. Minister of the Interior*, 1952 (2) SA 428 (A). Cf. Erwin N. Griswold, "The 'Coloured Vote Case' in South Africa", 65 *Harv. L. Rev.* 1361 (1952); the foreword by E.C.S. Wade to Dicey, *supra* note 34, at LVII–LXII.

[160]High Court of Parliament Act, no. 35 of 1952.

[161]*Minister of the Interior v. Harris*, 1952 (4) SA 769 (AD). Cf. Erwin N. Griswold, "The Demise of the High Court of Parliament in South Africa", 66 *Harv. L. Rev.* 864 (1953).

[162]Senate Act, no. 53 of 1955; Appellate Division Quorum Act, no. 27 of 1955.

[163]South Africa Act Amendment Act, no. 9 of 1956.

> than an Act which repeals or amends or purports to appeal the
> [entrenched language provisions].

Courts could conduct neither strong, nor weak review, as it was made clear
that they could not "enquire into" or "pronounce upon" the validity of laws,
and even if they could they had no bill of rights which to apply. The 1961
Constitution left no uncertainty as to the role of the courts, they had to
interpret and obey the law and not question it. Judicial boldness in attempt-
ing to reign in parliament had failed, as the National Party got its way in
steering the country's political and constitutional future as it saw fit. The
scene was now set, more so than ever before, for the government to further
its apartheid policies of racial segregation in all spheres of life.

62 In this regard, the concept of self-governing territories, or homelands, for the African population was brought to life. The National States
Citizenship Act assigned citizenship of the different homelands, for internal purposes, to the African population on an ethnic basis.[164] This was
carried through irrespective of the fact whether people were born or resided
in the territory assigned to them. Furthermore, once "independence" had
been granted to such a territory by the parliament of South Africa, the
people associated with that specific territory were stripped of their South
African nationality. This was something that happened to millions of people. Separate political institutions were also formed for the "coloured" and
Indian communities respectively.[165] Yet these institutions enjoyed little
powers, and even less legitimacy, and were abolished again by 1984.

Despite all its failures and irrespective of internal and external opposition to the discriminatory and oppressive policies of apartheid, the
government's response was simply to implement racial segregation regardless. The government tightened its grip on the country by suppressing
dissent, such as disallowing numerous political parties and rallies, as well
as banishing and jailing opponents.[166] However, instability increased as
political opposition intensified, especially after the Soweto Riots of 1976.

63 The government sought to broaden the social base of its institutions
in order to shore up support and consolidate its power by introducing limited reform in the shape of yet a new constitution, the Republic
of South Africa Constitution Act of 1983.[167] The main feature of the
1983 Constitution, and the reason behind its adoption, was to extend the

---

[164]National States Citizenship Act, no. 26 of 1970.

[165]Coloured Persons Representative Council Act, no. 49 of 1964; South African Indian
Council Act, no. 31 of 1968.

[166]Cf. Dugard, *supra* note 157, at 53–202.

[167]Republic of South Africa Constitution Act, no. 110 of 1983.

franchise to the "coloured" and Indian communities for elections to a tri-cameral parliament.[168] Each chamber of parliament was designated to the white, "coloured" and Indian population groups respectively, in order to allow them jurisdiction over their own affairs. Actual power was retained, nonetheless, by the white House of Assembly, which continued to dominate the political landscape. Moreover, the 1983 Constitution retained the principle of parliamentary sovereignty, and again did not contain a bill of rights. The bar on judicial review as it was formulated in the 1961 Constitution was qualified though by allowing the courts to test whether an act of parliament had been adopted in accordance with the prescribed legislative procedure. In other words, the coming about of an act of parliament could be checked, but not its substance. The idea was not to depart from parliamentary sovereignty as constitutional law's guiding light, but really to enable the courts to better recognise an enactment formally in order to give full effect to the sovereign will its content expressed.

64   The fact remained though that the 1983 Constitution together with some limited reforms could not alter, nor remedy the fundamental injustices that characterised South African society. As violent opposition became virtually uncontrollable in the 1980s, so did the proclamation of states of emergency increase. Thirty years of "low-level" violence, known as the struggle, between the liberation movements and the government had resulted in a costly stalemate, which saw large parts of South Africa hovering on the brink of anarchy. Apartheid had become too costly to maintain and could not be saved by cosmetic changes. Moreover, reform-minded leaders came increasingly to prominence in government, people who realised that white minority domination was a sinking ship without hope of salvage.

The dispensation faced a legitimacy crisis that could only be addressed by means of fundamental constitutional change. The *uhuru*, the wind of change over Africa of which then British prime minister Harold MacMillan had spoken of so many years before, could be felt with increasing intensity in South Africa.[169] The country was clearly in dire need of a new constitutional future.

---

[168]Heinz Klug, "Historical Background", in Matthew Chaskalson, Janet Kentridge, Jonathan Klaaren, Gilbert Marcus, Derek Spitz and Stuart Woolman (eds.), *Constitutional Law of South Africa* 2/10 (Kenwyn: Juta, Revision Service 5, 1999).

[169]Harold MacMillan delivered his famed "Wind of Change" speech to the South African parliament in Cape Town on 3 February 1960. In it, he accepted that the era of colonialism in Africa was coming to an end with the increase of national consciousness among the continent's peoples. This meant that apartheid was a doomed policy, as it negated the aspirations of the country's African population, something which the *Zeitgeist* would not tolerate forever.

2.4.2 Constitutional Supremacy and Full Democracy

65 The push towards full democratisation gained particular momentum with the release in 1990 of Nelson Mandela and the unbanning of the liberation movements, together with calls for multiparty negotiations.[170] There seemed to be consensus that democracy would prove the answer to the ills of the past, but deciding how this ideal had to be given flesh proved quite elusive.

The Convention for a Democratic South Africa (Codesa) was convened in 1991 and again in 1992 to address this very problem.[171] The forum was composed of most political organisations and other interest groups, assisted by working groups that had to ponder general constitutional principles and devise the process of writing a new constitution. It soon transpired that deep differences existed in relation to issues such as the form of the state, the extent of government interest in the economy, the protection of private property and political power sharing between the majority and minority.

66 Although general agreement was reached on the fact that a democratically-elected constituent assembly had to draft a new constitution, and that such a body would act as an interim parliament, positions diverged on the details of the process. Particular division existed as to how a new constitution had to reflect power relations in the country. The African National Congress (ANC), the largest liberation movement, insisted on fewer prior constraints on a democratically-elected assembly in drafting a constitution than the National Party government and smaller parties, who pleaded quite the opposite. Minority stakeholders were fearful that if a democratically-elected body were to be dealt a free hand, the constitution to be written would chiefly reflect the views of the victors, and not also of those who came second.[172] Although democracy was the answer according to all parties concerned, the difficulty in unlocking the promise it held for the country's future eventually led to Codesa's collapse.

---

[170]Willem de Klerk, "The Process of Political Negotiation: 1990–1993", in Bertus de Villiers (ed.), *Birth of a Constitution* 4 (Kenwyn: Juta, 1994).

[171]Motala and Ramaphosa, *supra* note 148, at 5–9; George Devenish, "The Interim Constitution in the Making", 60 *Tydskrif vir Hedendaagse Romeins-Hollandse Reg* 612 (1997).

[172]The negotiations faltered on the required majority with which the new constitution had to be adopted by an elected constitution-making body. The ANC supported a threshold of 70% for ordinary constitutional provisions and 75% for the bill of rights, while the National Party government insisted on 75% for the entire text. Matters were also complicated by the fact that the Inkatha Freedom Party went so far as to reject an elected constitution-making body altogether. Instead, it suggested Codesa as the appropriate forum to draft a consensus-based constitution, which would then have to be approved by referendum. For an overview, *see* Heinz Klug, "Participating in the Design: Constitution-making in South Africa", 3 *Rev. Const. Stud.* 18 (1996), at 31–39.

This state of affairs bred more political violence and instability. Intense national and international pressure came to bear on the main players to resume negotiation. Something they did in the form of the Multi-Party Negotiation Process, which reached a carefully negotiated political settlement.[173] This settlement resulted in the enactment by the tri-cameral parliament in 1993 of a comprehensive package of legislation that grounded and guided the transition of South Africa to a non-racial and multiparty democracy.

67   The most noteworthy piece of legislation included in the package was without doubt the historic Constitution of the Republic of South Africa Act of 1993 (the 1993 Constitution).[174] This document came to be referred to as the "interim" Constitution, as it had to lay the democratic groundwork necessary for the negotiation and adoption of the "final" Constitution. Its purpose was brought to life by the Preamble, which stated that:

> [T]here is a need to create a new order in which all South Africans will be entitled to a common South African citizenship in a sovereign and democratic constitutional state in which there is equality between men and women and people of all races so that all citizens shall be able to enjoy and exercise their fundamental rights and freedoms.

An explicit end was made to the doctrine of parliamentary sovereignty which had for so long been abused, and to this end section 4 decreed that the:

> Constitution shall be the supreme law of the Republic and any law or act inconsistent with its provisions shall (. . .) be of no force and effect to the extent of its inconsistency.

Giving teeth to this promise was the adoption, for the first time, of a justiciable bill of rights and the creation of a Constitutional Court as its ultimate guardian.[175]

68   The judiciary, powered by the new Constitutional Court, saw its role in society changed from a slavish follower of the letter of the law to a champion of its emerging human rights culture, as the 1993 Constitution was the

---

[173]Motala and Ramaphosa, *supra* note 148, at 9-12.

[174]Constitution of the Republic of South Africa Act, no. 200 of 1993. Cf. Lourens du Plessis and Hugh Corder, *Understanding South Africa's Transitional Bill of Rights* (Kenwyn: Juta, 1994); A.J. Steenkamp, "The South African Constitution of 1993 and the Bill of Rights: An Evaluation in Light of International Human Rights Norms", 17 *Hum. Rights Quart.* 101 (1995).

[175]Interestingly, the inclusion of fundamental rights stood in stark contrast to previous views held by many whites that recognising inalienable rights contradicted religion and was therefore unacceptable. Cf. Johannes A. van der Ven, Jaco S. Dreyer and Hendrik J.C. Pieterse, *Is There a God of Human Rights? The Complex Relationship between Human Rights and Religion: A South African Case* (Leiden: BRILL, 2004), at 307 et seq.

first in South Africa to assign an important role to the judiciary in constitutional affairs.[176] So important was the judiciary's new role that it could
overrule the final Constitution adopted by the Constitutional Assembly, if
the document did not respect a number of basic "Constitutional Principles"
which were contained in the interim Constitution. It was a radical and
novel invention to mandate the Constitutional Court to certify whether
the final Constitution was compatible with the 34 Constitutional Principles
contained in Schedule 4 of the 1993 Constitution.[177] These Constitutional
Principles, known as the "solemn pact", represented the core democratic
and constitutional standards that the final Constitution had to reflect in
order to become law. The principles centred on the establishment of a
democracy, which had to be characterised by equality and fundamental
rights and based on the separation of powers under the umbrella of a
supreme constitution. One of the reasons for this innovation was obviously
to put the white minority at ease that a new order in which their dominance was no longer guaranteed would be sympathetic to their interests
and rights.

69   The crowning glory of the interim Constitution was undoubtedly the
extension of the franchise to all South Africans regardless of their race.[178]
This meant that a new bicameral parliament, both houses of which would
comprise the Constitutional Assembly, could proceed with the important
duty of drafting and adopting the final Constitution. Peaceful elections in
1994 saw the composition of a non-racial interim parliament with the ANC
as victor and the start of the process that led to the final Constitution.[179]

---

[176]E.g. in *S. v. Makwanyane, supra* note 32, at par. 9, it was made clear that the
approach of the Constitutional Court had to be "generous" and "purposive" in giving
"expression to the underlying values of the Constitution". For a critique of the courts
traditional approach to textual interpretation, see Du Plessis and Corder, *supra* note
174, at 62–72, and on the way forward at 72–83; Christo Botha, *Statutory Interpretation*
(Cape Town: Juta, 4th ed., 2005), at 118–128.

[177]Cf. Francois Venter, "Requirements for a New Constitutional Text: The Imperatives
of the Constitutional Principles", 112 *S. Afr. L. J.* 32 (1995).

[178]The Constitutional Court made this point quite forcefully in *New National Party of
SA v. Government of the RSA*, 1999 (5) BCLR 489 (CC), 1999 (3) SA 191 (CC), at par.
120: "Many injustices of the past flowed directly from the denial of the right to vote
on the basis of race to the majority of South Africans. The denial of the right to vote
entrenched political power in the hands of white South Africans. That power was used
systematically to further the interest of white South Africans and to disadvantage black
South Africans. As South Africans, therefore, we should be aware of the power of the
franchise, and the importance of its universality."

[179]The transition also included a power-sharing arrangement that allowed smaller parties representation in the executive if they polled enough votes. Secs. 84, 88 of the
interim Constitution of South Africa (1993).

The drafting of the final Constitution by the Assembly proceeded in more ideal circumstances than the climate which characterised the political negotiations and drafting of the interim Constitution. This is because the proportionally elected non-racial parliament reflected for the first time the actual levels of support enjoyed by the political actors in the country, which was reflected in the composition of the Constitutional Assembly. The leadership of the Assembly bridged the divide between the ANC and the National Party by appointing a member of the former as its chair and selecting his deputy from the latter's ranks. In a country where governance based on legitimacy had been superseded by governance based on force for so long, much needed popular legitimacy was thus provided to the public institutions entrusted with constructing the new democracy and its final Constitution.[180] The Constitutional Assembly could now apply itself to the task at hand, namely that of agreeing on a final Constitution under the imperative of the Constitutional Principles without violence threatening to engulf the country. A constitutional text was adopted in 1996, after which it was sent to the Constitutional Court in order to be certified.

70   The certification function of the Constitutional Court was clearly without precedent.[181] Wisely, the Constitutional Court decided to opt for a purposive interpretive approach in order to avoid a rigid and textual examination in deciding whether the benchmarks of the Constitutional Principles were satisfied.[182] By choosing a contextual approach, the judges emphasised the crucial fact that the new dispensation had to be value-driven and not a mechanical slave to positivism – as had so often been the case in the past.

Certification, however, was denied due to ten shortcomings identified in the text presented to the Court.[183] These defects related to, among other issues, guaranteeing constitutional supremacy, the entrenchment of the bill of rights and the amendment of the Constitution. No stone was left unturned by the bench in ensuring that the resultant product would be a fully entrenched and justiciable constitution. The Constitutional Assembly responded by renegotiating and redrafting the affected parts of its text, after

---

[180]On public participation and the legitimacy it brought to the drafting of the new Constitution, *see* Klug, *supra* note 172, at 56–57.

[181]*Certification of the Constitution of the Republic of South Africa, 1996*, 1996 (10) BCLR 1253 (CC), 1996 (4) SA 744 (CC). Jeremy Sarkin, "The Drafting of South Africa's Final Constitution from a Human Rights Perspective", 47 *Am. J. Comp. L.* 67 (1999), at 72–77; Hirschl, *supra* note 6, at 184–187.

[182]*Certification of the Constitution of the Republic of South Africa, 1996*, *supra* note 181, at paras. 34, 36, 38.

[183]Ibid., at par. 482.

which it was certified by the Constitutional Court as meeting the requirements of the Principles.[184] The importance of the country's constitutional
rebirth was not lost on the Court, which proudly spoke of a "cataclysm"
having been avoided by negotiating a largely peaceful transition from a
"rigidly controlled minority regime" to a "wholly democratic constitutional
dispensation".[185]

71 South Africa's "final" Constitution had been adopted – an entrenched
document that ensured *constitutional supremacy and full democracy*,
in contrast to an old constitutional order predicated on *parliamentary
sovereignty and restricted democracy*.[186] A "negotiated revolution" had
taken place with the founding of a new dispensation predicated on the
values of human dignity, the achievement of equality and the general
advancement of human rights. Central to this new order is the Constitution,
a document which is not simply a set of guidelines, which may or may
not be followed by the political process, but an imperative document that
calls on the judiciary to settle constitutional disputes. Arthur Chaskalson,
the erstwhile President of the Court, captured the desired relationship
between the courts, the will of the people and the Constitution quite
succinctly:

> Public opinion may have some relevance to the enquiry (...), but in itself, it is no
> substitute for the duty vested in the Courts to interpret the Constitution and to
> uphold its provisions without fear or favour. If public opinion were to be decisive
> there would be no need for constitutional adjudication. The protection of rights
> could then be left to Parliament, which has a mandate from the public, and is
> answerable to the public for the way its mandate is exercised, but this would return
> to parliamentary sovereignty, and a retreat from the new legal order established
> by the 1993 Constitution.[187]

The Constitutional Court has risen to this challenge by actively trying to
determine the meaning of the Constitution in a host of matters ranging

---

[184]*Certification of the Amended Text of the Constitution of the Republic of South Africa,
1996,* 1997 (1) BCLR 1 (CC), 1997 (2) SA 97 (CC).

[185]*Certification of the Constitution of the Republic of South Africa, 1996, supra* note
181, at par. 10.

[186]Alfred Cockrell, "The South African Bill of Rights and the 'Duck/Rabbit'", 60 *Mod.
L. Rev.* 513 (1997); Peter N. Bouckaert, "The Negotiated Revolution: South Africa's
Transition to Multiracial Democracy", 33 *Stanford J. Int. L.* 375 (1997); Richard J.
Goldstone, "The South African Bill of Rights", 32 *Texas Int. L. J.* 1451 (1997); Rassie
Malherbe, "The South African Constitution", 55 *Zeitschrift für öffentliches Recht* 61
(2000).

[187]*S. v. Makwanyane, supra* note 32, at par. 88. Cf. Max du Plessis, "Between Apology
and Utopia: The Constitutional Court and Public Opinion", 18 *S. Afr. J. Hum. Rights* 1
(2002).

from the abolishment of the death penalty, [188] the enforcement of socio-economic rights[189] to the recognition of same-sex marriage.[190]

72 The judicial review of legislation as one of the cornerstones of the new order has come to reflect a principled preference for its perceived benefits over and above the idea that the political process was by itself the answer in having rights permeate society. On the other hand, the introduction of judicial review has also served as a political device to address the fears of the white minority that they might be sidelined by a new parliament which they could no longer dominate numerically.[191] This is because expanding the vote has meant changing the composition of political organs, which could in turn drown out the voice of the previously advantaged classes. Combined, these two reasons imply that judicial review was chosen not only because it presented a new substantive model for the country's future, but also because it served as a bridge to securing that new future.[192]

2.5 Identifying Trends

73 As the three countries studied illustrate, most modern societies strive to be democratic societies. Societies that realise the ideal of government of the people, by the people and for the people, to use the words of Abraham Lincoln's Gettysburg address of 1863. For instance, the culmination in the 1990s of the power struggle in South Africa had the extension of universal suffrage to the majority of the population at its base, an ideal that had long since been achieved in the United Kingdom and the Netherlands. In the United Kingdom the vehicle of parliamentary sovereignty links the people to government by allowing them a say through the ballot box, something which is also pursued in the Netherlands through the country's tradition of consensus democracy. Nonetheless, although there is agreement between the three countries on the need for the legislative branch to be democratically accountable, this does not mean that because of its accountability to the electorate this branch is to be isolated from other forms of control.

74 When the constitutional orders of the United Kingdom, the Netherlands and South Africa are compared, a distinctive trend in judicial review can be identified. All three countries have experienced a greater involvement

---

[188]*S. v. Makwanyane, supra* note 32.

[189]*Government of the RSA v. Grootboom*, 2000 (11) BCLR 1169 (CC), 2001 (1) SA 46 (CC).

[190]*Minister of Home Affairs v. Fourie; Lesbian and Gay Equality Project v. Minister of Home Affairs* (CC), *supra* note 25, at par. 114.

[191]Hirschl, *supra* note 6, at 92–93, 216–218.

[192]Ginsburg, *supra* note 5, at 55.

of the judiciary in reviewing the quality of legislation, although their exact approaches differ to varying degrees. The United Kingdom has experienced the careful involvement of the judiciary in deciding whether legislation is compatible with the fundamental rights norms laid down in the HRA without jeopardising parliamentary sovereignty in the process. Caution has also been the byword in the Netherlands where testing legislation against international norms has come to be accepted, although the question as to whether acts of parliament are to be constitutionally reviewed continues to be a contentious topic. South Africa, conversely, had a radical and far-reaching constitutional epiphany in allowing the judiciary to review the constitutionality of legislation. The country changed from a system that avoided any form of judicial review to one in which the judiciary has been greatly empowered to review and strike down legislation when it does not accord with the Constitution.

75 Considered against this background, there is no denying that the notion of bipolar constitutionalism is becoming all the more current. Judiciaries, whether they find themselves in established or young consolidating parliamentary democracies, are increasingly called upon to exercise control over the legislature. This brings to mind and affirms the questions posed in the introductory chapter, namely is this marked shift to judicial power to be desired, and what contours are there to be discerned in structuring judicial review? These questions will be addressed in the next chapters by drawing on what has thus far been learned of judicial review in each of the three countries.

Chapter 3
Judicial Review and Democracy

3.1 Counter-Majoritarianism

76 The fact that the United Kingdom, the Netherlands and South Africa have begun to interpret and apply the separation of powers in a way that allows the judiciary to check the exercise of legislative power, tells us very little about the justification of this development. A legal construction such as the judicial review of legislation needs to be justified if it is to enjoy any legitimacy. However, it is probably safe to say that justifying judicial review is a particularly vexing question that is unlikely ever to result in political or academic consensus. One of the main reasons for this is such review's perceived inconsistency with popular democracy.[193] Why are unelected judges to be allowed to test the constitutionality of laws passed by democratically-elected parliamentarians? In essence, should the will of majoritarian decision-making models be questioned or even overturned by models that do not ascribe to the same principle? Alexander Bickel famously referred to this as the "counter-majoritarian difficulty".[194]

77 Explaining the promise of majoritarian decision-making Aristotle argued in its defence against aristocratic governance that:

> [T]he principle that the multitude ought to be supreme rather than the few is one that is maintained, and, though not free from difficulty, yet seems to contain an element of truth. For the many, of whom each individual is but an ordinary person, when they meet together may very likely be better than the few good, if regarded not individually but collectively (...).[195]

---

[193]Lord Devlin, "Judges and Lawmakers", 39 *Mod. L. Rev.* 1 (1976), at 10.

[194]Alexander M. Bickel, *The Least Dangerous Branch: The Supreme Court at the Bar of Politics* (Indianapolis: Bobbs-Merrill, 1962); Barry Feldman, "The Birth of an Academic Obsession: The History of the Countermajoritarian Difficulty, Part Five", 112 *Yale L. J.* 153 (2002).

[195]*Politica*, Book III, Chap. 11, at 128b.

Much later, and in the context of judicial review, the well-known American judge Learned Hand, although not an opponent of judicial review, expressed his unease with it as follows:

> For myself it would be most irksome to be ruled by a bevy of Platonic Guardians, even if I knew how to choose them, which I assuredly do not. If they were in charge, I would miss the stimulus of living in a society where I have, at least theoretically, some part in the direction of public affairs. Of course I know how illusory would be the belief that my vote determined anything; but nevertheless when I go to the polls I have the satisfaction in the sense that we are all engaged in a common venture.[196]

78 This somewhat vague statement on the part of Learned Hand is open to more than one interpretation, yet the crux of his argument seems to be twofold.[197] To start with, he seems to believe that, as the influence exercised by the electorate on court decisions in constitutional matters will always be minimal, there should likewise be little scope for such decisions. He therefore takes the view that people are presented with a greater possibility or chance of participating in matters that concern them through democratic rather than judicial means. Learned Hand also appears to be claiming that it is unacceptable for people to be governed by a body which has not been elected by them. As a consequence, the personal democratic legitimacy of judges is much less direct than that of parliamentarians. In Learned Hand's comment, two sides of the democratic coin, namely election and accountability, come together. According to this view, the most essential aspect of a democracy is that an elected assembly respects the will of the majority of the people, and as a consequence decisions so arrived at should not simply be set aside by the judiciary. When the three systems under study were surveyed, it became clear that similar arguments stressing the virtue of majoritarian democracy have often been put to use against the cause of judicial review in the United Kingdom and the Netherlands.[198]

79 Although since the Second World War most systems have opted for judicial review of legislation in some shape or another, its democratic credentials still remain a problem for some.[199] A recent, and probably best-known, critic of allowing the judiciary to strike down acts of parliament has

---

[196]Learned Hand, *The Bill of Rights: The Oliver Wendell Holmes Lectures* (Cambridge, MA: Harvard University Press, 1958), at 73–74.

[197]For a similar treatment, *see* Adams and Van der Schyff, *supra* note 147, at 405–406.

[198]*See* §§ 24, 28, 53.

[199]Feldman, *supra* note 194, at 155, captures it quite clearly: "Before, the central obsession was the inconsistency between judicial review and democracy. Now, it is the inconsistency between judicial review and democracy." *Consider* also Lord Devlin, *supra* note 193, at 16, who holds that: "It is a great temptation to cast the judiciary as an élite which will bypass the traffic-laden ways of the democratic process. But it would only apparently be a bypass. In truth it would be a road that would never rejoin the highway but would lead inevitably, however long and winding the path, to the totalitarian state."

been the philosopher Jeremy Waldron.[200] He argues that well-functioning democracies based on universal suffrage and a commitment to individual and minority rights do not need strong review by the courts.[201] Waldron criticises the idea that rights can be treated as a given on which everyone agrees:

> It is puzzling that some philosophers and jurists treat rights as though they were somehow beyond disagreement, as though they could be dealt with on a different plane – on the solemn plane of constitutional principle far above the hurly-burly of legislatures and political controversy and disreputable procedures like voting.[202]

Rights-based issues such as enforcing affirmative action, legalising or criminalising abortion or drug use and the limits of religious expression and free speech are all matters on which reasonable people may and do disagree.[203] In solving these differences we are faced by the question as to what "would be a just and moral, or at any rate appropriate solution".[204] For Waldron this is decided on clear jurisdictional grounds by opting for either the legislative route or the judicial route, but not both. In choosing between these two jurisdictions he comes out very strongly in support of the legislature:

> The appeal of majority-decision is that it not only solves the difficulty that [general disagreement] generates, but it does so in a respectful spirit (…).[205]

Therefore, fundamental differences in society about the translation of rights to legislation are to be settled by majoritarian means and not by allowing the judiciary to overturn legislative wisdom.

80   Jeremy Waldron's views seemingly come very close to advocating parliamentary sovereignty in the classic Westminster mould where parliament can make any law it so wishes and to what Tim Koopmans has called the "parliamentary model" of rights protection.[206] Such views would mean that the South African courts would have to be stripped of their far-reaching powers, thereby ignoring the carefully negotiated settlement reached in the country. The Constitutional Court, which has become one of the country's cornerstones, would have to be abolished as well. Moreover, the Halsema Proposal in the Netherlands which is aimed at allowing binding judicial review of selected rights in the Constitution would have to be abandoned, as would any ideas to expand the British courts' newly acquired powers

---

[200]Waldron, *supra* note 7, at 1354.

[201]Ibid., at 1346, 1363–1367.

[202]Jeremy Waldron, *Law and Disagreement* (Oxford: Oxford University Press, 1999), at 12.

[203]Ibid., at 112–113.

[204]Ibid., at 118.

[205]Ibid. *See also* Jeremy Waldron, "Judges as Moral Reasoners", 7 *Int. J. Const. L.*2 (2009).

[206]Koopmans, *supra* note 6, at 15–20.

under the HRA. Carried to its logical conclusion, Waldron's majoritarianism may even come to question the entrenchment of rights as something that undermines democratic legitimacy by expressing mistrust in the wisdom of future elected legislators.[207] This is something which Richard H. Fallon has rightly criticised by arguing that rights such as free speech and the franchise actually shore up democratic legitimacy and are therefore often justifiably entrenched.[208]

81 Jeremy Waldron only aims his attack against the strong review of legislation by focusing on courts overturning legislation, while remaining silent about the host of options presented by models of weak review.[209] However, this distinction is somewhat immaterial for our current enquiry. This is because the distinction relates to fixing the scope of judicial review. In other words, what sort of judicial review is to be decided on?[210] Yet, the core question whether it is justified in the first place for the judiciary to question legislative wisdom remains the same, irrespective of whether a system opts for strong or weak judicial review. Put differently, can the positive picture presented by the apologists of majoritarianism be accepted, or should the shift to counter-majoritarianism be welcomed? On another point, the distinction between strong and weak review is also less valid when one considers that such a bright line is often difficult to draw. These labels cannot be viewed as binary alternatives, but should instead be understood as stations along a range of possibilities when it comes to characterising judicial review more closely.[211]

---

[207]Waldron, *supra* note 202, at 221–222: "To embody a right in an entrenched constitutional document is to adopt a certain attitude towards one's fellow citizens. That attitude is best summed up as a combination of self-assurance and mistrust: self-assurance in the proponent's conviction that what he is putting forward really *is* a matter of fundamental right and that he has captured it adequately in the particular formulation he is propounding; and mistrust, implicit in his view that any alternative conception that might be concocted by elected legislators next year or in ten years' time is so likely to be wrong-headed or ill-motivated that *his own* formulation is to be elevated immediately beyond the reach of ordinary legislative revision." Although later he expressly made no assumption, but left open the question, whether a society that is committed to rights and has adopted "an official written bill or declaration of rights" ought to entrench it, or not. *See* Waldron, *supra* note 7, at 1365.

[208]Fallon, *supra* note 7, at 1724.

[209]Waldron, *supra* note 7, at 1353–1355.

[210]This topic will be addressed in later chapters.

[211]Fallon, *supra* note 7, at 1733–1734; David Dyzenhaus, "Are Legislatures Good at Morality? Or Better at it Than the Courts?", 7 *Int. J. Const. L.* 46 (2009), at 48.

3.2 Democratic Participation

82 The problem with the thought of Learned Hand and likeminded thinkers, is that it rests on a narrow and rather outdated conception of democracy. For Learned Hand sees greater possibilities of citizen participation through elections than through judicial means. But, this is simply no longer a reality, if ever it was. Access to the courts is often far easier for people than access to political bodies.[212] For example, section 38 of the South African Bill of Rights allows a wide variety of persons to approach a competent court to seek relief if they allege that one of their rights has been infringed:

(a) anyone acting in their own interest;
(b) anyone acting on behalf of another person who cannot act in their own name;
(c) anyone acting as a member of, or in the interest of, a group or class of persons;
(d) anyone acting in the public interest; and
(e) an association acting in the interest of its members.

This stands in stark contrast with the right to vote, which can only be exercised every few years. Even though universal suffrage eventually arrived in South Africa, one could also argue that the long and complete exclusion of the majority from any real participation in the country's affairs warranted radical measures to ensure their active participation in the future, instead of simply relying on the franchise.

83 Arguably the emphasis, or even overemphasis, on electoral participation in the "old" democracies of the United Kingdom and the Netherlands has sidelined other methods of allowing people to unlock the possibilities that fundamental rights bring. Although important, electoral democracy became a mantra that promised more than it could always deliver. One only has to consider the remarks by the Supreme Court of the Netherlands, made in 1989, that people's rights were not adequately protected in the existing constitutional constellation.[213] This is quite revealing, given that the remarks were critical of a system that restricts constitutional review of acts of parliament in favour of an emphasis on electoral democracy.

84 Moreover, political bodies only allow the participation of those with clear political rights, something which is not a prerequisite for seizing courts, thereby also extending direct protection to non-citizens. And there

---

[212]Mauro Cappelletti, *The Judicial Process in Comparative Perspective* (Oxford: Clarendon Press, 1989), at 46; Mauro Cappelletti, "Judicial Review of the Constitutionality of State Action: Its Expansion and Legitimacy", *J. S. Afr. L.* 256 (1992).
[213]*Harmonisation Act* judgment, *supra* note 105, at par. 3.4. *Compare* also the views expressed in the Dutch Senate, that the answer in enhancing the protection of people's rights, lies not in judicial review, but in more democracy. *Parliamentary Proceedings I*, 2004–2005, 28 331, B, at 7.

are of course also the advantages that judicial fora present in allowing near permanent and structural minorities to be heard, who would otherwise have to rely on the altruism of political majorities in staking their claims.[214] Instead, they can now have their day not only in parliament, but also and possibly more effectively in court. This is particularly relevant in South Africa where the voice of smaller groupings may be drowned out by the near total dominance of one political party, and where the Constitutional Court has committed itself not to allow matters of principle to be eroded by public opinion.[215] Similarly, in the United Kingdom minorities can easily be sidelined by a political system that traditionally only favours two political parties due to its constituency voting. This becomes all the more clear given the fact that in the twentieth century most British governments were either Conservative or Labour, although these parties hardly ever attained an absolute majority of the votes cast.[216] While not creating obvious minorities in the Netherlands, the country's characteristically rich composition of parliament as far as the number and range of political parties is concerned, has not stopped the Supreme Court from suggesting that education laws unfairly violated students' legitimate interests in the *Harmonisation Act* case.[217] Political participation, however broad, is never an absolute guarantee that all groups' interests will be factored in as they should be.

85   The danger thus exists that by overemphasising majoritarianism it becomes an end in itself, democracy simply becomes the counting of heads and looses any real purpose of ensuring participation in allowing diverse voices to be heard. Similarly, Ronald Dworkin holds that democratic decision-making can only lay claim to legitimacy where all voters are regarded with equal worth by their peers.[218] Participation must be grounded in political equality in that people must have their worth recognised by others, notably the majority of the day. Otherwise prejudice might win the day and lead to people's rights being abused, which in turn

---

[214]Cf. Lever, *supra* note 7, at 290–293, who argues that even where people generally care about the rights of others, such rights can still be harmed by legislation.

[215]*See* § 71 where reference was made to *S. v. Makwanyane, supra* note 32, at par. 88. In South Africa the ruling African National Congress has seen its comfortable majorities increased in nearly every general election since coming to power in 1994.

[216]E.g. in the 2001 general election the Labour Party secured 62.5% of the seats, although it could only count on 41% of the votes. While in the 1983 general election, a share of 27.6% of the votes meant 209 seats for Labour, whereas 25.4% of the votes meant a mere 23 seats for the Alliance of Liberals and Social Democrats. Cf. Feldman, *supra* note 37, at 101, 231; Parpworth, *supra* note 31, at 120–122; David Denver, *Elections and Voters in Britain* (Basingstoke: Palgrave Macmillan, 2003).

[217]*Harmonisation Act* judgment, *supra* note 105, at par. 3.1.

[218]Ronald Dworkin, *Freedom's Law: A Moral Reading of the American Constitution* (Cambridge, MA: Harvard University Press, 1996), at 132.

will lead to people losing faith in democracy itself. In achieving such equality, so Dworkin argues, democracy by no means insists that judges should not have the power to exercise judicial review.[219] In other words, democracy is not by definition repugnant to the idea of judicial review, as review can enhance the legitimacy of and participation in a country's democracy. Far then from obstructing meaningful political participation, judicial review can actually bolster the participation of everyone in a democracy by guaranteeing their equal worth irrespective of a majority's leanings. Democracy, as Baroness Hale stated in *Ghaidan v. Godin-Mendoza*, "values everyone equally even if the majority does not", a noble ideal judicial review can stand in service of.[220]

3.3 Democratic Legitimacy of Laws

86 A related problem with majoritarianism arises from the fact that, as explained, its supporters value the democratic legitimacy it gives to laws, a quality which the judiciary supposedly cannot impart.[221] But, this premise rests on the erroneous belief that laws are backed-up by sound democratic majorities. In other words, there is a tangible link between what a legislature decides and the law that is applied to individuals. This view of laws as being democratically legitimised is quite a romantic one to say the least.

87 It is a reality in many states that parliaments are not the great sources of democratic debate and thought that the supporters of majoritarianism would have us believe. They are in fact strongly influenced by executive branches, to the extent even that the relationship between many executive and legislative branches can be described as monist with a clear executive dominance. This has been the case in the United Kingdom under prime ministers such as Margaret Thatcher and Tony Blair whose governments came to symbolise the heavy hand of the executive.[222] As Lord Steyn noticed quite forcefully:

> The power of a government with a large majority in the House of Commons is redoubtable. That has been the pattern for almost 25 years. In 1979, 1983 and 1987 Conservative governments were elected respectively with majorities of 43, 144 and 100. In 1997, 2001 and 2005 New Labour was elected with majorities

---

[219]Ibid., at 7.

[220]*Ghaidan v. Godin-Mendoza*, [2004] UKHL 30, [2004] 2 AC 557, at par. 132.

[221] E.g. Michael Mandel, *The Charter of Rights and the Legitimization of Politics* (Toronto: Thompson Educational Publishing, 1994), at 458, argues that allowing judicial review is a "travesty", as judges are unelected and therefore unaccountable. Judicial review excludes all democratic legitimacy, according to Mandel, as it prevents people from deciding for themselves.

[222]Cf. Ewing and Gearty, *supra* note 76, at 255–257; Burkens et al., *supra* note 13, at 241.

of respectively 177, 165 and 67. As Lord Hailsham explained in *The Dilemma of Democracy* (Collins, London, 1978), 126 the dominance of a government elected with a large majority over Parliament has progressively become greater. This process has continued and strengthened inexorably since Lord Hailsham warned of its dangers in 1978.[223]

In South Africa the ANC's dominance of the political process warrants similar questions. The centralising tendencies of the ANC are such that the national executive's powers have even come to overshadow political initiative and independence at provincial level, even though provincial legislatures and governments enjoy their own constitutional powers and democratic mandates.[224]

88 Moreover, modern societies such as the three studied here are very complex entities where the link between applicable laws and democratic majorities often becomes wafer-thin and even pure theory. Too heavy a reliance on the democratic legitimacy of laws ignores the fact that vast masses of legislation are in fact delegated legislation.[225] In other words, many pieces of legislation are not wholly acts of parliament, but based on such acts and decided upon by the executive. The previous decennia have seen an explosion of delegated legislation because as the reach of the state increased so too did the need for extra and more precise legislation. Such legislative regulation is then often so intricate and specific that it requires precision drafting by the executive, thereby not increasing legislatures' already heavy burdens. The result is obviously that the initial democratic legitimation bestowed on legislators by voters gets lost in the whole process, as actual responsibility for drafting subordinate legislation shifts from the legislature with its democratic credentials to the executive and its indirect legitimation.[226]

89 It also makes little sense to allow the judicial review of delegated legislation but not of acts of parliament in trying to compensate for

---

[223]*Jackson v. Her Majesty's Attorney General*, *supra* note 93, at par. 71. Cf. Bingham, *supra* note 2, at 391.

[224]Nico Steytler, "Concurrency and Co-operative Government: The Law and Practice in South Africa", 16 *SA Pub. L.*241 (2001), at 245; Rassie Malherbe, "Centralisation of Power in Education: Have Provinces Become National Agents?", *J. S. Afr. L.* 237 (2006), at 250–251.

[225]Cappelletti (1989), *supra* note 212, at 14, speaks in this regard of the transformation of the "welfare state" into an "administrative state" and "bureaucratic state".

[226]H.J. Hoorweg, "Delegatie", in P.W.C. Akkermans and C.J. Bax, *Interpretatie in het staatsrecht* (Rotterdam: Erasmus University, 1985), at 67, 69. Cf. Hermann Pünder, "Democratic Legitimation of Delegated Legislation – A Comparative View on the American, British and German Law", 58 *Int. Comp. L. Quart.* 355 (2009), who argues the need for public participation during the drafting of delegated legislation.

the former's lack of democratic credentials, as suggested by Waldron.[227] Experience in the Netherlands has shown that where courts may review delegated legislation but not acts of parliament because of the bar in section 120 of the Constitution, they actually end up reviewing very little, if anything, out of fear for intruding on the legislative domain.[228] In effect, this means that an already powerful executive in the Netherlands, with indirect democratic legitimation, becomes even more powerful in steering legislation while the government's parliamentary majority is quite hesitant in questioning its rather dominant executive.

The reality is actually quite closer to what Ronald Dworkin and Martin Shapiro have argued.[229] One should not be too hasty to apply "democratic" and "undemocratic" labels to particular decisions or bodies, as actual decision-making does not (always) reflect a particular majority, but is instead the result of compromise between various competing interests.[230] In fact, many democratically arrived at decisions may be just as much void of any majority will as delegated legislation, thereby begging judicial control. The late parliamentarian Tim Fortescue drove the point home after a long career in Westminster by remarking of the legislative process that: "It's a self-perpetuating oligarchy, there is no nonsense about democracy."[231]

3.4 Legitimacy of Judicial Decisions

90 A variant of the majoritarian argument focuses not so much on the democratic legitimacy of legislators, but instead takes aim at the fact that

---

[227]Waldron, *supra* note 7, at 1353–1354. In defining judicial review, he states that this essay is "about judicial review of legislation, not judicial review of executive action or administrative decisionmaking". By way of explanation, he notes that "it is almost universally accepted that the executive's elective credentials are subject to the principle of the rule of law, and, as a result, that officials may properly be required by courts to act in accordance with legal authorization".

[228]Cf. Rechtbank 's Gravenhage (The Hague District Court) of 18 January 1995; G. Leenknegt, "Hoe lang is de arm van artikel 120 Gr.w.?", *Regelmaat* 65 (1995); Jurgens, *supra* note 117, at 68–69. Leenknegt argues that delegated legislation must be open to full judicial scrutiny, as the legislature decided not to exercise its legislative powers itself. Whereas Jurgens argues for narrower scrutiny, in order not to offend the will of the legislature as applied by the executive in making delegated legislation. The latter view is prevalent in the Dutch legal order.

[229]Martin Shapiro, *Freedom of Speech: The Supreme Court and Judicial Review* (Englewood Cliffs, NJ: Prentice Hall, 1966), at 24–25; Ronald Dworkin, "The Forum of Principle", 56 *N.Y. Univ. L. Rev.* 469 (1981), at 517.

[230]Cf. Eric A. Posner and Adrian Vermeule, "Legislative Entrenchment: A Reappraisal", 111 *Yale L. J.* 1665 (2002), at 1686; *A. and Others v. Secretary of State for the Home Department*, [2004] UKHL 56, [2005] 2 WLR 87, at par. 42, where Lord Bingham of Cornhill argued the case for the courts' democratic mandate.

[231]*The Times*, Obituary (1 October 2008).

judges are unelected and therefore devoid of democratic legitimacy.[232] The argument goes something like this, legislators although imperfect are at least still accountable to their voters, something which cannot be said of judges. The logical conclusion would of course be that judges are to be denied the power of review, as such an instrument is not to be left in hands that are essentially illegitimate. The pitfall of this view is that it chooses to limit the legitimacy to that bestowed in elections. Yet this is overly narrow and runs the risk of placing all one's eggs into one basket when it comes to potentially serious and sensitive decisions.

91   Legitimacy can be derived from various sources. And thankfully so, as we have seen that the democratic legitimacy of laws leaves much to be desired at times. Just as legislators have to give account to the electorate every so many years, so too must judges render account, but in their case through the clear motivation of their judgments.[233] In this regard, Robert Alexy pleads for judges to give as clear an account as possible of how they balance competing rights and interests to explain to the affected parties which principles were at play and how they were dealt with.[234] Courts are quite often also part of a greater judicial structure that allows for decisions to be appealed and reconsidered by another court, thereby putting a matter back on the agenda for review. A case in point is the South African Constitutional Court that discourages litigants from seeking direct access to the court in bypassing lower courts, as this robs the bench of the benefit of lower judgments while its own decision is final and not capable of being appealed.[235]

92   The bench not only has to render account internally to strengthen the legitimacy of its choices, but also externally.[236] For example, decisions that persistently strike a wrong chord can nearly always be countered by the constitutional processes of the legal system concerned. Consider for instance the possibility of revising a constitutional document. The judiciary

---

[232]*Consider* again the views of Mandel, *supra* note 221, at 458.

[233]Cf. Peter Birks (ed.), *English Private Law* (Oxford: Oxford University Press, 2000), at paras. 1.01–1.04.

[234]Robert Alexy, *A Theory of Constitutional Rights* (Oxford: Oxford University Press, 2002), at 212–213.

[235]*Bruce v. Fleecytex Johannesburg CC*, 1998 (4) BCLR 415 (CC), 1998 (2) SA 1143 (CC), at paras. 7-8.

[236]E.g. Lawrence M. Friedman, *The Legal System: A Social Science Perspective* (New York: Russell Sage Foundation, 1977), at 194, explains that an external and internal legal culture can be distinguished. The internal legal culture refers to people who perform specialised legal tasks, who are in other words part of "the magic circle of the legal system". Yet, this is not the only dynamic the legal system must contend with, as litigants make use of the court system and society as a whole views the system in a particular light – the external perspective.

may be entrusted with interpreting a constitutional document, but the legislature or constitutional assembly may still choose to alter the contents of such a document.[237] This may put the mind of the persistent sceptic at rest, who not being content with the legitimacy sourced from internal accountability of the judiciary still requires some external and preferably democratic check. The Dutch and South African Constitutions are indeed not set in stone and can always be amended by following specific procedures usually involving special majorities, while the HRA is only subject to an ordinary parliamentary majority.[238] In other words, constitutional legislatures in all three countries set the agenda, which is then to be interpreted and given effect by the courts. If one happens to find that entrenched provisions are too difficult to amend, the reason for their entrenchment must be reconsidered as well as alternatives in amending such provisions, the answer lies not in discarding judicial review. It may very well be necessary to place certain topics more outside the reach of legislatures than others. These shifts in emphasis can be accommodated by entrenching some provisions in a bill of rights more than others, while not denying the judiciary a role in reviewing the legislature's actions. The fact of the matter is that both the legislature and the judiciary are organs that can be held to account, albeit by different means. Yet, their purpose remains the same, namely as methods with which to question and control state power for the sake of constitutionalism.

93 Judicial review is also increasingly seen as a method that invites discussion and dialogue in important matters such as fundamental rights, especially in the constitutional thought of Canada.[239] The legislative and judicial functions are no longer portrayed as mutually exclusive, but as communicating vessels. The legitimacy of court decisions then resides in the judiciary maybe not enjoying final authority or pretending to possess ultimate wisdom when it comes to understanding higher law. A legislative response may be included in the constitutional scheme of things, for instance. The HRA presents a good example in this regard by calling on

---

[237] Constitutional revisions are also often put before the people in referenda, thereby allowing a direct link between the people and the constitution which governs them. Cf. L.F.M. Besselink, "Constitutional Referenda in the Netherlands: A Debate in the Margin", 11 *Elect. J. Comp. L.* (2007), http://www.ejcl.org/111/art111-2.pdf (last accessed on 19 November 2009); Gerhard van der Schyff, "Referenda in South African Law", 13 *Tilburg Foreign L. Rev.* 125 (2006), at 133, regarding referenda as a method to solve constitutional deadlock.

[238] E.g. s. 74(2) of the South African Constitution requires a two-thirds majority in the National Assembly and the support of at least six of the nine provinces in the National Assembly for the Bill of Rights to be amended. *See* also the other provisions in s. 74 regarding amendments. As to amending the Dutch Constitution, *see* its s. 137, and § 53.

[239] *Consider* the seminal article by Peter W. Hogg and Allison A. Bushell, "The Charter Dialogue Between Courts and Legislatures", 35 *Osgoode Hall L. J.* 75 (1997).

parliament to reconsider its choices without nullifying those choices from the bench. It is then up to the political process to settle the matter as it deems fit. Something similar is possible in the Netherlands, where the bar on constitutional review in section 120 of the Constitution does not seem to exclude weak review, although the courts make little use of this opportunity. On one of the few occasions that this power was used, in the *Harmonisation Act* case, the Supreme Court indicated that an act of parliament regulating student grants violated national higher law.[240] In this way, the Court communicated its unease to parliament while still applying the legislation.

94 Importantly, systems of strong review also allow opportunities for dialogue even though the constitutional system creates no formal means for such interaction to take place. For instance, the South African Constitutional Court established that the right to equality meant that same-sex marriage had to be allowed, but left parliament ample time and room to decide how it wished to honour this constitutional commitment without simply imposing change.[241] In this instance the Constitutional Court established judicial legitimacy by recognising that although it could impose change by itself, a partnership with the legislature was judged more appropriate in allowing political representatives to mould the law in accordance with the Constitution. The important question of constitutional dialogue and interaction between the legislature and the judiciary will be canvassed more extensively later in this study.[242]

In sum, it would be wrong to characterise the judiciary as a remote and isolated body that lives to preys on democratic majorities. Various sources of legitimacy exist that strengthen the idea of judicial review.

3.5 Trias Politica Re-configurated

95 The strong emphasis on the democratic legitimation of laws by the majoritarian argument also overlooks the reality of the *trias politica*. Such an emphasis views the *trias* as a *separation* of powers in a very literal way. Legislatures are to pass laws, while judiciaries are to follow the plain meaning of the enacted words. Waldron, for example, states that an absence of judicial review would mean that the application or non-application of a law to a particular case is something to be derived from such a law's own terms, and that its effect may not be modified in a way not foreseen by the

---

[240]*Harmonisation Act* judgment, *supra* note 105, at par. 3.1.

[241]*Minister of Home Affairs v. Fourie; Lesbian and Gay Equality Project v. Minister of Home Affairs* (CC), *supra* note 25, at paras. 139, 157–161.

[242]Cf. Chap. 7.

law itself.[243] Although not stated in so many words, this implies a strict division between law and politics, the law then as a product of a political process which is firmly divorced from any judicial activity apart from its application to a dispute.[244]

Yet, judges by necessity also make law. It cannot be expected of judges to only apply the so-called literal meaning presented to them in a legislative text. Words do not speak for themselves, but require a contextual injection of meaning if they are to be intelligible.[245] Even in jurisdictions with a traditional insistence on simply applying what parliament decides numerous interpretive maxims and presumptions have been developed to ameliorate the negative effects of legislation and correct its flaws.

96   The interpretive approach to rights protection in the United Kingdom illustrates this. As explained earlier, in *R. v. Lord Chancellor, Ex parte Witham*, a case predating the HRA, the court chose an interpretation of the Supreme Court Act that favoured access to justice, although other reasonable interpretations were quite possible.[246] South African courts too, when still labouring under parliamentary sovereignty, interpreted legislation, mostly in non-political cases it must be added, in such a way that it did not result in unreasonable and unjust consequences.[247] A case in point being *Freeman v. Colonial Secretary* where a public railway company expropriated private land for which no compensation was paid, as the relevant legislation did not make any provision for this.[248] Nonetheless, the court ruled that compensation was necessary, as the legislation also did not expressly exclude payment. It was therefore reasonable to compensate the plaintiff whose common law right to property had been limited quite severely. Vivid examples of controlling the state's legislative power through judicial action.

Similarly in the Netherlands, the Supreme Court held already in 1972 that outdated provisions in an act of parliament needed not be applied by the courts, even though such provisions were still valid law.[249] This

---

[243]Waldron, *supra* note 7, at 1354.

[244]Maurice Adams, *Recht en democratie ter discussie: Essays over democratische rechtsvorming* (Leuven: Universitaire Pers Leuven, 2006), at 243.

[245]Cf. Stanley Fish, *Is There a Text in this Class? The Authority of Interpretive Communities* (Cambridge, MA: Harvard University Press, 1980), at 284, 334, explains that: "A sentence that seems to need no interpretation is already the product of one." Also: "It is within the assumption of a context – one so deeply assumed that we unaware of it – that the words acquire what seems to be their literal meaning."

[246]*See* § 26.

[247]Cf. Christo Botha, *Wetsuitleg* (Kenwyn, Juta, 3rd ed., 1998), at 69–71.

[248]*Freeman v. Colonial Secretary*, 1889 NLR 73.

[249]Hoge Raad, 3 March 1972, *NJ* 1972, 339. *Consider* also Hoge Raad, 28 November 1978, *NJ* 1979, 93, where it was decided that pornography could be distributed among

decision would not have been so remarkable, had it not been for the fact that it was achieved in a system that apart from treaty review, which was not the basis for the decision, does not allow the strong review of acts of parliament. Interestingly, the decision achieved a result that reeks of progressive constitutional interpretation by contradicting an enforceable law. The bench clearly interpreted the law with reference to principles extraneous to the text in what can probably best be termed judicial review by stealth.

97 Such judicial activity is not to be criticised, but properly provided for and channelled. Courts are by necessity fora of principle, as will be explained below. This becomes all the more clear when it is considered that legislative provisions are characterised by often vague and open statements that require extensive judicial interpretation.[250] This is because a law taken on its own terms can mean different things to different interpreters without exceeding the bounds of reason. It is therefore wrong to ignore the fact that judges also shape the law, and that they do not simply apply the at times very elusive and confusing plain meaning in which a legal rule is expressed. The judiciary has an important role in not only applying legislative policy, but also in crafting such policy by applying interpretive principles.

Without such judicial activity the law becomes an inoperable wasteland that erects an artificial wall between the legislature and the judiciary that can simply not be maintained. Insisting on maintaining this wall does nothing to advance good constitutionalism by seeking effective ways to check state power, but simply elevates majority rule to an end in itself that can bedevil good governance.

98 The answer, however, is not to attack the doctrine of the separation of powers as such, but to query its interpretation and application. Separating powerful forces in a state is certainly healthy to avoid an overconcentration of power, but a strict separation is decidedly unhealthy as well. This is because such a strict separation leaves little room for checks and balances between the various forces and can lead to an overconcentration of power with one of those forces. Thereby creating the exact same problem that the separation was designed to remedy in the first place.

---

consenting adults, irrespective of the fact that a general legislative ban existed on pornography which did not include such an exception but actually contradicted it. R.J.B. Schutgens, "Het voorstel-Halsema en de toelaatbaarheid van de wet", *Regelmaat* 12 (2007), 22, calls this the "re-interpretation" of acts of parliament.

[250]Cf. G.J. Wiarda, *Drie typen van rechtsvinding* (Zwolle: W.E.J. Tjeenk Willink, 3rd ed., 1988), at 21–31, explains that a strict separation of powers is not possible the more one deals with unclear provisions, as judges are by definition called upon to ensure clarity, which may even include extending a provision's literal meaning.

A historical interpretation of the thought underlying the separation of powers, as conceived by its great champion Montesquieu, also shows that he never intended a strict separation of powers.[251] Instead, he advocated a *gouvernement modére*. The separation of powers has to moderate the possible excesses of government, instead of separating powers only to create fiefdoms impervious to each other's watchful eye.

In addition, as explained above, a near blind faith in democratic majorities is not enough to guard against possible legislative mistake or excess without other checks built into the system. As a matter of fact, it could very well contribute to such problems, as legislatures often have to limit rights and other constitutional guarantees, while being called to protect these interests at the same time.[252] Such an anomaly is unacceptable in modern societies where the need to protect ordinary people against the might of the state has resulted in viewing the *trias politica*as a *duas politica*, or bipolar constitutionalism in other words.[253] This bipolar approach sees the judiciary as a necessary counterweight against the combined force of the, often intertwined, legislature and executive.

99 The separation of powers is certainly useful in achieving good constitutionalism, but can damage that very project by losing sight of its ultimate aim, namely that of limiting state power. However, advocating judicial constitutional review within the separation of powers does not mean to say that the powers involved are assigned the same duties. Far from it. What such a plea says is that the legislature does not enjoy a legislative monopoly, but legislative primacy.[254] This means that the legislature takes the initiative while the judiciary follows in checking the quality of the initiative. A point which was made quite clear in the Halsema Proposal for example, whose stated aim is not to displace the legislature, but to augment it where necessary.[255] This amounts to a different, yet nonetheless important role to that of the legislature.

3.6 Fora of Principle

100 Wojciech Sadurski is undoubtedly correct in arguing that the parliamentary protection of fundamental rights might in theory be just as effective as the judicial protection of such rights, but unfortunately we

---

[251]Cf. Adams, *supra* note 244, at 244.

[252]Ibid., 253.

[253]Koopmans, *supra* note 6, at 245–251.

[254]Adams, *supra* note 244, at 244, 251.

[255]*Parliamentary Proceedings II*, 2002–2003, 28, 331, no. 9, at 14.

do not live in a perfect world.[256] A pertinent concern when it comes to majoritarianism is that its supporters present the world with an idealised view of political decision-making and its benefits.[257] Judicial review is sidelined only to opt for politicians who often act with short-term gain in mind, and quite often personal gain at that.[258] For laws to be inviolable on account of their democratic legitimation would suppose a political process that is in touch with the views and needs of voters. Yet surveys often find that ordinary citizens have more faith in the judiciary than in political organs. For example, as the presidential election saga in 2000 between George Bush and Al Gore unfolded, opinion polls in the United States showed that 60% of the population wanted the Supreme Court to be involved in deciding the election as opposed to only 38% wanting Congress or the Florida legislature to play a role.[259] This raises questions as to the wisdom of waging too much on democracy and the legitimacy it supposedly brings to the law while choosing to view the courts with suspicion, whereas in fact the legislature's legitimacy may be much weaker than some would like to admit. What should also be made of the consistently low opinion poll ratings enjoyed by many politicians who are entrusted with making our laws?

101 This is exactly where the added worth of judicial review becomes apparent. Courts can provide the sort of reliable consistency necessary in

---

[256]Wojciech Sadurski, "Judicial Review and the Protection of Constitutional Rights", 22 *Oxford. J. Legal Stud.*275 (2002). Sadurski also argues that there is little difference between courts applying constitutional rights and other legal rules, which again makes judicial review of legislation more justifiable. If courts can be trusted with other branches of the law, why not constitutional law? Wojciech Sadurski, "Rights and Moral Reasoning: An Unstated Case Assumption – A Comment on Jeremy Waldron's 'Judges as Moral Reasoners' ", 7 *Int. J. Const. L.*25 (2009).

[257]E.g.*consider* the radical democratic views of Allan C. Hutchinson, "A 'Hard Core' Case Against Judicial Review", 121 *Harv. L. Rev. Forum* 57 (2008), at 63, who argues for more popular participation in "micro-communities" instead of judicial review or conventional political institutions.

[258]J. van der Hoeven, "Toetsen aan de Grondwet. Hoe en door wie?", *Nederlands Juristenblad* 784 (1991), at 785, argues that political parties in the Netherlands are sometimes more concerned with keeping coalition governments together and maintaining party unity than representing their voters and articulating their best interests.

[259]Cf. Charles Krauthammer, "The Winner in Bush v. Gore", *Time Magazine*(18 December 2000). The Supreme Court did eventually play an important role in deciding the outcome of the presidential election, *see Bush v. Gore*, 531 US 98 (2000). More recently on 30 June 2009 the Supreme Court also settled an election contest for one of Minnesota's two Senate seats, *see State of Minnesota, Sheehan and Coleman v. Franken*, no. A09-697.

checking democratic decision-making that the latter often lacks itself.[260]
As Roscoe Pound argued:

> Judicial finding of law has a real advantage in competition with legislation in that
> it works with concrete cases and generalizes only after a long course of trial and
> error in the effort to work out a practicable principle. Legislation, when more
> than declaratory, when it does more than restate authoritatively what judicial
> experience has indicated, involves the difficulties and the perils of prophecy.[261]

Frank Michelman argues in similar fashion, and in direct contrast to Jeremy
Waldron, that where there is persistent disagreement on fundamental issues
courts are much better placed than legislatures to handle the "full blast" of
competing views in deliberating such disagreement.[262]

102   One could say that judicial review makes use of courts' potential as
"fora of principle", in the words of Ronald Dworkin.[263] When courts focus
on principle and try to determine what rights individuals have, political
morality is transformed from a mere political power game to something
more worthwhile and durable. A focus on principle is something that by
their very nature legislatures can never fully achieve themselves, thereby
requiring a judicial injection from time to time. Far from detracting from
democratic legitimacy, this function of judicial review might very well add
to it, provided that the process is "designed to reach generally sensible
substantive decisions while making infringements of individual rights as
unlikely as reasonably possible".[264]

103   This is precisely what happened when South Africa's newly created
Constitutional Court was entrusted with certifying whether the final draft of
the 1996 Constitution satisfied a number of constitutional principles before

---

[260]Fallon, *supra* note 7, at 1718. Cf. Jörg Paul Müller, "Fundamental Rights in
Democracy", 4 *Hum. Rights L. J.*131 (1983), at 136–137: "[D]emocracy itself needs an
institution which thinks in broader time dimensions than a legislator operating for its
term of office and an administration bound up with day-to-day problems usually do. This
does not discredit democratic processes at all. It is simply reminded of the limits of the
suitability of democratic procedure and its machinery of decision-making. Democracy
also needs a long-term body whose thinking revolves around fundamental rights. This
is widely agreed as expressed in the fact that rulings by constitutional courts, which
in basic matters of human rights run counter to the dominant political tendency, are
usually accepted without being set aside, and are even carried into effect." Footnotes
omitted.

[261]Roscoe Pound, *The Formative Era of American Law* (Boston: Little Brown, 1938),
at 51.

[262]Frank Michelman, *Brennan and the Supreme Court* (Princeton, NJ: Princeton
University Press, 1999), at 59.

[263]Dworkin, *supra* note 229, at 469; Ronald Dworkin, *A Matter of Principle* (Cambridge,
MA: Harvard University Press, 1985), at 33, 69–71. See also the criticism of Waldron,
supra note 7, at 1385.

[264]Fallon, *supra* note 7, at 1718.

it could become the country's supreme law.[265] Although the various political actors had agreed on these principles as minimum requirements for a new constitutional dawn, they considered it wise to enlist judicial help in deciding whether they had met those benchmarks in drafting a constitutional text. The Constitutional Court was clearly thought of as a body which could detach itself from the political debate and focus on the principles at stake. A clear case of judicial review having to evaluate a political outcome, if under somewhat unique circumstances, to ensure that a society as divided as South Africa was unified in respecting certain basic constitutionalist principles. This is a classic example of what the United States Supreme Court explained as follows:

> The very purpose of a Bill of Rights was to withdraw certain subjects from the vicissitudes of political controversy, to place them beyond the reach of majorities and officials and to establish them as legal principles to be applied by the courts. One's right to life, liberty, and property, to free speech, a free press, freedom of worship and assembly, and other fundamental rights may not be submitted to vote; they depend on the outcome of no elections.[266]

104 Alec Stone Sweet has also shown that legislators have come to consider and use the principles distilled by judges in formulating and debating policy matters.[267] A case in point would be parliamentary debates in the Netherlands on anti-terrorism legislation. In their debates members of parliament continually referred to treaty rights, which are enforced by judges in that country, as opposed to constitutional rights, which may not be enforced by the judiciary.[268] This has fuelled claims that the country's Constitution has become all but a dead letter, often disregarded by parliament and in need of judicial review in order for it to be taken seriously by politics.[269] Decisions such as the *East African Asians* case referred to earlier, also show that parliament's protection of fundamental rights in the United Kingdom is not always as sound as many would have us believe.[270] The HRA was therefore justified in wanting to ensure greater judicial involvement in deciding whether the important principles embodied by fundamental rights are indeed being respected. Although technically

---

[265]*See* §§ 68, 70.

[266]*West Virginia State Board of Education v. Barnette*, 319 US 624 (1943), at par. 3.

[267]Alec Stone Sweet, *Governing with Judges: Constitutional Politics in Europe* (Oxford: Oxford University Press, 2000), at 201–203.

[268]Cf. Albers and Schlössel, *supra* note 139, 2526.

[269]*See* again § 51. *Sed contra* C.B. Schutte, "De verwarring van rechtsstaat en rechtersstaat. Kanttekeningen bij constitutionele rechtspraak volgens het voorstel-Halsema", *Regelmaat* 93 (2004), at 98.

[270]*See* § 29.

intact, parliamentary sovereignty is no longer an "empty vessel" for political victors to fill as they wish when it comes to Convention rights, to use the words of Conor Gearty.[271]

However, it would be wrong to conclude that courts have all the answers or that legislatures should play second fiddle to them as a matter of course. The crux of the matter is that courts and legislatures have different but interlinked roles to fulfil in coming to decisions that can be described as generally fair, after having considered all relevant angles to a case, instead of simply equating something with fairness because "the majority said so".

105   A related argument deals with the development of the common law. Legal systems with a common law base, such as the United Kingdom and South Africa, as opposed to civil law systems such as the Netherlands, have always realised the importance of the judiciary as a forum of principle. This is because the rules of the common law are developed by the judiciary in so far as they have not been supplanted by legislation. The adoption of bills of rights did not change this position. Instead, it provided judges with a set of values to be used in developing the common law to ensure that it reflects contemporary notions of justice. This is something which is reflected in section 39(1)(a) of the South African Bill of Rights which states that:

> When interpreting any legislation, and when developing the common law or customary law, every court, tribunal or forum must promote the spirit, purport and objects of the Bill of Rights.

The adoption of the HRA has also given fresh impetus to the development of the English common law by presenting judges with rights with which to model this body of law.[272]

Thus, by allowing the judicial review of legislation, one simply expands a function already familiar to and enjoyed by many courts. If the courts can be entrusted with infusing the common law with principle, they might as well be entrusted with doing the same when it comes to legislation. Especially, as the democratic credentials of legislative fora, one of the main arguments in disallowing the judicial review of legislation, are not always watertight, thereby adding to the appeal of judicial fora of principle.[273]

---

[271] Gearty, *supra* note 84, at 23. Cf. Elliott, *supra* note 93, at 549–551, illustrating why parliamentary sovereignty is not simply an untouchable political fact, but is itself subject to the United Kingdom's unwritten constitution.

[272] The courts are less reticent in applying the HRA to the common law than legislation. This is because the common law is a clear judicial domain whose development rests with the judiciary. Cf. *Douglas v. Hello! Ltd*, [2001] QB 967; *A. v. B. plc and another*, [2002] ECWA Civ 337, [2003] QB 195; Gearty, *supra* note 84, at 157–164, on the expanded protection of rights which the HRA brought to the common law.

[273] *See* §§ 86–89 above on the democratic legitimacy of legislation.

3.7 Benefit to Democracy

106 The trouble with the majoritarian argument is also that it fails to realise that democracy is not simply a political project in a narrow parliamentary sense, but that democratic governance can benefit from the input of other institutions such as the judiciary. Jeremy Waldron, for example, argues that fundamental difference in society should only be solved by democratic majorities, yet this is an overly positive view of democratic decision-making and an overly negative view of the bench's role. For instance, the European Court of Human Rights has helped to concretise human rights norms in a very substantial way in the last few decades. It is very doubtful whether any elected organ would have had a similar success rate given the vast expanse covered by the Council of Europe.[274] One only has to think of the Court's consistent high regard for freedom of expression, especially in a political context. *Castells v. Spain* provides ample evidence of this, a case where in the interest of a well-functioning democracy, the Strasbourg Court refused to accept limits imposed on a politician's freedom of speech.[275] Far from detracting from democratic governance, the Court has actually become an agent in defence of electoral politics by giving flesh to minimum or important requirements necessary for a healthy democracy. The Preamble to the European Convention on Human Rights explains it well when it states that fundamental freedoms, being the foundation of justice and peace, require not only effective political democracy in order to be enforced, but also a common understanding of human rights, something which the Convention and its judicial enforcement aim to bring about.

107 It is this notion of a necessary partnership between democratic organs and the judiciary that is not fully appreciated by the proponents of majoritarianism. Yet, its necessity is very clearly illustrated in federal states. For example, in Belgium proposals were mooted to solve legislative disputes between the various legislatures by handing the final word to the houses of parliament when the country started moving towards federalism. However, the proposals were soon abandoned in favour of creating a constitutional

---

[274]Steven Greer, "What's Wrong with the European Convention on Human Rights?", 30 *Hum. Rights Quart.*680 (2008), acknowledges the Convention as "the most successful experiment in the transnational, judicial protection of human rights in the world". So successful has it been in protecting people's rights, that its case overload is described as a "savage indictment of the Council of Europe's effectiveness", at 701.

[275]*Castells v. Spain* of 23 April 1992, *Publ. Eur Court of H.R.*, Series A, no. 236, at para. 42: "While freedom of expression is important for everybody, it is especially so for an elected representative of the people. He represents his electorate, draws attention to their preoccupations and defends their interests. Accordingly, interferences with the freedom of expression of an opposition member of parliament, like the applicant, call for the closest scrutiny on the part of the Court."

court to adjudicate such disputes.[276] This is a clear case of where political disputes simply had to be turned into judicial questions in order to ensure the smooth functioning of democratic organs that would otherwise incessantly have been at loggerheads with each other.

108 Of the three countries studied, South Africa presents the best example in this regard. The drafters of South Africa's new constitutional dawn accepted that the health of the new democracy could not simply be left to party politics, but that it had to be checked by the judiciary as well. It was decided that the country's future depended on a new constitutional system, which meant not just replacing old political masters with new ones. Etienne Mureinik captured this shift quite vividly when he wrote that the new dispensation had to be a bridge to a culture of justification at all levels of government, with the bill of rights as its chief strut, and not simply a culture of authority as had been the case under parliamentary sovereignty and apartheid.[277] This logic became abundantly vivid in *Doctors for Life International v. Speaker of the National Assembly*.[278] The Constitutional Court held that the upper house of parliament had neglected to follow the constitutional procedure for adopting legislation, as the house's consultation process left much to be desired, with the consequence that the legislation was struck down leaving parliament to respect the democratic process more closely. On the day, political will was not stronger than sound constitutionalism thanks to judicial intervention.

109 It may be true though that a strong and sudden shift to totalitarian dictatorship may not be stopped or countered by judicial intervention, but this is no reason to deny the judiciary a role in constitutional matters. If it were a reason to deny the judiciary a role, it would miss a very important point. Namely, that judicial review can contribute to the fostering of a human rights culture in emphasising basic values. This is something which may end up saving democracy by preventing authoritarianism and even totalitarianism from gaining popularity and taking hold in the first place. Although established democracies such as those in the United Kingdom and the Netherlands are not faced by such immediate threats, the need to nurture a human rights culture cannot be underestimated. This is also very true for a relatively young democracy such as South Africa, where a respect for rights still needs to be created and consolidated in many respects.

---

[276]R. Leysen and J. Smets, *Toetsing van de wet aan de Grondwet in België* (Zwolle: W.E.J. Tjeenk Willink, 1991), at 23.

[277]Etienne Mureinik, "A Bridge to Where? Introducing the Interim Bill of Rights", 10 *S. Afr. J. Hum. Rights* 31 (1994), at 32.

[278]*Doctors for Life International v. Speaker of the National Assembly*, 2006 (12) BCLR 1399 (CC), 2006 (6) SA 416 (CC).

110 If then, as it is generally agreed, that a human rights culture is necessary for a well-functioning democracy; it is quite strange for democracy to be its own and only arbiter as to whether it meets these standards. In this respect, the late Mauro Cappelletti captured the need for judicial review quite strikingly:

> [T]here is the lesson of history and comparative analysis. It demonstrates that no illiberal, dictatorial regime has ever accepted an effective system of judicial review. The experiences in Nazi Germany, in *Anschluss*Austria, in Franco's Spain, in Salazar's Portugal, are full evidence for the incompatibility of judicial review with unbound authority.[279]

Far from being, at best, useless to democracy, or at worst, its enemy; sensible judicial review might just serve the best interests of democracy by emphasising the requirements necessary for continued sound democratic governance.

3.8 Charting the Middle Ground

111 It should be clear from the above that majoritarianism poses a number of difficulties and risks that need mitigation and checks in modern states. Comparing the experience of the United Kingdom, the Netherlands and South Africa shows that there is a lot to be said for judicial review in each of the three systems. Only taking refuge in the will of a democratic majority is no longer good enough by itself. Modern states and societies are too complex to leave important matters to the sole discretion of legislatures. Essentially, majoritarianism must accept the principle of counter-majoritarian constraints. However, this statement calls for some explanation.

Counter-majoritiarianism is not to be confused with the dreaded spectre of a *gouvernement des juges*. The idea is not to replace legislative decision-making by an overly domineering judicial model. Instead, counter-majoritarianism advocates sensible governance that realises the weaknesses of electoral democracy and the potential of the judiciary in this regard. One might say that the "middle ground" is defended.

112 Middle ground means that the legislature and judiciary are not to be viewed as mutually exclusive extremities, but rather as two communicating

---

[279]Cappelletti (1992), *supra* note 212, at 266. Similarly, Carla M. Zoethout, "The End of Constitutionalism? Challenges to the Ideal of Limiting Governmental Power", in P.W.C. Akkermans, D.J. Elzinga and E. Pietermaat-Kros (eds.), *Constitutionalism in the Netherlands* 9 (Groningen: Groningen University Press, 1995), at 18, comes to the conclusion that only "when the decisions of the majority are limited, can democracy as such exist".

vessels. Each has its own place and responsibilities in a reasoned system, instead of allowing a situation of distrust and even fear to prevail by banishing each to its own corner. A well functioning democracy, as emphasised by Jeremy Waldron, is indeed then to be valued as the bedrock of modern states. However, this may never be at the cost of sound and responsible decision-making in the form of an additional check by the judiciary where desirable. The aim is to seek ways to control the state, and a blinding focus on just one actor, such as the legislature, can very well endanger that aim by confusing the means with the ends. Wisdom then teaches that political control by the voters over the legislature and self-control by the legislature are to be augmented by judicial control. This approach sits well with the perception of the separation of powers that was set out earlier in this discussion, as judicial review can make good an imbalance in the relationship between the state and its subjects. Nevertheless, the judiciary retains its own role and character, as it may only act in the wake of the legislature's actions or inactions. Therein also resides an essential and permanent difference between these two bodies – the legislature holds the initiative, while the judiciary may respond to the initiative's handling.[280]

113 On a terminological but also substantive note, care should be taken not to characterise *middle ground* as *judicial deference*. This is because the phrase judicial deference implies a somewhat negative role for the courts in relation to the legislature, as the judiciary seemingly has to restrict its appropriate constitutional role to appeasing and pandering to the legislature, something which is not intended here. In contrast, middle ground emphasises that each has equally vital roles to fulfil in achieving constitutionalism, but roles that are essentially different. Making a similar point, Ronald Dworkin argued that legislatures articulate utilitarian goals expressed as "policy", while the courts apply "principles" in the form of moral rights to such policies.[281] Or, as Lord Hoffmann explained convincingly in *R. (on the application of Pro-Life Alliance) v. BBC*:

> My Lords, although the word "deference" is now very popular in describing the relationship between the judicial and other branches of government, I do not think that its overtones of servility, or perhaps gracious concession, are appropriate to describe what is happening. In a society based upon the rule of law and the separation of powers, it is necessary to decide which branch of government has in any particular instance the decision-making power and what the legal limits of that power are. (...) Likewise, when a court decides that a decision is within the

---

[280]A case in point being *Broniowski v. Poland* of 22 June 2004, *Reports of Judgments and Decisions*, 2004-V, at par. 189, where the Grand Chamber of the European Court of Human Rights characterised its actions as a response to a "malfunctioning of Polish legislation and administrative practice".

[281]Ronald Dworkin, *Taking Rights Seriously* (London: Duckworth, 1978), at 22.

proper competence of the legislature or executive, it is not showing deference. It is deciding the law.[282]

114 The essential question therefore to be addressed is not whether there *must* be judicial review and therefore middle ground, but centres instead on *charting* such ground. It is generally appreciated that majoritarian democracy goes a long way towards legitimising legislation, but in itself and unaided by some form of judicial review it proves to be insufficient to satisfy the ideal of constitutional governance. Even the House of Lords seemed to have warmed to this view in the face of a theoretically sovereign parliament, as Lord Steyn opined in *Jackson v. Her Majesty's Attorney General* that:

> In exceptional circumstances involving an attempt to abolish judicial review or the authority of the courts, the Appellate Committee of the House of Lords or a new Supreme Court may have to consider whether this is a constitutional fundamental which even a complaisant House of Commons cannot abolish.[283]

Put differently, it may be said that judicial review as such is desirable, which moves the enquiry to whether it can be said that the extent of its scope is appropriate.

115 Similarly, Mark Tushnet opines that:

> Although pure parliamentary supremacy has few defenders today (...), the precise contours of the constraints on legislative power are to some degree controversial.[284]

Tushnet is correct – although judicial review might be desirable, the way in which it is given shape differs from case to case as not all societies choose the same form of review. This prompts the question, how the design and scope of judicial review are to be determined once it is realised that the legislature *and* the judiciary have a shared responsibility when it comes to the quality of legal norms? The answer lies in understanding a particular society's attitude to majoritarianism because judicial review is conceived as an instrument with which to counter a majority. Demarcating the middle ground between the legislature and the judiciary is therefore an exercise that must happen with reference to majoritarianism. As different societies have different experiences of majoritarianism, so their approach to fashioning judicial review in relation to it will differ. In other words, because not all democratic societies are identical, it would make little sense to impose

---

[282]*R. (on the application of Pro-Life Alliance) v. BBC*, [2003] UKHL 23, [2003] 2 WLR 1403, at paras. 75–76. Cf. Jeffrey Jowell, "Judicial Deference: Servility, Civility or Institutional Deference", *Pub. L.*592 (2003).

[283]*Jackson v. Her Majesty's Attorney General*, *supra* note 93, at par. 102.

[284]Mark Tushnet, "Judicial Review of Legislation", in Peter Cane and Mark Tushnet (eds.), *The Oxford Handbook of Legal Studies* 164 (Oxford: Oxford University Press, 2003), at 165.

a common standard of review on all such societies. One could say that the scope of review in a given case should be responsive to the needs of that particular system. This means that the scope of review must be refined to fit the purpose that judicial review was designed to fulfil in a certain instance.

116 To say the least, although accepting the principle of judicial review, the three countries have had to contend with very different conceptions and experiences of majoritarianism in each fashioning their review. The history of American constitutionalism, as studied by Bruce Ackerman, might be able to help conceptualise this difference in context.[285] Ackerman identified three "constitutional moments" in the United States' history over the last two centuries.[286] Such moments denote profound events and signal discontinuity and transformation in constitutional law.[287] One could say that everyday politics is supplanted, at least for a while, by constitutional politics which impacts on how everyday politics will be conducted in future. The legacy of such moments is nothing short of a watershed in the framework according to which a society is steered and governed from then onwards. Change generated during constitutional moments is then obviously very infrequent and may be abrupt when such moments do occur. Ackerman chiefly uses the force released by these moments to justify the judicial application of higher law created during such events.[288] However, the current purpose in speaking of constitutional moments is not so much to justify judicial review, but instead to show differences in the frequency of constitutional change that may come to influence the shape of review.[289] Simply put, having accepted the principle of judicial review, the particular constitutional setting must be brought to bear in giving flesh to the scope of review.

117 Applied to the three systems concerned, it quickly becomes clear that South Africa experienced a constitutional moment of great consequence in the 1990s when the old dispensation, bankrupted due its democratic deficit and violation of people's basic rights, was replaced by an order wanting to remedy the ills of the past by charting a new constitutional future for the country. Mahomed J. captured the moment thus:

---

[285] Bruce Ackerman, *We the People: Foundations* (Cambridge, MA: Belknap Press, 1991); Bruce Ackerman, "Revolution on a Human Scale", 108 *Yale L. J.* 2279 (1999).

[286] The foundation of the United States, the Civil War and the New Deal.

[287] *See* Neil Walker, "The Legacy of Europe's Constitutional Moment", 11 *Constellations* 368 (2004), for a succinct exposition; Gerhard van der Schyff, "Constitutional Review by the Judiciary in the Netherlands: A Bridge Too Far?", 11 *German L. J.* 275 (2010), at 284–285.

[288] For criticism of constitutional moments as a means of justifying judicial review, *see* Hirschl, *supra* note 6, at 189–190.

[289] On the constitutional effects of change, *see* also Ruti Teitel, "Transitional Jurisprudence: The Role of Law in Political Transformation", 106 *Yale L. J.* 2009 (1997).

In some countries, the Constitution only formalizes, in a legal instrument, a historical consensus of values and aspirations evolved incrementally from a stable and unbroken past to accommodate the needs of the future. The South African Constitution is different: it retains from the past only what is defensible and represents a decisive break from, and a ringing rejection of that past (...). The contrast between the past which it repudiates and the future to which it seeks to commit the nation is stark and dramatic.[290]

The process of constitution-making could evidently garner enough consensus and momentum to effect such radical change. A central feature in bringing about change was the agreed need to limit legislative power through judicial review. The excess of apartheid left its mark on constitutional thought in South Africa by illustrating the divisive and harmful effect wrought by legislation. Although universal suffrage solved the problem of legislation's legitimacy, it did not reach far enough in securing constitutional governance in the eyes of the Constitution's drafters. Taking stock of the past meant not only an acceptance of majoritarianism, but importantly also meant a condemnation of parliamentary sovereignty as the model that made the whole-scale abuse of people's rights possible in the first place. Institutional failure was to be remedied by drastic counter-majoritarianism and not put in jeopardy by half-measures, a purpose that would logically have to be reflected in the design of review. Apart from remedying defects in the constitutional system, counter-majoritarianism also had to reassure the white minority that the tables would not be turned on them once they relinquished political power to the majority.[291] Judicial review therefore had to help nurture a culture of rights and not revenge by checking majoritarianism where necessary.

118 In comparison, the HRA probably attests more to what may be termed constitutional serialism or incremental development than to a definite constitutional moment.[292] It could be argued that the change wrought by the Act is a link in a chain of constitutional events, and although of significance it does not warrant the description of constitutional moment. The HRA had to fit the strictures of the existing constitution as much as possible without really calling into question the constitutional arrangements as they had evolved over time.[293] Far from also speaking the language of

---

[290]*S. v. Makwanyane, supra* note 32, at par. 262. *See* also Van der Schyff, *supra* note 287, at 285–286.

[291]Hirschl, *supra* note 6, at 92–97, 216–218.

[292]Samantha Besson, "The Many European Constitutions and the Future of European Constitutional Theory", in Philippe Mastronardi and Dennis Taubert (eds.), *Staats- und Verfassungstheorie im Spannungsfeld der Disziplinen* 160 (Stuttgart: Franz Steiner Verlag, 2004), at 172, describes constitutional serialism as "a semi-permanent dialogue and revision process".

[293]*See* the remarks by the then Home Secretary, Jack Straw, *Hansard*, HC, 16 February 1998, col. 769.

radical change, T.R.S. Allan chose to write that public law "gained in coherence with the gradual disappearance of rigid doctrinal barriers to judicial review".[294] Conor Gearty observed that:

> The Human Rights Act 1998 has a dialectical tension at its core. On the one hand the measure presents itself as establishing a new, justiciable language of human rights; on the other it declares itself to be still in thrall to the fundamental constitutional principle of Parliamentary sovereignty.[295]

A state of affairs that judges may not forget in applying the Act, he concludes.[296] In other words, far from signalling a radical break with the past, the HRA sought to appease tradition and contradict it as little as possible. This is all but confirmed when the references to tradition in the discourse surrounding the HRA are given thought.[297] Emphasising the idea of serialism, Vernon Bogdanor speaks of the HRA as part of a piecemeal process of reform, the end-point of which is unclear.[298] And even if the HRA were a fundamental break with the past and generated a constitutional moment, that moment will undoubtedly be judged of a lower frequency than the one experienced by South Africa where the idea of parliamentary sovereignty was firmly rejected.[299] In contrast, judicial review in terms of the HRA had to be shaped in a way that did not undermine parliamentary sovereignty, but which tried to augment the protection already given to people's rights by this form of majoritarianism.

119 Viewing the Halsema Proposal in a similar light, one could pose the question whether a potential constitutional moment lurks in its wish to amend the bar on judicial review. Will the lifting or substantial amendment of the bar in section 120 of the Dutch Constitution, the topic of much debate and political wrangling since its inclusion in 1848, evidence an event that attests to transformation and discontinuity? The answer offered to this is, no. The change of direction desired by the Proposal and its novelty pale somewhat when one considers that it will not introduce the principle of judicially reviewing acts of parliament, but will upgrade the courts'

---

[294]T.R.S. Allan, "Human Rights and Judicial Review: A Critique of 'Due Deference'", 65 *Camb. L. J.*671 (1996).

[295]Conor Gearty, "Reconciling Parliamentary Democracy and Human Rights", 118 *L. Quart. Rev.*248 (2002).

[296]Ibid., at 269.

[297]E.g. White Paper, *Rights Brought Home*, supra note 74, at paras. 2.13, 2.16, made it very clear that it still attached importance to parliamentary sovereignty, a mainstay of British constitutional practice, and added that the HRA should not be entrenched as it "could not be reconciled with our constitutional traditions".

[298]Vernon Bogdanor, "Our New Constitution", 120 *L. Quart. Rev.*242 (2004), at 246.

[299]The title of an article by Arthur Chaskalson, the first president of the Constitutional Court of South Africa captures the fundamental change which South Africa underwent quite vividly: "From Wickedness to Equality: The Moral Transformation of South African Law", 1 *Int. J. Const. L.*590 (2003).

powers from the weak to strong judicial review of selected rights in the Constitution. Strong or binding review is also no novelty, as it is already required in the case of international law. The modest reach of the Proposal by limiting itself to some and not all rights guaranteed in the Constitution while still discounting the review of operative provisions such as those pertaining to the legislative process, fuels the case against identifying a constitutional moment. The Proposal sees its role not as the motor of great change, but more as an additional check being added to existing political and judicial processes.[300] The ambition of the Proposal becomes all the more clear when one considers P.A.M. Mevis' lament that the bill is "stingy", whereas in his opinion it should have heralded a "revolution" instead of simply wanting to "supplement" that which already exists.[301] This careful ambit can probably be ascribed to a lack of any real political will to turn the settled relationship between the legislature and the courts on its head, a reluctance which is traceable to the absence of any pressing need comparable to that of South Africa to effect critical and tangible constitutional change, for instance. Comparably, Vernon Bogdanor remarked of the constitutional reforms in the United Kingdom of the 1990s, of which the HRA formed a part, that there was "neither the political will nor the consensus to do more".[302] An attitude not uncommon in the Netherlands when it comes to bringing about constitutional reform, and something which typifies a country blessed by few political crises that require urgent attention.[303] However, if by a stretch of the imagination a constitutional moment is still to be identified in the Netherlands, it too, will be of a different magnitude than that of South Africa's constitutional reforms of 15 years ago.[304]

120 The purpose of this excursion is to show that while South Africa's transition can rightly be described as a negotiated revolution, the reform of judicial review in the United Kingdom and the Netherlands comes closer to semi-revolutions, if not fundamental constitutional evolution. Essentially,

---

[300]*Parliamentary Proceedings II*, 2002–2003, 28, 331, no. 9, at 14.

[301]P.A.M. Mevis, "Constitutioneel toetsingsrecht: Zuinigheid in plaats van revolutie", 32 *Delinkt en Delinkwent* 933 (2002), at 934–935.

[302]Bogdanor, *supra* note 298, at 246.

[303]Although constitutional amendments do occur from time to time, far-reaching changes are rare. Even the grand revision of 1983 (and the subsequent amendments in 1987) focused more on "tidying up" and "structuring" the Dutch Constitution than overhauling it in any major way. Cf. Adams and Van der Schyff, *supra* note 147, at 405; Bense, *supra* note 147, at 89.

[304]Similarly, W.J. Witteveen, "Nomoi: Hamilton, Koopmans en Ackerman over constitutionele toetsing", *Regelmaat* 177 (2006), at 182, makes the point that constitutional change in the Netherlands is incremental, rather than governed by "constitutional moments". Witteveen sees little difference between "constitutional" and "ordinary" Dutch politics, something which is necessary for such moments to occur. *See also* Van der Schyff, *supra* note 287, at 286–290.

judicial review in the United Kingdom and the Netherlands serves to strengthen the long-established, if imperfect, culture of rights in the two countries without upsetting majoritarian structures too much. Judicial review in South Africa on the other hand has to help build and consolidate a fledgling rights culture in a country that has known great strife and conflict for so long.[305] The simple point is that although the shared purpose behind this judicialisation of legislation may be the desire to protect people's liberty by not relying solely for this on the political process anymore, different circumstances may lead to different results in ultimately designing review. In South Africa a factor in designing review was to address the white minority's fears that the passing of political power to the majority might leave their vested and future interests unprotected. This concern was, and is, of no actual importance in the United Kingdom and the Netherlands, as in both countries thoughts about the design of review centred around refining existing political and judicial levels of protection.

There is no denying that one is dealing with different political and constitutional settings, which might conceivably lead to a different balance being struck between the legislature and judiciary in each case. It is this difference in context that must be kept in mind when studying judicial review in each of the three countries to determine how diverging constitutional landscapes may influence the eventual scope of review.

121   Mindful of the constitutional nature and character of the United Kingdom, the Netherlands and South Africa, the scope of judicial review adopted in each country will be explained, studied and compared in the following chapters. This is achieved by paying attention to the judicial fora granted the power of review.[306] Is review limited to a special court, or may most or all courts review legal norms against the background of higher law? This question is important, as review is not only dependent on the manner in which it is conducted, but also on the structural arrangements that guide its everyday application. Having established the institutional setting, attention will be turned to gauging the modalities according to which legal norms are reviewed.[307] Are courts restricted to considering enacted law (a posteriori review), or may bills also be subjected to scrutiny (a priori review)? Related to the timing of review, is the question of how a court looks upon norms. May norms be reviewed in abstract contexts or is review primarily the settling of concrete disputes through the application of higher law?

---

[305]In *Shabalala v. Attorney General of the Transvaal*, 1995 (12) BCLR 1593 (CC), 1996 (1) SA 725 (CC), at par. 26, the Constitutional Court stressed that the new order sought to achieve "a constitutionally protected culture of openness and democracy and universal human rights" in contrast to established political and legal systems that already enjoy sufficient legitimacy in this regard.

[306]Chap. 4.

[307]Chap. 5.

Although having explored a fair bit of judicial review's ambit by this stage, little remains said of the content of review.[308] What is it that is actually tested? May a norm's legality, the manner in which it formally came about, be tested, or only the reasonableness or necessity in deciding the law, its legitimacy in other words? And finally, some thought will be devoted to the consequences of review.[309] Does a judgment endeavour to leave the legislature room to respond or act, or is the intention that of handing the last word to the judiciary? In studying these elements that populate the scope of judicial review, each country's approach in giving flesh to the middle ground between its legislature and judiciary will become clear.

---

[308] Chap. 6.
[309] Chap. 7.

Chapter 4
Fora of Review

4.1 Introduction

122 In cultivating a proper understanding of judicial review, attention is not only to be paid to the structure and reasoning of a *judgment*, but also to the *court* handing down the judgment and its place in the judicial system. The principle distinction that is usually made in characterising courts is that between *centralised* and *decentralised* (or diffuse) review. In other words, does a system have a special constitutional court and what is its relation to other courts when it comes to its adjudicative powers? A wide middle ground is possible, as a system can allow for total centralisation or decentralisation with a host of options in between. First, a terminological point is in order though. While decentralisation is often referred to as the American model and centralisation as the European model, as a token to their geographical origins, this study prefers the systemic description of (de-)centralisation of review.

123 Decentralisation is the older of the two options in organising the judiciary when its comes to powers of review. It originated, as hinted to above, in the United States of America. In that country:

> [A]ny judge of any court, in any case, at any time, at the behest of any litigating party, has the power to declare a law unconstitutional.[310]

Empowering all judges in this manner is rooted in the United States' open attitude to judicial review. This attitude was evidenced early on in the well-known decision of *Marbury v. Madison*, when in 1803 the Supreme Court interpreted the Constitution to imply not only the power of judicial review but also constitutional jurisdiction for all courts.[311] An interesting decision, especially because the trend in Europe at the time was to affirm the strict

---

[310]Martin J. Shapiro and Alec Stone, "The New Constitutional Politics of Europe", 26 *Comp. Pol. Stud.* 397 (1994), at 400.

[311]*Marbury v. Madison, supra* note 17.

separation of powers, and because the American Constitution was silent on the topic of review, let alone decentralised review.

124 Nonetheless, as the principle of judicial review became increasingly tenable in the twentieth century, the winds of change were also increasingly felt on the Continent, raising questions about the way forward. Hans Kelsen proposed bridging the gap between the strict separation of legislative and judicial power in many civil law jurisdictions by centralising judicial review.[312]

This solution entailed dividing the middle ground, between politicians who were not willing to accept the review of legislation and scholars contemplating far-reaching decentralised review, by concentrating powers of review in a single constitutional court instead. In this approach ordinary courts are unburdened by constitutional questions, thereby leaving them able to pursue their traditional adjudicative role, while the institution of a constitutional court serves to protect the integrity of the constitution as the logical apex of the legal system.

Initially, Kelsen's solution did not find favour, except in the 1920s in his native Austria and the newly founded Czechoslovakia. His views were judged too conciliatory to the legislature by some, especially by those favouring strong decentralised review; whereas others feared the creation of a "supra-legislature" and not a real court.[313] Nonetheless, the emphasis in the aftermath of the Second World War on fundamental rights as co-enforced by legislatures *and* judiciaries meant that constitutional government was no longer the sole preserve of elected politics, but came alive to the possibilities presented by judicial review. This "new constitutionalism" led to a variety of jurisdictions adopting centralised review with vigour.[314]

125 However clear-cut these two models of review may seem, the distinction between them is to be thought of as a spectrum and not as two unconnected poles. Legal systems can choose to combine features of both models, often referred to as mixed or hybrid models of review. This usually means that a constitutional court is instituted, while other courts also have powers of review, such as in Portugal.[315] A constitutional court then usually retains exclusive jurisdiction over the most important topics qualifying for

---

[312]Cf. Hans Kelsen, "La garantie juridictionnelle de la Constitution", 44 *Revue de Droit Public* 197 (1928).

[313]Cf. Carl Schmitt, *Verfassungsrechtliche Aufsätze aus den Jahren 1924–1954* (Berlin: Duncker and Humblot, 1958), at 77–90; Stone Sweet, *supra* note 267, at 36–37.

[314]E.g. Belgium. Cf. Patrick Peeters, "Expanding Constitutional Review by the Belgian 'Court of Arbitration'", 11 *Eur. Pub. L.* 475 (2005); Stone Sweet, *supra* note 267, at 37–38.

[315]S. 207 read together with secs. 225 and 277 of the Constitution of Portugal (1976).

review and also acts as the highest court in all matters related to review, but recognises the role and input of other courts as well. In this regard, voices can be heard arguing for centralised systems of review to allow for more elements of decentralisation to be introduced in order to keep judicial review effective and the court system well balanced.

126 Stating the case, Victor Ferreres Comella argues that ordinary courts in centralised jurisdictions should be allowed to review legislation when there are clear constitutional court precedents to guide them, while putting preliminary questions to the constitutional court only where uncharted waters are concerned.[316] This means decentralised review in that lower judges can decide most matters before them without having to suspend proceedings for referral to the constitutional court. On the other hand, "hard cases" can only be dealt with by the constitutional court, which ought to be the best experienced in settling such matters. Mixing models of review in this way can be seen as streamlining the decision of constitutional cases by not implicating the constitutional court as a matter of course.

As this introduction has shown, decentralisation and centralisation present various possibilities and combinations according to which the fora exercising review can be designed. In what follows, a closer look will be taken at how the scope of judicial review is characterised in the United Kingdom, the Netherlands and South Africa in relation to judicial fora of review.

4.2 The United Kingdom: Following Tradition

127 A discussion of the United Kingdom's judicial organisation is a complicated exercise at the best of times, with the division of jurisdiction between the former Appellate Committee of the House of Lords and the Judicial Committee of the Privy Council once having been described as "of Byzantine complexity and obscurity".[317] Since this remark was made, a new Supreme Court has been created that has brought a clearer structure to delineating judicial jurisdiction in the United Kingdom.[318] This new

---

[316]Victor Ferreres Comella, "The European Model of Constitutional Review of Legislation: Toward Decentralization?", 2 *Int. J. Const. L.* 461 (2004), at 476.

[317]Aidan O'Neill, "Judging Democracy: The Devolutionary Settlement and the Scottish Constitution", in Andrew Le Sueur (ed.), *Building the UK's New Supreme Court: National and Comparative Perspectives* 23 (Oxford: Oxford University Press, 2007), at 46.

[318]Constitutional Reform Act 2005 (c.4). Cf. the consultation paper of the Department of Constitutional Affairs, *Constitutional Reform: A Supreme Court for the United Kingdom*, CP 11/03 July 2003; David Hoffman and John Rowe, *Human Rights in the UK: An Introduction to the Human Rights Act 1998* (Harlow: Pearson Longman, 2nd ed., 2006), at 38–40; Johan Steyn, "The Case for a Supreme Court", 118 *L. Quart. Rev.* 382

Court incorporates the House of Lords' erstwhile judicial function and hears appeals from all three of the United Kingdom's legal systems including devolution issues, but excluding Scottish criminal appeals that are still heard by Scotland's High Court of Justiciary. In addition, the reforms also entail the creation of the Judicial Appointments Commission, an independent body that must advise on most judicial appointments, thereby securing and strengthening the professional nature and independence of the bench even more than has so far been the case.[319]

However, the purpose here is not to repeat all there is to be said in this regard about the recent reforms, but to investigate the structure of the court system when it comes to reviewing legislation in terms of the HRA.

128 The main purpose of the HRA in incorporating various provisions of the European Convention on Human Rights was to make the judicial protection of fundamental rights a reality for the inhabitants of the United Kingdom more than had previously been the case.[320] This ideal was achieved not only by the number and range of rights that were incorporated, but also by making the HRA as widely applicable before judicial fora as possible. Section 6(1) of the Act makes it unlawful for a public authority to act in a way which contradicts one of the Convention rights, and by including courts and tribunals under the definition of such authorities it is clear that the judiciary as a whole is bound to consider legislation in the light of the HRA's guarantees. Although British constitutional law does not generally speak in these terms, this jurisdiction of the courts will be classified as decentralised review for present purposes. To this a qualification must be added, in that although all courts are to follow the Act's lead in protecting fundamental rights where possible, not all courts enjoy the same powers under it. Whereas section 3 makes it clear that "primary and subordinate legislation" must be interpreted and given effect to in a way which is compatible with the Convention rights, section 4 reserves the power to issue declarations of incompatibility only for the more senior courts. This power of a court to indicate to government where legislation is at fault, leaving any correction to the political process, is awarded the following courts in section 4(5) of the Act:

In this section "court" means-

(a) the Supreme Court [formerly the House of Lords];
(b) the Judicial Committee of the Privy Council;

(2002); G. van der Schyff, "Het nieuwe Britse Supreme Court belicht", 1 *Tijdschrift voor Constitutioneel Recht* 69 (2010).

[319]Cf. John Bell, *Judiciaries within Europe: A Comparative Perspective* (Cambridge: Cambridge University Press, 2006), at 310–311.

[320]Cf. White Paper, *Rights Brought Home*, *supra* note 74, at paras. 1.18–1.19. *See also* § 30.

(c) the Courts-Martial Appeal Court;
(d) in Scotland, the High Court of Justiciary sitting otherwise than as a trial court or the Court of Session;
(e) in England and Wales or Northern Ireland, the High Court or the Court of Appeal.

Thus, although the courts differ in the extent of their jurisdiction in terms of the HRA, the fact remains that each and every bench must review legislation in the light of its provisions before simply applying it, and in the process preference must be given to the HRA without violating parliament's sovereignty.

129 The HRA's decentralised application is further aided by the fact that standing under it is particularly wide, although a superficial reading of the Act will probably lead to the opposite conclusion.[321] Section 7(1) reads:

> A person who claims that a public authority has acted (or proposes to act) in a way which is made unlawful by section 6(1) [the duty of public authorities to act in accordance with Convention rights] may –
>
> (a) bring proceedings against the authority under this Act in the appropriate court or tribunal, or
> (b) rely on the Convention right or rights concerned in any legal proceedings, but only if he is (or would be) a victim of the unlawful act.

Firstly, this provision is not aimed at those instances where the courts are to exercise weak review of acts of parliament, as parliament does not qualify as a public authority.[322] This means that the normal rules of standing remain unaffected in such cases in that an applicant must show that they have a sufficient interest in bringing a matter before a court. Instead section 7(1) refers to typical cases of executive action being reviewed using the HRA. For example, where a remedy such as a quashing order of some or other executive action is claimed, such as the issuing of a building permit, and not where a court bid is aimed at securing a declaration of incompatibility regarding an act of parliament.[323] The effect of section 7(1) is to require that applicants must prove that they were victims in such administrative law cases. The term "victim" was borrowed from article 34 of European Convention on Human Rights, and must be interpreted in the

---

[321]Cf. Wadham et al., *supra* note 57, at 79–80; Mark Elliott, "The Human Rights Act 1998 and the Standard of Substantive Review", 60 *Camb. L. J.* 301 (2001); Danny Nicol and Jane Marriott, "The Human Rights Act, Representative Standing and the Victim Culture", *Eur. Hum. Rights L. Rev.* 730 (1998); Joanna Miles, "Standing Under the Human Rights Act 1998: Theories of Rights Enforcement & The Nature of Public Law Adjudication", 59 *Camb. L. J.* 133 (2000).

[322]S. 6(3) of the HRA.

[323]See *R. v. Her Majesty's Attorney General (Appellant) Ex parte Rusbridger (Respondent)*, [2003] UKHL 38, par. 21; Wadham et al., *supra* note 57, at 95.

same way as the Strasbourg organs do.[324] However, the range of parties able to litigate in such cases under the Act is limited by this requirement when compared to the possibilities under the normal rules of standing in the United Kingdom.[325] A strange situation could arise, in that the HRA although intending to bring "rights home", might actually restrict the scope of those able to claim relief under it. But this conclusion is incorrect. The fact that all courts are to give effect to the HRA as is required of other public authorities as well, means that even if a party cannot claim to be a "victim" in the meaning of section 7, courts must consider any applicable Convention right in adjudicating cases before them.[326] This broadens the application of the HRA more than the victim requirement might suggest at first glance.

130 It is tempting to think that this exposition of the fora of review under the HRA confirms a radical break with the past in the United Kingdom. Not only has the HRA placed the doctrine of parliamentary sovereignty in a new light, but importantly for this discussion, all courts have become agents in guaranteeing the Act's enforcement while a number may issue declarations of incompatibility. For would it not have been more appropriate and predictable had the power of review under the HRA been centralised in a Kelsenian fashion by awarding it to a special constitutional court, given its apparent novelty and constitutional significance? To this can be answered, that far from signalling an end to tradition, the current choice serves to confirm the constitutional traits of the United Kingdom and was to be expected for a number of reasons.

131 Centralised review is usually founded on the strict separation of powers, as the idea that courts are not to test legislation because this carries the danger of them usurping the legislative function.[327] However, the separation of powers so characteristic of French law after the Revolution of 1789 has not been repeated in British constitutionalism. In the United Kingdom there was even a debate as to whether the constitutional order can be described as resting on the doctrine of separation, and although since recognised by the courts, it certainly fails to attest to a strict separation by any measure.[328] Instead, British law's traditional concern has been more about balancing government power than necessarily separating different powers from each other. In this, it resembles the thought of John

---

[324] S. 7(7) of the HRA. Cf. Parpworth, *supra* note 31, at 427–428.

[325] Elliott, *supra* note 321, at 322–323; Wadham et al., *supra* note 57, at 80–82.

[326] *See* Elliott, *supra* note 321, at 325–334.

[327] Cappelletti (1989), *supra* note 212, at 137–138.

[328] *Consider* the various views and arguments cited by Parpworth, *supra* note 31, at 29–31, which although illustrating the weight of opinion in favour of the separation of powers, also show the difficult position of the doctrine in British constitutionalism.

Locke to a degree.[329] For although Locke identified different powers which he called the legislative, the executive and the federative, he recognised that their exercise was more often than not concentrated in the hands of the same person. Interestingly, a separate judiciary even lacked from his thought. Controlling government power was not so much to be achieved by separating its exercise from the exercise of other powers, but through cross-checks and the notion of a social contract based on the people's trust in their political masters. Which amounts to a rather distinct view from the strict Montesquieuan separation of powers as a way to protect people's liberty against a powerful state.

132 This occasional ambivalence towards the separation of powers, is illustrated by the fact that the jurisdiction of the House of Lords as the highest court in most matters, was only recently transferred to the newly created Supreme Court to achieve a visible separation between the legislative and judicial functions. This reform was first considered in the 1870s, but only came to fruition in 2009 and for the most part probably only to satisfy the European Court of Human Rights that an acceptable separation of powers was maintained which did not endanger the right to a fair trial in article 6 of the Convention on Human Rights.[330] Previously, a separation was achieved by constitutional convention instead, where members sitting on the House of Lord's Appellate Committee refrained from engaging in non-judicial political debate, even though their membership allowed for it.[331]

In considering the HRA in this light, it becomes clear that the real issue was not so much creating or selecting a special court to apply the Act in maintaining a clear separation of powers, as it was in balancing competing powers. For instance, while the Act enjoins all courts to interpret legislation in conformity with its provisions, it prevents them from striking

---

[329]Cf. Paul Joseph Kelley, *Locke's Second Treatise of Government: A Reader's Guide* (London: Continuum, 2007); Parpworth, *supra* note 31, at 19.

[330]E.g. in *Procola v. Luxemburg* of 29 September 1995, *Publ. Eur. Court H.R.*, Series A, no. 326, the European Court of Human Rights decided that Luxemburg's Council of State was not an independent and impartial tribunal in the meaning of art. 6 of the Convention (right to a fair trial), as it members also fulfilled an advisory role in the legislative process. Similarly, the Court held that the President of Guernsey's States of Deliberation (the island's parliament) was not qualified to later also sit as the sole judge in matters to be decided according to legislation in whose passing he had participated, *McGonnell v. The United Kingdom* of 8 February 2000, *Reports of Judgments and Decisions*, 2000-II.

[331]In emphasising this, the judicial members of the House of Lords made the following statement: "[F]irst, the Lords of Appeal in Ordinary do not think it appropriate to engage in matters where there is a strong element of party political controversy; and secondly, the Lords of Appeal in Ordinary bear in mind that they might render themselves ineligible to sit judicially if they were to express an opinion on a matter which might later be relevant to an appeal in the House", *Hansard*, HL, 22 June 2000, col. 419.

down legislation where such an interpretation is not possible, instead only allowing the more senior courts to issue declarations of incompatibility.[332] This immediately places the courts' powers in perspective as something different from centralising the power of review to avoid ordinary courts from considering politically sensitive issues such as fundamental rights. Weak review became the compromise for decentralising review in balancing the distribution of legislative and judicial power.

133 Decentralising review is also concomitant with other traits of the United Kingdom's legal order, such as not recognising a hierarchy of legal norms.[333] In legal systems with a distinct hierarchy, such as that of Germany, the notion of constitutional law as embodying higher law quickly develops. It is then but a small step to consider it appropriate that the enforcement of such special laws should be centralised somehow. In *A Supreme Court for the United Kingdom*, the consultation paper published in 2003 by the Department for Constitutional Affairs, it is explained that as higher law does not exist it serves no purpose to create a special court for its application. Legal theory only recognises the law as such, something which is to be applied by all courts:

> A Supreme Court along the United States model, or a Constitutional Court on the lines of some other European countries would be a departure from the UK's constitutional traditions. In the United States, the Supreme Court has the power to strike down and annul congressional legislation, and to assert the primacy of the constitution. In other countries, for example Germany, there is a federal constitutional court whose function it is to protect the written constitution. In our democracy, Parliament is supreme. There is no separate body of constitutional law which takes precedence over all other law. The constitution is made up of the whole body of the laws and settled practice and convention, all of which can be amended or repealed by Parliament. Neither membership of the European Union nor devolution nor the Human Rights Act has changed the fundamental position. Such amendment or repeal would certainly be very difficult in practice and Parliament and the executive regard themselves as bound by the obligations they have taken on through that legislation, but the principle remains intact.[334]

However, arguments that deny higher law may not be as relenting as they appear. As the quote also alludes to by conceding that any change to laws such as the HRA might be very difficult in practice, thereby signalling their special character. Add to this the judicial policy of treating the HRA as a constitutional statute that may only be amended expressly by parliament and not by implied repeal and the idea higher of law becomes a de facto

---

[332] S. 3 of the HRA. *See* also § 31 and Chapter 7.

[333] For a succinct exposition, *consult* Feldman, *supra* note 37, at 44.

[334] Par. 23 of the Department of Constitutional Affairs' consultation paper, *Constitutional Reform: A Supreme Court for the United Kingdom*, *supra* note 318. *See* also White Paper, *Rights Brought Home*, *supra* note 74, at par. 2.4, putting a similar case, but in respect of the HRA.

reality if not a *de iure* one, yet.[335] For current purposes though, the quote certainly confirms tradition by shying away from the notion of higher law, thereby justifying the HRA's decentralised application.

134 The doctrine of *stare decisis* or binding precedent, so characteristic of the United Kingdom, can also be mentioned as a factor that stimulated the adoption of decentralised review.[336] The fact that an apex court directs all other courts in the same hierarchy promotes legal unity and minimises the risk of such other benches adopting divergent approaches in adjudicating matters as important as people's rights.[337] Although helpful in understanding judicial review in the United Kingdom, care should be taken not to overstate the significance of precedent in deciding whether a system chooses decentralised review or not. While the argument based on binding precedent might be useful in explaining judicial review in systems that follow it, the opposite might not always hold true. This is because lower courts in some civil law systems that do not hold judicial precedent to be binding still tend to follow the decisions of higher courts, even though they are not formally required to do so.[338] Experience in the Netherlands also shows that the absence of binding precedents has not really featured in the debate about whether constitutional review by the judiciary is to be centralised or not. Instead, the Halsema Proposal seems to have an air of pragmatism about it, as will be explained shortly.

135 In addition, the absence in the United Kingdom of traditional civil law signposts pointing to centralised review, such as codified law and legal argumentation based on syllogism, are sometimes advanced as reasons to allow all courts the power of review.[339] The argument goes that civil law judges are more attuned to viewing the law as something to be logically deduced, than as something whose meaning is to be reasoned, and this makes it unlikely that these judges will be particularly competent at balancing the competing values of higher law. Conversely, their common law counterparts traditionally enjoy wider powers of interpretation and have

---

[335]*Thoburn v. Sunderland City Council*, *supra* note 88, at par. 63. *See* again the discussion in § 33.

[336]On binding precedent, *see* Feldman, *supra* note 37, at 92–96.

[337]One of the arguments raised by the Department of Constitutional Affairs in its consultation paper, *Constitutional Reform: A Supreme Court for the United Kingdom*, *supra* note 318, at par. 20.

[338]Cf. D. Neil MacCormick and Robert S. Summers, "Further General Reflections and Conclusions", in D. Neil MacCormick and Robert S. Summers (eds.), *Interpreting Precedents: A Comparative Study* 531 (Aldershot: Ashgate, 1997), at 531–532; M. Adams, "Precedent Versus Gravitational Force of Courts Decisions: Between Theory, Law and Facts", in E. Hondius (ed.), *Precedent and the Law* 149 (Brussels: Bruylant, 2008).

[339]Michel Rosenfeld, "Constitutional Adjudication in Europe and the United States: Paradoxes and Contrasts", 2 *Int. J. Const. L.* 633 (2004), at 635.

already tasted "judicial law-making" by developing the common law to meet new and modern needs and factual situations.[340] Although these arguments explain the ease with which decentralised review was adopted in the United Kingdom, they are not as convincing as they used to be in justifying centralised review in many civil law jurisdictions, as many civil law benches have ever-increasing experience in applying treaty law in a decentralised way, such as those in France and Belgium. This point is also emphasised by the Halsema Proposal in the Netherlands, which argues for the decentralised review of the Constitution on the basis of the courts' experience in applying higher law in the form of treaties.

Even so, the fact remains that the fora of review entrusted with applying the HRA were concomitant with the United Kingdom's legal tradition, even to the extent of affirming it. Instead of breaking with the past, review under the Act was crafted to harmonise with tradition and not to turn its back on it.

4.3 The Netherlands: Pragmatism First

136 Although surfacing from time to time, debates regarding the characterisation of fora of review have never been a particularly pressing matter in the Netherlands. This is probably due to the rather limited scope of judicial review, given the bar in section 120 of the Constitution enjoining the courts to apply acts of parliament even when they are unconstitutional. Where judicial review is allowed, think of section 94 of the Constitution for example, such review is very much decentralised. While section 94 recognises that domestic laws, including acts of parliament, must be reviewed for conformity with applicable international law, it is silent on the fora fit to conduct review. This would seem to imply the judiciary as a whole, but also the executive, as its apparatus too is entrusted with applying laws and respecting the hierarchy of legal norms.

Interestingly, a brief experiment with what would today be called a constitutional court was conducted in the Netherlands between 1802 and 1805. During this time a body comprising three members of the judiciary, called the National Syndicate, exercised centralised constitutional

---

[340]*Consider, Indyka v. Indyka* [1976] 2 All E.R. 689 (HL), at 701 (*per* Lord Reid): "Parliament has rarely intervened in the matter of recognition of foreign matrimonial decrees. The existing law is judge-made and I see no reason why that process should stop." And on the relationship between common and civil law jurisdictions on the topic of "judge-made" law, *see* H.R. Hahlo and E. Kahn, *The South African Legal System and Its Background* (Cape Town: Juta, 1968), at 305.

review.[341] More recently, the tabling of the Halsema Proposal has rekindled the debate about the appropriate fora of review were section 120 to be amended.

137 Judicial organisation in the Netherlands presents a rather complicated picture and stands on the eve of a number of reforms, the intricacies of which need not detain us here.[342] Suffice it to say that the court system traces its roots to the Napoleonic Occupation of nearly two centuries ago and today recognises four highest courts each with its own distinct jurisdiction. These are the Supreme Court (*Hoge Raad*),[343] the Administrative Law Section of the Council of State (*Afdeling Bestuursrechtspraak van de Raad van State*),[344] the Central Appellate Council (*Centrale Raad voor Beroep*),[345] and finally the Appellate Chamber for Economic Affairs (*College van Beroep voor het Bedrijfsleven*).[346] In this, the Dutch system is typical of civil law jurisdictions by having various courts of final instance depending on the nature of the legal dispute. Yet, it differs by not having an entirely separate court system for administrative law such as in France or Belgium, or labour courts as in Germany. Instead, these matters are – with some exceptions – heard by ordinary courts, while appeals make their way to each of the specialised benches for a final decision.[347] As there is no body similar to a constitutional court, each of the four benches mentioned also functions as the final instance in interpreting and applying applicable higher law. Consequently, judicial review of legislation is always conducted by ordinary judges who also hear other disputes and is not reserved for specialised members of the bench.[348]

---

[341] Cf. A.M. Elias, *Het Nationaal Sijndicaat 1802–1805* (Bussum: Fibula-Van Dishoeck, 1975).

[342] The outline of the judiciary is determined for the most part by Chap. Six of the Constitution and the Wet op de rechterlijke organisatie, 18 April 1827. Cf. A.F.M. Brenninkmeijer, "Judicial Organization", in Jeroen Chorus, Piet-Hein Gerver and Ewoud Hondius (eds.), *Introduction to Dutch Law* 53 (Alphen aan den Rijn: Kluwer Law International, 4th ed., 2006); Maria Ijzermans, "Dutch Ways of Doing Justice", in Sanne Taekema (ed.), *Understanding Dutch Law* 59 (The Hague: Boom Juridische Uitgevers, 2004), at 61–69.

[343] The highest jurisdiction in civil, criminal and tax law.

[344] As its name suggests, the final instance in administrative law.

[345] The highest jurisdiction in social security law and matters related to the civil service.

[346] This body deals with a range of commercial law matters.

[347] On the ordinary courts, see Brenninkmeijer, *supra* note 342, at 56–59.

[348] Presiding officers are normally career judges who have followed legal training upon joining the judiciary. See Erhard Blankenburg, "Dutch Legal Culture", in Jeroen Chorus, Piet-Hein Gerver and Ewoud Hondius (eds.), *Introduction to Dutch Law* 13 (Alphen aan den Rijn: Kluwer Law International, 4th ed., 2006), at 22–23; Ijzermans, *supra* note 342, 69–70; C.A.J.M. Kortmann, *Constitutioneel recht* (Deventer: Kluwer, 5th ed., 2005), at 256–285.

Clearly, judicial review is very much treated as part and parcel of the judicial function and is mostly incidental in deciding a case and thus on the whole concrete in nature.[349] This means that the normal rules of standing and causes of action apply in unlocking review.

138 Although the Halsema Proposal is largely concerned with defending the idea of allowing courts a binding power to review the constitutionality of acts of parliament, it also pays attention to which fora are to conduct the scrutiny. The Proposal comes out in support of decentralised review.[350] This means that were it to be successful in amending the Constitution, all courts would then apply the rights exempted from the bar in section 120 in passing judgment over parliament's legislation. Decentralised review has been put forward as the most logical option in structuring review because this is also the method employed in shaping the review of international law under section 94. As the Proposal perceives decentralised review to function properly in the context of international law, it was felt unnecessary to experiment with a different approach regarding constitutional review. As a matter of fact, the Proposal even warns against introducing a system of review other than decentralised review for section 120, as this would create two different systems next to each other which may cause confusion and disruption. Allowing both centralised and decentralised review would mean that even though a single right such as that to freedom of expression may be at issue, two trajectories are to be followed in the same matter if a party pleads its right both as it appears in the Constitution and the European Convention on Human Rights, for instance. In settling the case's constitutional aspects, the court would then have to refer the question to a special court for decision, while it might settle the international side itself given section 94's decentralised working. This state of affairs was thought unhelpful as it would slow down decision-making and be unjustifiably at odds with the current judicial organisation.[351]

139 In emulating treaty review, the Proposal displays as much pragmatism as it shows the limits of classic theory in a modern context when it comes to constitutional review. Theory would have us believe that civil law systems will typically centralise the review of their constitutions.[352] This preference

---

[349] The modalities of review are discussed separately, *see* §§ 187–197.

[350] *Parliamentary Proceedings II*, 2002–2003, 28, 331, no. 9, at 16–18.

[351] What is remarkable is that decentralised *weak* review under the Constitution is mentioned nowhere in the Proposal as a reason to also allow for decentralised *strong* review of constitutional guarantees. Instead the Proposal draws on the courts' experience with treaty review. This is probably because weak review under the Constitution is not a power of similar consequence and, given its infrequent appearance, not as sure a guide in deciding the shape of constitutional strong review as treaty review is.

[352] E.g. constitutional review in France, Belgium and Germany; Cappelletti (1989), *supra* note 212, at 136–146.

is seated in the fear that decentralising the application of a constitution would expose the judiciary to unnecessary political questions and consequently confuse the strict separation of powers which is at the heart of civil law theory.[353] As has been shown, these fears are much less prevalent in a common law jurisdiction such as the United Kingdom. However, where civil law systems are also monist in relation to international law, there is traditionally much less hesitation to decentralise the review of treaties, such as European Convention on Human Rights.[354] This is seen as a way to give full effect to the idea of monism and promote the integrity of international law.[355]

140 Historically, international law was also of less importance in everyday affairs than national constitutions, which lowered resistance to decentralising treaty review. For instance, while the Dutch Constitution has included an express bar on constitutional review ever since 1848, the duty of all courts to apply treaty provisions over and above legislation has remained largely uncontested. Yet, the tables have been turned. International law, especially the fundamental rights guaranteed by it, has increased markedly in importance since the Second World War.[356] An increase even to the extent of matching the role of constitutions in protecting people's rights, while at the same time doing so in a decentralised manner.[357] Predictably, this weakens the traditional resolve to centralise constitutional review, especially where such review is conducted of rights and not for instance of the unitary or federal distribution of power in a state. The reason is that civil law judges, whose ability in applying fundamental rights was usually subject to serious doubt, have gained valuable experience in balancing competing interests and applying fundamental rights given their jurisdiction to apply international law.[358] This reality has forced civil law systems with centralised constitutional review and decentralised treaty review to rethink

---

[353] Cappelletti (1989), *supra* note 212, at 137–138.

[354] E.g. France and Belgium, where treaty review is decentralised, in contrast to constitutional review, which is centralised. *See* also Heringa and Kiiver, *supra* note 15, at 97–98.

[355] As a matter of fact, European Union law even requires its decentralised application for similar reasons. Cf. Margot Horspool and Matthew Humphreys, *European Union Law* (Oxford: Oxford University Press, 4th ed., 2006), at 171 et seq.; Heringa and Kiiver, *supra* note 15, at 97–100.

[356] On the increased role of international law in the Netherlands' legal order, *see* Burkens, *supra* note 13, at 327–363; G.P. Kleijn and M. Kroes, *Mensenrechten in de Nederlandse rechtspraktijk* (Zwolle: W.E.J. Tjeenk Willink, 1986).

[357] Charting the rise of international law's importance in the Netherlands' constitutional order, *see* F.C.L.M. Crijns, *Het Europese perspectief van het Nederlandse staatsrecht* (Zwolle: W.E.J. Tjeenk Willink, 2nd ed., 1989).

[358] E.g. Hoge Raad, 10 May 1996, *NJ* 1996, 578, at paras. 3.2–3.4, is a good example of balancing competing interests in the context of the right to freedom of expression in art. 10 of the European Convention on Human Rights. For an exposition of the traditional

their position.[359] It is exactly this change of heart that has gradually come about over the years in thinking about the structure of review in some civil law systems that the Halsema Proposal taps into by arguing that review under section 120 must mirror that of section 94 of the Constitution.

141 This is not the end of the matter. The Proposal also considers the question of whether the various highest courts are a good thing in the context of judicial review. Should there be only one highest court in constitutional matters? Viewed from a different angle, one could probably speak of "horizontal" centralisation, as opposed to the "vertical" decentralisation discussed thus far. The benefits of legal unity in combining adjudication under section 120 in a single highest court, so as not to run the risk of different highest courts handing down conflicting judgments, was not found to be persuasive enough by Halsema. Instead, it was argued that the current organisation of the court system entails that such conflicts may and do arise in various fields of law.[360] This is usually corrected over time in that the courts harmonise their views on a specific issue without being forced to do so.[361] Maintaining separate highest courts was even praised in the Proposal as encouraging judicial review to be adopted, as various highest courts counter a *gouvernement des juges* by spreading judicial authority in sensitive constitutional issues over more than one court without leaving parliament challenged by a unified judicial force.[362] A clear case of structuring review sensitive to the role of democratically-elected organs.

142 It is important to note though, that in choosing decentralised review and maintaining the various highest courts, the Proposal elected not to change anything but to leave intact the current distribution of judicial power in the Netherlands. These forms of review will not become entrenched even if the Constitution is to be amended as proposed, which means that parliament is still free to legislate as it sees fit in structuring these aspects of judicial review. Nothing forbids the legislature to opt for a single highest court in constitutional matters and to decide to centralise review by depriving lower courts of jurisdiction in constitutional matters, as the Council of State also pointed out in rendering advice on the Proposal.[363]

---

deficiencies of civil law benches in applying higher law, *see* Cappelletti, *supra* note 212, at 142–143.

[359]*Consider* again Ferreres Comella, *supra* note 316, who argues that the time has come for centralised systems to introduce more elements of decentralised review.

[360]*Parliamentary Proceedings II*, 2002–2003, 28, 331, no. 9, at 17.

[361]Cf. Van Houten, *supra* note 107, at 297; G.K. Schoepen and K. Teuben, "Rechterlijke samenwerking", in E.R. Muller and C.P.M. Cleiren (eds.), *Rechterlijke macht* 403 (Deventer: Kluwer, 2006).

[362]Drawing on the views of C.A.J.M. Kortmann, "Advies van prof. mr. C.A.J.M. Kortmann", 17 *NJCM-Bull.* 305 (1990), at 306.

[363]*Parliamentary Proceedings II*, 2002–2003, 28, 331, no. 9, at 17–18; 2002–2003, 28, 331, A, at 2.

143   Legal and political opinion in the Netherlands is not unanimous in supporting the idea of decentralising the judicial review of the Constitution and the argument that various highest courts are in fact a good thing. In 1991, the then cabinet foresaw a prejudicial procedure which would refer constitutional questions to the Supreme Court for decision, instead of leaving them to the ordinary and other highest courts when a decision of unconstitutionality was likely to be handed down.[364] In this it would have resembled the present setup in South Africa, where findings of *un*constitutionality must be confirmed by the Constitutional Court. The Dutch cabinet foresaw centralisation not only for national law, but also international law, something which is not possible in the context of European Union law if it were to imply debarring other courts from applying such law at all. However, nothing came of this political initiative.[365]

144   More recently, the National Convention supported the idea of instituting a constitutional court with semi-centralised powers as the single highest bench in reviewing whether legislation conflicted with the rights in the Constitution and deserved application or not.[366] Although the idea was not really worked out in great detail, it was argued that a special court would have the advantage of concentrating constitutional expertise in a single body. This, the Convention hoped, would stimulate debate over fundamental rights protection in general and serve to bolster the quality of their implementation.

145   Jan-Willem Sap, one of the members responsible for drafting the Convention's report contemplating the Constitution's future, later further developed the idea of a constitutional court.[367] Sap chiefly modelled his views after the example of the Constitutional Court of Belgium. For instance, he argued that a special court should at first only be allowed to apply a few selected rights, such as those to equality, non-discrimination, education and the *nulla poena* principle, in order to overcome political reluctance in allowing strong constitutional review. The range of rights could be expanded over time once the principle of review had become more accepted by the legislature, as happened in Belgium. As to deciding who had to sit on the bench, his aim was to maximise experience by including

---

[364] On this, *see* C.A.J.M. Kortmann, *supra* note 362; A.W. Heringa, "Rechterlijke toetsing in Nederland", 17 *NJCM-Bull.* 235 (1992).

[365] Around the same time, the Netherlands Society of Lawyers published studies on the possible introduction of judicial review, which included some thoughts on the fora of review, *see* L. Prakke, T. Koopmans and J.M. Barendrecht, *Handelingen Nederlandse Juristen-Vereniging: Toetsing* (Zwolle: W.E.J. Tjeenk Willink, 1992), at 31, 69–80, 125–128.

[366] Hoekstra, *supra* note 135, at 9, 47. *See* also the working group's preparatory report listing a few possibilities, Zoethout et al., *supra* note 136, at 34.

[367] Jan Willem Sap, "De aanbeveling van de Nationale Conventie om een constitutionele hof in te stellen", 32 *NJCM-Bull.* 590 (2007).

senior judges, academics, and former politicians.[368] The Court's jurisdiction would attest to a hybrid arrangement, as ordinary judges would only have to refer prejudicial questions to the constitutional bench if their own judgment was not open to appeal unless they felt it to be necessary anyway.[369] The idea behind this set-up was to preserve legal unity while still allowing a measure of decentralised review. In passing, the idea was also floated to allow political organs, such as the cabinet or a fixed number of parliamentarians to seize the Court in asking it to review a law.[370] Altogether quite different from the Halsema Proposal.

146 However, Sap's ease in using Belgium as a model for structuring review in the Netherlands is open to some doubt, as E.A. Alkema also points out.[371] While Belgium experienced strong political impulses which stimulated the adoption of a constitutional court, the same cannot be said of the Netherlands. The Netherlands is still a unitary state, while Belgium embarked on a process of far-reaching federalisation in the 1970s which called for a special judicial authority to settle jurisdiction disputes between the country's various regions and linguistic communities. Adding the adjudication of constitutional rights to the Belgian Constitutional Court's portfolio was not the main reason for its creation, but initially only of secondary importance. In the Netherlands, on the other hand, the function of judicial review as envisaged by the Halsema Proposal is on the whole less ambitious. Its aim is to serve as an extra check on the legislative process.[372] The Proposal is not so much intended to stop the legislative process dead in its tracks, as it is to carefully add to the courts' existing powers of review under section 94 without wanting to needlessly upset the institutional balance of power.

147 Although correctly dismissive of the Belgian model's comparative worth given its dissimilar context, Alkema is quick to point out other

---

[368]Strangely, ministers were excluded from Sap's model, while members of parliament were expressly included. Ministers were seen as representing the executive, not the legislature, and this position would justify barring them from membership of a constitutional court. Not only is this line of reasoning dubious, it also contains a factual inaccuracy. From s. 81 of the Constitution it is clear that parliament and the government jointly constitute the legislature.

[369]Sap, *supra* note 367, at 599. This is also what the working group of the National Convention proposed, *see* Zoethout et al., *supra* note 136, at 36.

[370]Ibid.

[371]E.A. Alkema, "Repliek: Toetsing door een speciaal constitutioneel hof", 32 *NJCM-Bull.* 792 (2007), at 793–794.

[372]*Parliamentary Proceedings II*, 2002–2003, 28, 331, no. 9, at 14, where the Proposal argues that the primary duty to review legislation still rests with the legislature, while *judicial* review is to be complimentary.

reasons for rethinking the system of highest courts in the Netherlands.[373]
He pleads for creating a single highest court that would have the final word
not only on the interpretation and application of the Constitution, but also
on how Dutch courts and other state organs are to discharge their duty in
applying binding international law. The idea, it seems, is not so much to
centralise review by ousting other courts' jurisdiction, something which is
impossible in the context of EU law, but to create a central appellate body.

In contrast to Alkema, E.M.H. Hirsch Ballin considers the European
Court of Human Rights in Strasbourg and the European Court of Justice in
Luxemburg as sufficient guiding lights for Dutch courts on the topic of international and EU law without warranting a new domestic highest court.[374] In
his view, the same though cannot be said of the Constitution which is bereft
of such a "guiding light", thereby creating the need for a single bench to
steer case law on the Constitution. In achieving this, Hirsch Ballin favours
the creation of a special chamber as part of the Council of State as the only
court competent to pronounce on the Constitution, which would mean that
other courts would have to pose prejudicial questions on constitutionality to the new chamber.[375] The hidden danger in this, and here Belgian
experience *is* comparable, is that by introducing a highest constitutional
bench without giving it the last word in applying international law domes-
tically can lead to an unhealthy competition between it and the courts of
final instance for international law. The Belgian Constitutional Court is not
the highest bench in applying international law, a privilege reserved for the
Court of Cassation, something which leads to artificiality and tension as
the two courts are protective of their prestige and consequently reluctant
to refer matters to the other for final decision.[376]

---

[373]Alkema, *supra* note 371, at 796–797; E.A. Alkema, *Over implementatie van
internationaal recht – de internationale rechtsorde is de onze nog niet*, inau-
gural address as professor at Leiden University, 18 October 2005, 17 p. Cf.
https://openaccess.leidenuniv.nl/handle/1887/3764/ (last accessed on 19 November
2009). See also *Een meerkeuzetoets: De rechter en de internationale rechtsorde* (Zwolle:
Tjeenk Willink, 1985).

[374]E.M.H. Hirsch Ballin, "Een levende Grondwet", *Regelmaat* 161 (2005), at 164–165.

[375]E.M.H. Hirsch Ballin, "Constitutionele toetsing van wetten als bijdrage aan de recht-
sontwikkeling", in Willem Konijnenbelt (ed.), *Rechter en wetgever* 47 (The Hague:
Council of State, 2001), at 58–61. Hirch Ballin sees the creation of a special chamber as
a synthesis of centralised and decentralised review, yet, it seems to be more centralised,
as other courts must refer constitutional questions to this bench.

[376]*See* Eva Brems, "Belgium: The Vlaams Blok Political Party Convicted Indirectly of
Racism", 4 *Int. J. Const. L.* 702 (2006), at 709–711; P. Popelier, "Constitutionele toetsing
van wetgeving in België", *Regelmaat* 116 (2006), at 131; Jan Velaers, "De samenloop
van grondrechten in het Belgische rechtsbestel", in A.J. Nieuwenhuis et al., *Samenloop
van grondrechten in verschillende rechtsstelsels, multiculturaliteit in het strafrecht &
schuldsanering en collectieve schuldenregeling* (The Hague: Boom Juridische Uitgevers,
2008), at 81.

148   The lack of urgency driving any reform of judicial review and its organisation in the Netherlands probably explains why so many views have blossomed over the years on whether review must be decentralised or centralised. It is quite easy to contemplate various options from a position of comfort without being compelled to act. However, this lack of any real sense of change being urgently required may very well also explain why the Halsema Proposal has chosen the route of least resistance, namely that of leaving things as they are in deciding on the judicial fora to conduct constitutional review.

4.4   South Africa: A New Beginning

149   Before the advent of the new South African constitutional order, the emphasis on parliamentary sovereignty excluded the possibility of judicial review and with it any thought of how to structure it. As Didcott J. remarked in 1976:

> [U]nder a constitution like ours, Parliament is sovereign (. . .). Our courts are constitutionally powerless to legislate or veto legislation. They can only interpret it, and then implement it in accordance with the interpretation of it.[377]

The 1983 Constitution qualified the principle somewhat by allowing the various divisions of the Supreme Court to decide whether an act of parliament had come about in accordance with the correct legislative procedure while still leaving its substance sacrosanct.[378] Nothing much came of this power in practice, as it only concerned the manner and form of an act's adoption and could not be used to review its substance, thereby still safeguarding parliamentary sovereignty.

However, the start made in the 1980s towards democratisation and the idea of entrenching fundamental rights meant that their enforcement needed to be rethought. Initially, the focus rested on non-judicial means of asserting rights in the legal order and in society at large.[379] Ideas were mooted such as enjoining a parliamentary commission or other non-judicial organ to oversee the implementation of rights rather than entrusting this task to the judiciary.[380] Although the mood changed and the number of supporters of judicial review increased, opinions continued to differ as to

---

[377]*Nxasana v. Minister of Justice*, 1976 (3) SA 745 (D), at 747G.

[378]See also the discussion in § 63.

[379]Johann van der Westhuizen, "The Protection of Human Rights and a Constitutional Court for South Africa: Some Questions and Ideas, with Reference to the German Experience", 24 *De Jure* 1 (1991), at 3.

[380]Albie Sachs, *Protecting Human Rights in a New South Africa* (Cape Town: Oxford University Press, 1990), at 20–21.

whether a special constitutional bench had to be instituted and what its relationship with the ordinary courts should be.

150   By the "ordinary courts" is meant the two branches of the judiciary, namely the Supreme Court and the Magistrates' Courts.[381] The latter were never really considered an option for conducting review, as they were considered too low on the judicial ladder. Instead, attention centred on the Supreme Court. This court, contrary to its name, did not consist of a single bench, but had a court in each of the then four provinces headed by a judge president, while a number of local divisions were also created where a particular provincial bench was not able to handle the workload alone. Appeals were heard by the Appellate Division of the Supreme Court, presided over by the Chief Justice. These courts still exist today, with the difference that the local and provincial divisions have been renamed High Courts, while the Appellate Division is now called the Supreme Court of Appeal and operates under the stewardship of a President.[382]

151   These existing courts were considered unsatisfactory by many and not up to the task of exercising judicial review and cultivating the necessary respect for the new constitution. The erosion of basic rights and freedoms under apartheid meant that the courts did not enjoy the support of most South Africans, as they were seen at worst as parliament's allies and at best as turning a blind eye to apartheid.[383] Although there were moments of some judicial recalcitrance in the face of ever tightening security legislation over the years, the courts eventually became bound up in narrow and naive positivist interpretations that inevitably favoured public power. As Hugh Corder explains, the Appellate Division:

> [D]istinguished itself by its craven submission to executive discretion in the individual-State relationship, and it even appeared that the Chief Justice was forming panels of judges to hear such cases in a way that a "safe" outcome for the government was likely, if not ensured. The record of the superior courts under colonialism and apartheid can safely be described as technically competent but overwhelmingly submissive to legislative and executive fiat.[384]

---

[381] For an overview, *see* Hugh Corder, "Judicial Activism of a Special Type: South Africa's Top Courts Since 1994", in Brice Dickson (ed.), *Judicial Activism in Common Law Supreme Courts* 323 (Oxford: Oxford University Press, 2007), at 326–328.

[382] Constitution of the Republic of South Africa Amendment Act, no. 34 of 2001.

[383] Van der Westhuizen, *supra* note 379, at 5; Hugh Corder, "South Africa's Transitional Constitution", *Pub. L.* 291 (1996), at 293–294; Mark S. Kende, *Constitutional Rights in Two Worlds: South Africa and the United States* (Cambridge: Cambridge University Press, 2009), at 45.

[384] Corder, *supra* note 381, at 327. Cf. Hugh Corder, *Judges at Work: The Role and Attitudes of the South African Appellate Judiciary, 1910–50* (Cape Town: Juta, 1984); C.F. Forsyth, *In Danger of Their Talents: A Study of the Appellate Division of the Supreme Court of South Africa from 1950–80* (Cape Town: Juta, 1985).

The courts were perceived to be part of the oppressive and draconian state of affairs that prevailed under apartheid and which allowed a minority parliament to dictate the country's fate.[385]

152 Adding to the courts' legitimacy woes was the fact that their composition did not sufficiently reflect the population's make-up in order for them to be entrusted with the important task of exercising judicial review once it had been introduced.[386] The Supreme Court was almost exclusively populated by white male judges who were drawn from the small world of the bar.[387] This meant that such judges were often seen as out of touch with broader society and the people whose cases they had to hear, and although very experienced, they were not versed in engendering a human rights culture through their judgments. This is something which South Africa was in dire need of at the time. Johann van der Westhuizen explained the task ahead quite strikingly by pointing out that the judiciary had to help destroy the remnants of apartheid, while Albie Sachs stressed that the bench had to expand democracy and not restrict it.[388]

153 These and similar considerations served to justify a completely new structure to embody constitutional justice and serve as a potent symbol of nation-building and common pride among all South Africans.[389] This was the appointed route instead of simply sprucing up the existing bench, for example, by adding a special constitutional chamber to the Appellate Division.[390] Such a chamber would have run the risk of suffering from a legitimacy deficit for being too closely associated with the symbols from the old order.

As a matter of fact, it would have been quite odd if the existing bench had had the last word in deciding whether democratically-made laws had to be overturned or not. This is because it would have meant that a new and non-racial parliament had to explain its actions to a judiciary which dated largely from undemocratic times. An important case in point was the adoption of the final Constitution in 1996, as the document accepted by the Constitutional Assembly had to be submitted for judicial certification based on a number of core constitutional principles, before it could become the

---

[385]Carole Lewis, "Reaching the Pinnacle: Principles, Policies and People for a Single Apex Court in South Africa", 21 *S. Afr. J. Hum. Rights* 509 (2005), at 510.

[386]Sachs, *supra* note 380, at 20; Jeremy Sarkin, "The Political Role of the South African Constitutional Court", 114 *S. Afr. L. J.* 134 (1997).

[387]Van der Westhuizen, *supra* note 379, at 5; Lewis, *supra* note 385, at 510.

[388]Sachs, *supra* note 380, at 17–19; Van der Westhuizen, *supra* note 379, at 8.

[389]Cf. Van der Westhuizen, *supra* note 379, at 7.

[390]This was proposed by Michael Corbett, the then Chief Justice; Lewis, *supra* note 385, at 511.

country's new supreme law.[391] Quite a heavy responsibility for any court, let alone courts in all likelihood tainted by a difficult and controversial history. Clearly, constitutional and political reform meant that business as usual was out of the question for the judicial branch. Furthermore, the institutional structure of the state was also about to change from a unitary model to a federalised one, something which quite often not only justifies judicial review but also the introduction of a special court to hear jurisdiction disputes, such as in Germany and Belgium.[392]

154 In meeting these needs, a constitutional court was established by the interim Constitution of 1993, and given its current form by the final Constitution of 1996.[393] The essence of the new constitutional scheme retains the Supreme Court of Appeal (as the Appellate Division was renamed) as the highest court in *non-constitutional* matters, while the Constitutional Court became the highest authority in *constitutional* matters. However, although a certain degree of centralisation was chosen and some matters assigned solely to the Court's jurisdiction, such as conducting abstract review of legislation upon the request of a fixed number of legislators, the Court is not a classic example of centralised Kelsenian review.[394] This is evident from the fact that where the Supreme Court of Appeal or one of the High Courts (the new name for the various divisions of the Supreme Court) finds that an act of parliament is constitutional, its decision is final and only subject to appeal.[395] Were such a court to find the opposite, its decision can only become final once the Constitutional Court confirms it. This means that the legal system is based on a presumption of constitutionality, the finding of which does not warrant the Constitutional Court's gaze as a matter of course. The number of cases making it to the Constitutional Court are reduced in this way, while still allowing litigants to argue their case before the law without denying them their generous constitutional right to access justice when their rights are threatened.[396]

---

[391]Cf. §§ 68, 70; Andrew S. Butler, "The Constitutional Court Certification Judgments: The 1996 Constitution Bills, Their Amending Provisions, and the Constitutional Principles", 114 *S. Afr. L. J.* 703 (1997).

[392]Cf. Peeters, *supra* note 314, at 476.

[393]S. 98 of the interim Constitution; s. 167 of the Constitution. For critical appraisals of the Constitutional Court since its inception, *see* Lynn Berat, "The Constitutional Court of South Africa and Jurisdictional Questions: In the Interests of Justice?", 3 *Int. J. Const. L.* 39 (2005), at 48–55, 59–76; Corder, *supra* note 381, at 328–362; Du Plessis and Corder, *supra* note 174, at 194–200.

[394]S. 98(3) of the interim Constitution determined the Court's exclusive jurisdiction over a range of matters.

[395]This relates not only to the constitutionality of acts of parliament, but also to decisions regarding whether the president acted constitutionally, s. 167(5) of the Constitution.

[396]On the right to access *see*, Currie and De Waal, *supra* note 31, at 703–736.

155 Apart from appealing a case to the Constitutional Court or having a decision referred to it for confirmation, litigants can approach the Court directly when the interests of justice so require.[397] The Court takes a narrow view of this exception, as granting it deprives the bench of the benefit of lower courts' reasoning and litigants of any possibility of appeal.[398] The effect is to firmly entrench the Court as part of the judiciary and its appellate function and not as something foreign to it that will occasionally strike like a bolt from the blue. The doctrine of binding precedent further ensures the Court's ultimate authority over matters where it may happen to share jurisdiction with other courts, apart from the fact that its supremacy is guaranteed in the Constitution as well.

156 Importantly, the Constitution requires that the composition of the Constitutional Court reflect the racial and gender heterogeneity of South African society, which ensures much needed legitimacy and a bench very different from that which South Africa was accustomed to in the past.[399] Of the 11 judges making up the Court, at least four must have been serving judges prior their appointment. All members are appointed by the President of the Republic from a list of candidates prepared by the Judicial Services Commission, and after a round of consultation with the Chief Justice and the leaders of the political parties represented in the National Assembly.[400] The exceptions being the Chief Justice and Deputy Chief Justice, who are not appointed from a list of candidates. This break with the past, when the pool of candidates for judicial appointment was quite small and the process not as transparent, has meant that the demography of the constitutional bench more closely reflects the society whose rights it has to uphold. Involving a representative body such as the Judicial Services Commission, which is composed of judges, politicians, members of the legal profession and academia, means in addition that the process of selection is open to scrutiny and not confined to backroom wrangling.[401] The idea is for the members of the Constitutional Court to be professionals with a specialisation in constitutional law matters, and not a collection of elder statesmen and former politicians as is often the case with the French Constitutional Council and the Belgian Constitutional Court.

---

[397] S. 167(6)(a) of the Constitution.

[398] *Bruce v. Fleecytex Johannesburg CC, supra* note 235, at paras. 7–8.

[399] S. 174(2) of the Constitution. Judges are appointed for a term of 15 years.

[400] S. 174(4) of the Constitution.

[401] S. 178 of the Constitution; Hugh Corder, "Judicial Authority in a Changing South Africa", in Guy Canivet and Mads Andenas (eds.), *Independence, Accountability, and the Judiciary* 187 (London: British Institute of International and Comparative Law, 2006), at 196–200 on the JSC's benefits.

157   It can therefore rightly be said that the Constitutional Court is more a court of law, than a body designed to be a political extension with judicial credentials or some arbiter or other between the branches of the *trias politica* which fails to nail its colours to the mast. This has become clearer in recent years when the Court's ideal role in the judicial scheme of things is considered. For example, the initial justification for a special court with an exclusively constitutional focus has decreased somewhat. The ills of the past have been remedied in many respects, as most courts in South Africa are beginning to reflect the country's demographics.[402] This means that the reason for creating a special court to fill a legitimacy gap is no longer as important as it used to be when the interim Constitution was adopted in 1993. The break with the past, at least as far as the judiciary is concerned, has been made and is becoming more marked with the passage of time. Given the current judicial landscape, the focus is shifting to the Constitutional Court's future.

158   In this regard, questions have been raised as to whether the Court should not be integrated further into the judicial system by making it the country's apex court in all matters. This would mean that the Constitutional Court would also be the country's highest court in *non-constitutional* matters, whereas the Supreme Court of Appeal is the body of last instance in such cases at present. One of the main problems fuelling the argument for reform has been the at times difficult and confusing decision to be made between whether a matter is constitutional or not.[403] A problem which is also experienced in other countries with similar distinctions in jurisdiction.[404] In 2005, a constitutional amendment was proposed that retained the Supreme Court of Appeal, but allowed the Constitutional Court to hear any matter as and when required by the interests of justice.[405] In practice, most matters of a non-constitutional nature would still stop at the Supreme Court of Appeal, but a limited number of special cases could make their way to the Constitutional Court for the final

---

[402]Lewis, *supra* note 385, at 519.

[403]E.g. in *Phoebus Apollo Aviation CC v. Minister of Safety and Security*, 2003 (1) BCLR 14 (CC), 2003 (2) SA 34 (CC), the Constitutional Court was careful not to make a constitutional issue of the doctrine of vicarious liability, as did happen in *K. v. Minister of Safety and Security*, 2005 (3) SA 179 (SCA).

[404]E.g. the Belgian Constitutional Court only adjudicates constitutional disputes. While the other courts in the country, such as the Court of Cassation, adjudicate applicable international law, but not the Constitution. This has led to tension between the two courts. Cf. Brems, *supra* note 376, at 709–711; Lech Garlicki, "Constitutional Courts Versus Supreme Courts", 5 *Int. J. Const. L.* 44 (2007).

[405]Cf. Lewis, *supra* note 385, at 509 et seq.; http://www.pmg.org.za/ (the Parliamentary Monitoring Group – last accessed on 19 November 2009). *See* also the recommendations by Jonathan Lewis, "The Constitutional Court of South Africa: An Evaluation", 125 *L. Quart. Rev.* 440 (2009), at 466.

word on them. However, to date not much has come of the proposal, and this can probably be explained by the fact that the Department of Justice conducted very little consultation with the courts and the legal profession before tabling the bill. Although the approach has been criticised, many stakeholders might still be in favour of the envisaged change.[406]

159 The introduction of the Constitutional Court has proved invaluable for South Africa. Not only did this special body help to make constitutional justice acceptable in the eyes of many South Africans, it has also been a driving force in embedding a narrative based on fundamental rights in the country's legal thinking.[407] The fact that the Court, although enjoying ultimate and sometimes exclusive constitutional jurisdiction, was not neatly severed from the rest of the court system means that the Constitution is not seen as something reserved for special judges removed from everyday reality. Deciding on a hybrid structure of shared jurisdiction between the Constitutional Court and other courts has proved very useful in constructing the scope of judicial review in South Africa. Two purposes are served, that of severing ties with the past and that of encouraging existing courts to participate in bringing about fundamental change. Moves towards an apex court are also to be seen in this light, namely that of strengthening legal unity while not sacrificing constitutional wisdom.

4.5 Concluding Remarks

160 What is immediately apparent from comparing the three systems, is the different way in which each has approached the organisation of its bench. While the United Kingdom and the Netherlands come closest to full decentralised review, South Africa employs a hybrid model of centralisation. This diversity in approach confirms that despite the general acceptance of the principle of judicial review, the way in which it is shaped or given form is often a matter of disagreement and debate. Sir Otto Kahn-Freund even went so far as to warn against the worth of comparing matters of procedure and judicial organisation, preferring instead comparison that focuses on issues of substantive law.[408] Although this observation is true under some circumstances, its blanket application would undoubtedly be an exaggeration.

161 This is illustrated by the combined experience of the three systems, the worth of which is to emphasise the relationship between the purpose

---

[406]E.g. Lewis, *supra* note 385, at 522–523.

[407]*Compare, Shabalala v. Attorney General of the Transvaal, supra* note 305, at par. 26.

[408]O. Kahn-Freund, "On Uses and Misuses of Comparative Law", 37 *Mod. L. Rev.* 1 (1974), at 20.

in introducing judicial review on the one hand and shaping the judiciary
to conduct such review on the other. When adopting judicial review, the
less its purpose is to upset the relationship between the legislature and
the judiciary, the more probable it becomes that hitherto established patterns of judicial organisation will be followed in designing review. Patterns
which meant decentralised review both under the HRA and according to
the Halsema Proposal. The more radical the change in the relationship
between the legislature and the judiciary envisaged by introducing review,
the greater the importance of a particular political setting becomes as a
guide over and above a reliance on established patterns of awarding jurisdiction. If South Africa's experience is anything to go by, systems will be
more inclined to experiment with centralisation under such circumstances
in order to formalise and drive radical change, instead of leaving such a
project to a judiciary that might not share in the political mood, or at least
not as vigorously.

162 Incorporating the European Convention on Human Rights in the
United Kingdom is a good example of where allowing fundamental rights
to be judicially applied to legislation did not mean that traditional theory on judicial organisation had to be displaced in the process. The extent
of that system's constitutional reform in adopting the HRA was not justified in upsetting the relationship between the legislature and the judiciary.
Although it was recognised that the European Convention on Human Rights
had to be incorporated to secure people's rights more effectively, this had
to happen in conjunction with conventional theory.[409] Something which
meant its decentralised application.

Decentralised review, as has become clear from the discussion, is concomitant with the United Kingdom's traditional denial of higher law, which
means that there exists no separate body of law to be applied by a court
created especially for that purpose.[410] Similarly, the absence of a strict
separation of powers sits easier with the idea that all courts may engage
in actions that attest to judicial law-making and not only the legislature or
a constitutional court. The law is there to be applied by all courts, with the
real question centring not so much on which courts are to apply the law,
but what constitutes law. And where this liberal attitude to which courts
may apply the rights guaranteed by the HRA might put judicial certainty
in jeopardy, the doctrine of binding precedent ensures that lower courts
follow the lead of higher courts in fostering a common approach to legal
doctrine. Even though some of these factors might have to be taken with
a pinch of salt in today's legal theory – such as the idea that higher law

---

[409]Elizabeth Wicks, *The Evolution of a Constitution: Eight Key Moments in British
Constitutional History* (Oxford: Hart Publishing, 2006), at 132, speaks of the Act as
being a "compromise" between conventional theory and the wish for reform. *See* § 118.
[410]*See* § 133.

is not a characteristic of common law systems – the combined strength of these factors is to champion decentralised review over centralised review. The introduction of judicial review under the HRA then did not come as a shock to the system in the United Kingdom, but came with the reassurance that its implications for the bench's organisation confirm tradition more than they contest it.

163 In comparison, the Halsema Proposal's wish to introduce decentralised review of the Constitution may seem quite strange at first, as many of the very characteristics that encouraged decentralised review in the United Kingdom are absent from the Netherlands' legal system. For a start, Dutch legal thought never really grappled with the idea of higher law, having accepted the idea in its Constitution ever since the nineteenth century by including fundamental rights and entrenching their protection. Related to this is the relatively strict separation of powers in many civil law jurisdictions. Combined, this sits uneasy with the idea that ordinary judges be allowed to apply higher law, as it might amount to too much judicial law-making by questioning the province of the legislature and because it might also engage questions of a political nature.[411] Yet, the idea to allow for decentralised review under the Halsema Proposal is not all that surprising. Granted, other voices can be heard arguing the case for a constitutional court with varying degrees of centralised powers to be instituted, but opinion is very divided on the issue.[412] The simple fact is that centralised constitutional review may not be the best option judged from the perspective of current judicial practice and accumulated experience over the years. As the Proposal argues, courts are used to applying applicable rules of international law in a decentralised fashion, and have been doing so for many decennia with ever-increasing frequency and without any real problems to date. On this view, the practical and safe route would be to also decentralise the constitutional review of acts of parliament.[413]

164 One might even say that the Proposal is the result of a gradual reappraisal of the Netherlands' adherence to a fairly strict separation of powers regarding the review of legislation, and not simply the product of pure pragmatism. Either way, the effect that the decentralised review of legislation has generated over the years is that the onus now rests not so much on those wanting to decentralise review to prove their case, as it does on those wanting to centralise review to prove theirs. Breaking with this tradition of decentralisation might be quite difficult, as it would require sufficient need

---

[411] The relevance of such a strict separation of powers has already been criticised in this study and will not be repeated here, see §§ 95–99.

[412] See §§ 143–147 where the arguments in favour of a constitutional court are discussed.

[413] To use the words of Ginsburg, *supra* note 5, at 36, it can be argued that Dutch courts have gained sufficient "institutional credibility" to justify decentralised review.

matched with appropriate momentum to upset what has become accepted practice. In this regard, it could be argued that the Halsema Proposal cannot rely on enough momentum to also warrant introducing a new judicial organisation even if it wanted to do so. Political enthusiasm for the bill might not stretch that far. In contrast, the Netherlands' neighbouring countries, Germany and Belgium, have each experienced political and constitutional changes, constitutional moments if you will, that necessitated the centralisation of review. Germany wanted to make a clean break with its totalitarian Nazi past and realised that this could not be achieved by relying solely on the existing courts to stimulate a human rights culture, and in addition, like Belgium, needed a non-legislative body to adjudicate jurisdiction disputes arising from its newly created federation.[414]

165 The situation in the Netherlands is quite different. There the Halsema Proposal has gone to great lengths not to experiment with new approaches to review, but has stressed the ease with which judicial review can be combined with existing ways. Allowing the strong judicial review of acts of parliament against selected provisions in the Constitution can probably afford the luxury of trial and error in deciding on the ideal fora to carry out such review and the extent of its centralisation. This is because procedural problems can simply be addressed by ordinary legislation without a constitutional amendment being required as in the case of section 120, as pointed out in the discussion of the Netherlands' fora of review.[415] There is essentially no pressing need to expect of the Dutch parliament to pass the Proposal *and* reorganise the judiciary at the same time. On the whole, structuring the fora of review in the Netherlands and the United Kingdom presents a very different picture indeed to that of South Africa's experience.

166 In stark contrast, constitutional reform in South Africa did not ask the question how established patterns could be confirmed to ease the introduction of judicial review. The shape of reform was not driven by a need to follow legal traditions such as in the United Kingdom or settled practice in the Netherlands, but could only be justified against the ideal of what constitutional justice had to be. Nothing from the past could be considered "sacred" if it did not fit the aspirations of the new order. This also meant that the country's judicial organisation came under intense scrutiny. Arguably, South Africa's legal system would have been more inclined to decentralised rather than centralised review of its Constitution under normal circumstances.[416] This is because the court system was based on a single hierarchical structure with the erstwhile Appellate Division at its

---

[414]McWhinney, *supra* note 5, at 7; Kader Asmal, "Constitutional Courts – A Comparative Survey", 24 *Comp. Int. L. J. South. Afr.* 315 (1991), at 317–318.

[415]*See* § 142.

[416]Making a similar point, *see* Ginsburg, *supra* note 5, at 33.

apex, while the doctrine of binding precedent secured the Court's authority over the lower courts that had to adhere to its interpretation of the law.[417] These facts would obviously militate against the creation of a special court next to the existing court structure with the exclusive jurisdiction to review constitutional matters, because the power of review could simply be entrusted to the Appellate Division. This would have meant that the lower courts would have had to follow its lead in the field of constitutional interpretation.[418]

167   However, the constitutional trauma associated with apartheid and the illegitimacy of the existing bench in the eyes of many, meant that decentralised review or simply modifying existing structures presented no credible option.[419] The Constitution and the hope it embodied had to be entrusted to a new bench that was up to the task, a need which the creation of the Constitutional Court satisfied. The main purpose was that of securing constitutional justice that would be legitimate and actively further people's newly guaranteed rights. The tarnished state of democracy in South Africa meant that its primary exponent, parliament, needed radical reform, which also meant that the judiciary could not by way of course be shielded from real reform itself.[420] Embracing judicial review was not simply a question of adding to the existing configurations that characterised the relationship between the legislature and the judiciary, such as in the British and Dutch cases, but it meant creating a completely new constitutionalism from scratch. Such was the legal necessity and political reality that the existing judicial organisation could not satisfy.

168   Interestingly, although the South African experience may go some way towards affirming Ran Hirschl's theory that the device of judicial review allows waning centres of power to retain their hegemony in future by recourse to the courts if no longer the political process, it also shows ways of limiting such hegemony through properly structuring judicial review.[421] Fitting his explanation, it is plausible to argue that introducing judicial review in the country served to protect the white minority's economic and social, but not political, position from majoritarian intrusion – hence

---

[417]See § 150.

[418]The 1983 Constitution proved the point in a way by entrusting the (very limited) power to check the formal quality of an act of parliament to the various divisions of the then Supreme Court, instead of centralising it in any way. See §§ 61, 149.

[419]See §§ 151–154.

[420]Ginsburg, *supra* note 5, at 36, also makes the point that new democracies are often not equipped to allow decentralised judicial review.

[421]Hirschl, *supra* note 6, at 50–99, 216–218. See also Ran Hirschl, "The Political Origins of Judicial Empowerment Through Constitutionalization: Lessons From Four Constitutional Revolutions", *L. Social Inquiry* 91 (2000), at 134–138; Michael Mandel, "A Brief History of the New Constitutionalism, or 'How We Changed Everything So that Everything Would Remain the Same'", 32 *Israel L. Rev.* 251 (1998), at 277–281.

explaining partly this minority's support of review. However, the new court structure was geared not towards protecting the old order from the new by a continued reliance on a discredited judiciary. Instead it sought to emphasise and accelerate change by creating a specialised constitutional court. As a consequence, ruling through the bench and not through parliament became decidedly more difficult for the white minority. Semi-centralising review by devolving some powers to other courts reinforces this point, as it was appreciated that the Constitutional Court could not be cut off from the very court system whose motor for change it had to become, thereby justifying a departure from pure centralisation in most cases. Yet, pure centralisation was also rightly to be expected in those matters where political organs enjoy sole standing to initiate abstract review under the Constitution.[422] Where this is usually the case, a system nearly always chooses to centralise what has the potential of being very sensitive matters, for example in France, where only the Constitutional Council enjoys jurisdiction to test the constitutionality of parliamentary bills.[423] Conversely, where political organs lack sole standing, as experience in the United Kingdom and the Netherlands confirms, there may be one reason fewer to award constitutional jurisdiction to a single court.

169 Essentially, while the context of reform sought to confirm tradition in the United Kingdom and settled practice in the Netherlands, the South African experience evidenced a radical new constitutionalism. A new wind that did not turn to the past for any inspiration and security, but one which wanted to make a clean break with the past as it posed a threat to the future of reform. This situation meant creating a constitutional court with semi-centralised powers in South Africa, while the wish to secure the future by reference to the familiar, explains why the HRA and the Halsema Proposal opted for decentralised review.

The systems also show the living character of judicial organisation. Reform is only justified, and continues to be justified, as long as it corresponds to the needs of the legal system it is intended to serve. For instance, after the initial effort in bridging the gap between an undemocratic dispensation to a democratic one, thought in South Africa turned to more effective ways in which the relationship between the Constitutional Court and the Supreme Court of Appeal could be structured.[424] In other words, the priority of consolidating sound constitutional justice having largely been achieved, meant that room was created to consider streamlining the system. Similarly, in the Netherlands the Halsema Proposal makes it clear that other options must be engaged if the decentralised review it champions, turns out not to be answer in allowing constitutional review.

---

[422] See § 154.

[423] S. 61 of the French Constitution (1958).

[424] See § 158.

Chapter 5
Modalities of Review

5.1 Modalities of Review

170 The act of judicial review entails matching two norms against each other. The idea is to find out whether a legal norm fits the requirements of a set of higher norms.[425] In classifying ordinary legal norms, a distinction can be made between legislative and common law legal norms. As explained earlier, the focus of this study rests on investigating legislative norms, while reference to common law norms will be made where appropriate.[426]

In reviewing legislative norms, two major modalities can be distinguished. The first relates to the stage when review first becomes possible during the legislative process, while the second relates to whether norms may be reviewed in an abstract or concrete setting. These modalities can obviously have a far-reaching effect on the scope of judicial review by determining when and how legal norms are scrutinised.

171 As to the first modality of review, legislative norms capable of review need not necessarily be enacted law, but can also include bills.[427] In other words, it is possible for norms to be reviewed by the judiciary before they pass into law. While judicial review is usually exercised once the political process has taken its course (a posteriori review), prior review allows the judiciary a say in the norms still to become law (a priori review).

Prior review enhances the standing of a piece of legislation, because those who ultimately enact it, already know that the judiciary found it to be compatible with higher norms.[428] But the price of such legal certainty,

---

[425]*See* the definition of judicial review in § 8.

[426]This distinction is explained in § 13.

[427]Rautenbach and Malherbe, *supra* note 22, at 244–245.

[428]Van der Hoeven, *supra* note 258, at 787, considers that the abstract review of bills reduces the chance of difficult constitutional questions arising at a later stage.

G. van der Schyff, *Judicial Review of Legislation*,   107
Ius Gentium: Comparative Perspectives on Law and Justice 5,
DOI 10.1007/978-90-481-9002-7_5, © Springer Science+Business Media B.V. 2010

is that the legislative process is no longer the sole domain of the legislature, but may also be influenced by the courts. A posteriori judicial review of legislation, on the other hand, guarantees the legislature more room in deciding for itself what it considers sufficient to become law.

172 The prime example of prior judicial review is the French Constitution of 1958 which allows the Constitutional Council (*Conseil constitutionnel*) to test whether bills are constitutional or not.[429] Organic bills, in other words bills whose passing is mandated by the Constitution, *must* be submitted for prior review; while all other bills, the ordinary bills, *may* be reviewed. However, seizing the Council to review bills is still very much a political matter, as private parties enjoy no standing in this respect.[430] The judicial process is thus not open to all possible interested parties, but is restricted to political actors only. The idea is clearly to allow important office-holders and legislative minorities to call on the wisdom of judicial reason, where reasoning with their political colleagues has failed them.[431]

If the Council rejects a bill, it may not be promulgated in its present form. The upside of prior judicial intervention is of course that enacted legislation is unlikely to be challenged in the courts on constitutional grounds.[432] The reason for this being that legislation then enjoys a constitutional stamp of approval or *nihil obstat* as it were before it comes into force.[433]

173 The second modality of review that is distinguished relates to whether contested norms are reviewed in an *abstract* or *concrete* fashion.[434] Abstract review refers to cases where a court judges the compatibility of ordinary norms with higher norms without there being a factual dispute

---

[429]Cf. J.H. Reestman, *Constitutionele toetsing in Frankrijk: De Conseil constitutionnel en de grondwettigheid van wetten en verdragen* (Nijmegen: Ars Aequi Libri, 1996); Koopmans, *supra* note 6, at 34, 69–76; Allan R. Brewer-Carías, *Judicial Review in Comparative Law* (Cambridge: Cambridge Universtiy Press, 1989), at 251–260.

[430]According to s. 61 of the French Constitution (1958), an ordinary bill may be referred to the Council by the President of the Republic, the Prime Minister, the President of either the Senate or National Assembly; or, since 1974, by at least sixty members of either the Senate, amounting to 20% of its membership, or the Assembly, amounting to about 10% of its membership.

[431]Stone Sweet, *supra* note 267, at 198, explains: "The rules governing the exercise of constitutional review differ radically from the rules governing parliamentary decision-making. This difference is exactly what attracts the opposition to the court, since under majority decision rules, the opposition always loses".

[432]S. 62 of the French Constitution (1958).

[433]Until the constitutional reforms of 2008, the Council presented the archetypal model of prior review in that the constitutionality of legislation could never be challenged before the courts. However, it is now possible for other courts to refer constitutional issues that arise from legislation to the Council, thereby allowing for unforeseen circumstances to be judicially factored.

[434]Rautenbach and Malherbe, *supra* note 22, at 245.

between litigants. In other words, the judiciary is only called upon to evaluate a legal norm as such without applying the contested norm to solve any particular conflict at the same time. Concrete review involves matters where in order to solve a real conflict between parties a court has to test a legal norm in the process. For example, when parties complain that the state should never have enforced a law against them, by reason that the legislation violated a higher norm.

174   By definition, prior review is a type of abstract review, such as the review of bills by the French Constitutional Council. This is because a court has to judge a bill on its own merits without a concrete case being heard, as the bill still has to become law before it can be applied to everyday situations. However, abstract review can also be conducted of legislation already enacted, and not only bills. For instance, the German Basic Law allows for the compatibility of a federal or *Land* law to be reviewed by the Federal Constitutional Court on request of the federal government, a *Land* government or a third of the members of the lower house of parliament, the *Bundestag*.[435] Private parties may also request abstract review after having exhausted all other remedies, including concrete review.[436] Similarly, Belgian law allows the abstract review of legislation by the Constitutional Court on application of certain political organs, such as the Council of Ministers, or individuals and bodies to whom the contested legislation could be applied in future.[437] However, in Germany no time limit is fixed within which an application for the abstract review of legislation may be brought, while a similar application in Belgium must be brought before the Constitutional Court within six months of the contested legislation having come into force.[438] This means that although private parties do not have to exhaust all other remedies in Belgium as opposed to their counterparts in Germany, they have to act timeously in requesting abstract review.

175   Abstract review can take on many forms and combinations, depending on the particular system. Systems that allow the abstract review of *posited* norms, usually allow the concrete review of such norms as well, as

---

[435]S. 93(2) of the German Constitution (1949). Prior review is also allowed in Germany, but then in respect of treaties still to be ratified.

[436]S. 4 ibid. Cf. Brewer-Carías, *supra* note 429, at 210–211.

[437]S. 2 of the Special Majority Act on the Court of Arbitration of 6 January 1989. Even though political organs do not have to show a particular interest to enjoy standing, while private parties must show that the contested law could negatively affect them, the Belgian Constitutional Court does not exercise concrete control in the latter cases. The Court does not solve any dispute in such matters but only pronounces judgment on the constitutionality of the contested legislative norms.

[438]S. 3(1) of the Special Majority Act on the Court of Arbitration of 6 January 1989. Cf. Peeters, *supra* note 314, at 475 et seq.

is the case in Belgium and Germany.[439] In comparison, the Constitutional Council of France until recently only exercised the abstract review of bills and not either abstract or concrete review of enacted legislation in respect of the Constitution. Although a system's scope of judicial review may provide for both abstract and concrete modes of review, many systems emphasise the latter. Federal courts in the United States are a case in point, as they may only hear matters that present a "case or controversy".[440] This is taken to mean that there must be an actual dispute between adversarial parties which is capable of being resolved by a court, thereby excluding the possibility of applying to a court to review only a norm itself. Courts must refuse to hear cases where a controversy has not arisen yet and which are therefore "unripe", as well as cases that are "moot", which means that the controversy has been settled in the mean time.[441]

176 However, it would be rash to argue that abstract review is never possible in jurisdictions without special procedures and rules of standing. In conducting concrete review, American courts sometimes face situations that call for an abstract evaluation and hypothetical reasoning that devalue any supposed concrete application of higher norms, although this might not be readily admitted.[442] On this, Alec Stone Sweet and Martin Shapiro conclude after having studied various judgments that:

> However understood, the abstract review of statutes is alive and well in the United States. Indeed, it has become a "normal" technique of judicial lawmaking in the areas of free speech and abortion rights.[443]

It would therefore be better to speak of the abstract and concrete review of legislation as presenting a spectrum of possibilities, and not as distinct and unconnected categories. This is also the reason why definitions that equate abstract review *only* with prior review or rules concerning standing

---

[439]Brewer-Carías, *supra* note 429, at 211. The obligation of ordinary courts in many systems of judicial review to put a prejudicial question to a constitutional court, does not detract from the concrete nature of the review. This is because judicial review is still brought to bear on a particular dispute, if not by the same judge who has to decide the facts of the case between the parties.

[440]Concrete review is traced to art. III of the United States Constitution that extends the courts' jurisdiction to matters that involve either a case or controversy; Brewer-Carías, *supra* note 429, at 144–145.

[441]This power is interpreted as excluding advisory opinions, but not a declaration of rights.

[442]E.g. an exception of sorts was recognised concerning the constitutionality of abortion in *Roe v. Wade*, 410 US 113 (1973). The matter was heard, even though the judicial appeal process would have lasted longer than the average pregnancy. In other words, by the time a judgment was handed down, the pregnancy would have run its course, thereby rendering the question of whether abortion was constitutional purely academic.

[443]Cf. Alec Stone Sweet and Martin Shapiro, *On Law, Politics and Judicialization* (Oxford: Oxford University Press, 2002), at 352.

for political organs are not followed in this study.[444] These factors may indicate abstract review, but abstract review should not be confined to such examples.

177 In what follows the distinguished modalities of review will be investigated in the United Kingdom, the Netherlands and South Africa. Do these systems employ abstract review of bills and/or abstract or concrete review of legislation? And what may be the reasons for any differences found?

5.2 United Kingdom: Respecting Parliamentary Sovereignty

5.2.1 Abstract Review of Bills

178 As to the modalities of review, the HRA does not provide for the abstract review of bills. This is evidenced by the fact that the Act only makes reference to "legislation" and creates no special procedure that would allow for Westminster's parliamentary bills to be judicially reviewed.[445] An exclusive focus on the review of legislation is explainable given the strong tradition of parliamentary sovereignty in the United Kingdom. Interestingly, this tradition is confirmed by the fact that bills from the Scottish Parliament may be submitted for prior review in order to determine whether devolution laws were respected, so as not to undermine Westminster's supreme will.[446] However, this is of less importance for the current discussion as it relates to devolution and not the HRA.

179 Instead of enabling prior judicial review, the HRA places the duty squarely on the political process itself to ensure that it honours the requirements of the HRA. This is done by expecting of ministers who table

---

[444]*Consider* John C. Reitz, "Political Economy and Abstract Review in Germany, France and the United States", in Sally J. Kenney, William M. Reisinger and John C. Reitz (eds.), *Constitutional Dialogues in Comparative Perspective* 62 (Basingstoke: Macmillan, 1999), who defines abstract review as "facial challenges to the constitutionality of legislation at the behest of certain official parties with automatic standing".

[445]E.g. s. 3 of the HRA.

[446]S. 33 of the Scotland Act 1998 (c. 46): "(1) The Advocate General, the Lord Advocate or the Attorney General may refer the question of whether a Bill or any provision of a Bill would be within the legislative competence of the Parliament to the Supreme Court for decision. (2) Subject to subsection (3), he may make a reference in relation to a Bill at any time during- (a) a period of four weeks beginning with the passing of the Bill, and (b) any period of four weeks beginning with any subsequent approval of the Bill in accordance with standing orders made by virtue of section 36(5). (3) He shall not make a reference in relation to a Bill if he has notified the Presiding Officer that he does not intend to make a reference in relation to the Bill, unless the Bill has been approved as mentioned in subsection 2(b) since the notification."

legislation to publish or state before the second reading of a bill that is compatible with the requirements of the HRA. Were a minister unable to make such a statement, this must also be made known.[447] The motivation behind such statements is to force the government to consider and respect the rights guaranteed by the HRA, but also to be honest where this was not the case. This leaves parliament to decide whether it wants to support legislation that contradicts the Act's protection or not. Debating the desired impact of fundamental rights on legislation is so brought to the fore and not allowed to be skirted or kept silent about. The Joint Parliamentary Committee of Human Rights (JCHR), which consists of members of both legislative chambers and was appointed in 2001, serves an important function in this regard.[448] The JCHR considers matters relating to fundamental rights in the United Kingdom by scrutinising all government bills and giving further examination to those bills that have serious rights implications. In doing so, the JCHR has come to influence parliament on much debated pieces of legislation such as the Anti-Terrorism, Crime and Security Act of 2001 and the Terrorism Act of 2006. The JCHR has also been critical of the government's handling of people's rights on numerous other issues.[449]

The fact remains though that statements of compatibility and other initiatives such as the JCHR form part of the legislative process and do not amount to any prior judicial control.

5.2.2 Abstract or Concrete Review of Legislation

180 As the Mother of Parliaments, Westminster has been immune to all forms of external control, apart from regular elections, for centuries. Its measure has been its own integrity and judgment. Courts had to make do with holding legislation against the light of common law rights, but the doctrine of parliamentary sovereignty meant that legislation could be interpreted in the light of such rights only where the legislation itself was not gainsaid.[450] The HRA continues this interpretive tradition, but lends more force to judicial interpretation than has been the case traditionally. The

---

[447]S. 19 of the HRA. *See* also Robert Hazell, "Pre-legislative Scrutiny", *Pub. L.* 477 (2004).

[448]Cf. Wadham et al., *supra* note 57, at 13–14; David Feldman, "Parliamentary Scrutiny of Legislation", *Pub. L.* 323 (2002).

[449]Cf. JCHR, "The Committee's Future Working Practices", 23rd Report (2005–2006), August 2006; JCHR, "The Work of the Committee in 2007 and the State of Human Rights in the United Kingdom", 6th Report (2007–2008), February 2008, at 36–39. Available from http://www.parliament.uk/ (last accessed on 19 November 2009).

[450]On common law rights, *see* § 26.

Act, in section 3(2)(a), makes acts of parliament and delegated legislation capable of review. However, judicial review is not limited to these norms as such, as section 6 makes it unlawful for a public authority to act in contravention of the rights guaranteed by the HRA.[451] The definition of public authority excludes parliament, but includes courts, tribunals and persons exercising a function of a public nature. This means that all lawful action can in principle be interpreted and judged according to the dictates of the HRA, creating an impressive range of reviewable facts indeed.[452] Because section 6 makes no distinction as to the legal base of public authorities' actions, both actions with a legislative and common law origin reside under the Act. In particular, for the courts this means that they have to develop the common law by following the dictates of the HRA in shaping that body of law.[453]

181   In characterising the judicial review of legislation under the HRA as being either abstract or concrete it can be remarked that British courts have always been reluctant to decide legal issues that will not resolve concrete cases.[454] In *Gillick v. West Norfolk and Wisbeck Area Health Authority*, a case predating the HRA, it was said that courts may not speak or proffer "answers to hypothetical questions of law which do not strictly arise for decision".[455] This emphasis on concrete review is also evident in cases dealing with the HRA.

182   A good example is *R. (Burke) v. The General Medical Council*.[456] In this matter it was common cause that due to a debilitating illness, a patient would require artificial nutrition and dehydration treatment in future and that towards the end of his life he would probably not be competent to decide the course of his own treatment. Given this prospect, he feared that necessary artificial nutrition and hydration treatment might be withheld from him in future by doctors, leading him to die. This fear prompted him to claim judicial relief in assuring continued medical treatment, were he to need it.

The court *a quo* heard the matter and made six declarations after having interpreted the patient's rights in conformity with a number of

---

[451]Cf. Wadham et al., *supra* note 57, at 53, 70–76.

[452]S. 3 of the HRA read together with s. 6.

[453]Cf. Gearty, *supra* note 84, at 78–83, 157–167.

[454]John Bell, "Reflections on Continental European Supreme Courts", in Guy Canivet and Mads Andenas (eds.), *Independence, Accountability, and the Judiciary* 253 (London: British Institute of International and Comparative Law, 2006), at 260.

[455]*Gillick v. West Norfolk and Wisbech Area Health Authority*, [1986] AC 112, at 193–194.

[456]*R. (Burke) v. The General Medical Council*, [2005] EWCA Civ 1003.

Convention rights.[457] Three of the declarations related to the patient as such, while three related to a guidance document issued by the General Medical Council (GMC) regarding the treatment of patients who required artificial nutrition and hydration. In the process, the judge declared some parts of the GMC guidelines to be unlawful and considered general questions of medical law and ethics in great detail. The GMC appealed the decision wanting the declarations to be overturned.

183 The Court of Appeal allowed the appeal and set the six declarations aside. It noted that the relief claimed, extended far beyond what was necessary in allaying the patient's fears.[458] The Court also criticised the Official Solicitor, who having found that the facts would probably only lead to any real legal questions at a future date, went on to canvass issues which he considered to be of "general public importance" instead.[459] The Court observed that:

> There are great dangers in a court grappling with issues such as those that Munby J. [in the court *a quo*] has addressed when these are divorced from a factual context that requires their determination. The court should not be used as a general advice centre. The danger is that the court will enunciate propositions of principle without full appreciation of the implications that these will have in practice, throwing into confusion those who feel obliged to attempt to apply those principles in practice. This danger is particularly acute where the issues raised involve ethical questions that any court should be reluctant to address, unless driven to do so by the need to resolve a practical problem that requires the court's intervention.[460]

The Court continued:

> The first three declarations were extraordinary in nature in that they did not purport to resolve any issues between the parties, but appeared to be intended to lay down propositions of law binding on the world. The declarations as a whole go far beyond the current concerns [of the patient].[461]

The patient was then ensured that he enjoyed sufficient legal protection under the law as it stood, without legal action having been necessary to consider the broader questions raised by his plight.

184 The House of Lords' decision in *R. v. Her Majesty's Attorney General (Appellant) Ex parte Rusbridger (Respondent)* is another example of what can probably be described as a textbook case of concrete review.[462] In the matter, *The Guardian* newspaper published a series of articles arguing that

---

[457]Ibid., at par. 1.

[458]Ibid., at par. 16.

[459]Ibid., at paras. 17–18. An Official Solicitor defends the rights of those who are not capable of doing so themselves, such as children.

[460]Ibid., at par. 21.

[461]Ibid., at par. 22.

[462]*R. v. Her Majesty's Attorney General (Appellant) Ex parte Rusbridger (Respondent)*, *supra* note 323.

the monarchy had to be abolished peacefully. The newspaper, however, was concerned that its decision to promote republicanism might be punishable under the Treason Felony Act of 1848, even though no prosecution was brought against them. To allay its fears, the newspaper asked the courts for a declaration that given the requirements of the HRA, the 1848 Act did not apply to persons campaigning for a republic except in cases where such a campaign was waged unlawfully or through violence. Alternatively, a declaration of incompatibility was sought.[463]

185 In hearing the matter, Lord Steyn held that the newspaper's claims must fail, as:

> The part of section 3 of the 1848 Act which appears to criminalise the advocacy of republicanism is a relic of a bygone age and does not fit into the fabric of our modern legal system. The idea that section 3 could survive scrutiny under the Human Rights Act is unreal. The fears of the editor of The Guardian were more than a trifle alarmist. In my view the courts ought not to be troubled further with this unnecessary litigation.[464]

Other members of the House added that the judiciary's interpretive powers under the HRA and the possibility to issue declarations of incompatibility were not intended as a way to "spring clean" unwanted and outdated legislation where there was no pressing question of rights actually having been interfered with.[465] The House noted that although on the face of it the 1848 Act was undesirable and should probably have been abolished a long time ago, granting relief in terms of the HRA would only have symbolic value.[466] It was for parliament to review the wisdom of the law and not the courts if someone's rights were not under any real threat.

186 It is quite clear from the two judgments discussed above, that judicial attitudes to the HRA are weighted in favour of the concrete review of legislation. Concrete review seems therefore to be the norm in relation to the HRA. Although recognising this, David Feldman observes nonetheless that concrete review should not be an invariable rule.[467] He points to cases decided by the European Court of Human Rights which allowed claimants to attack legislation, even though it had not been applied to

---

[463]Ibid., at paras. 1, 9–10.

[464]Ibid., at par. 28.

[465]Ibid., at par. 36 (*per* Lord Hutton).

[466]Ibid., at par. 45 (*per* Lord Scott of Foscote), at paras. 61–62 (*per* Lord Walker of Gestingthorpe).

[467]David Feldman, "Institutional Roles and Meanings of 'Compatibility' Under the Human Rights Act 1998", in Helen Fenwick, Gavin Phillipson and Roger Masterman (eds.), *Judicial Reasoning under the Human Rights Act* 87 (Cambridge: Cambridge University Press, 2007), at 104–105.

them and in all likelihood would not have been applied to them either.[468]
Situations could therefore arise which might force British courts to look
more sympathetically at introducing an abstract element to their review
under the HRA.[469] While this could be argued, it may not be forgotten that the Strasbourg Court's approach in these cases was based on
the "victim" requirement in article 34 of the European Convention on
Human Rights, and as we have seen this requirement is not always applicable to all cases under the HRA.[470] The Act focuses on the victim
requirement in administrative law and not on constitutional law matters, which raises the question whether Strasbourg jurisprudence that
might resemble elements of abstract review must be followed by British
courts in cases where the victim requirement is not applicable according to the HRA.[471] Whichever way this question is addressed in future,
it is probably safe to say that as things stand British courts generally
use judicial review to address real threats to rights, leaving questions
regarding the desirability of legislation to parliament.[472] An approach
that sits well with traditional attitudes to judicial review in the United
Kingdom.

187   In sum, judicial review in the United Kingdom does not entertain any
possibility of the abstract control of bills. The focus falls on the concrete
review of posited norms, while review that veers towards abstract control
of such norms tends to be avoided by the courts. As a consequence of these
combinations, parliamentary sovereignty is very much respected, as the
legislative process is out of bounds for the courts while spurts of judicial
activism in reviewing a law may very well be curtailed by the facts of the
matter.

---

[468]E.g. *Dudgeon v. The United Kingdom* of 22 October 1981, *Publ. Eur. Court H.R.*,
Series A, no. 45. In this case a homosexual man successfully complained of laws that
criminalised homosexual acts although he was not prosecuted under them. Similarly,
see *Norris v. Ireland* of 26 October 1988, *Publ. Eur. Court H.R.*, Series A, no. 142.

[469]The stress lies on an *element* of abstract review, as the European Court of Human
Rights is adamant that its review does not amount to abstract review as such. *See Klass
v. Germany* of 6 September 1978, *Publ. Eur. Court H.R.*, Series A, no. 28, at par. 33.

[470]*See* again § 129.

[471]E.g. in *R. v. Her Majesty's Attorney General (Appellant) Ex parte Rusbridger
(Respondent)*, *supra* note 323, a declaration of incompatibility was sought in respect of
an act of parliament. Lord Steyn noted the generous approach taken by the Strasbourg
Court in deciding who was a "victim" in terms of the European Convention, but
nonetheless ruled that the requirement was not applicable to the facts before him (at
par. 21).

[472]*See* Wadham et al., *supra* note 57, at 95, who refer to *Taylor v. Lancashire County
Council and Secretary of State for the Environment, Food and Rural Affairs*, [2005]
EWCA Civ 284, (2005) HRLR 17.

5.3 The Netherlands: Emphasising the Review of Posited Norms

5.3.1 Abstract Review of Bills

188 While the review of *legislation* is clearly a feature of judicial review in the Netherlands as section 94 of the Constitution applies to "statutory regulations in force", the same cannot be observed of the abstract review of *bills*, as this is quite foreign to Dutch law.[473] The Constitution of the Netherlands does not make any provision for such review to take place, nor is any such power recognised by the courts. For example, some judgments take the view that the prohibition on review in section 120 of the Constitution is applicable once a bill is tabled, meaning that judicial review is also excluded during a bill's consideration and not only after its promulgation.[474] A good example was presented in the matter of environmental organisations that requested a court to intervene in the legislative process by reviewing a bill that sought to adopt the Eems-Dollard treaty.[475] However, the bill still had to be debated by the upper house of parliament. The court's response was to hold that it was not a judge's duty to intervene in the legislative domain, but that the legislature carried the sole responsibility for any actions in its own domain. Considering the importance that the judgment attached to the separation of powers it might also be questionable for a court to conduct weak review of *bills*, as it might be able to do with *acts of parliament*.[476] Albeit non-binding, such review would be a bridge too far given the delicate balance between the legislature and the judiciary when it comes to reviewing legislative acts.

189 Other judgments, notably of the Supreme Court, go even further in stressing a strict separation by refusing to intervene where rules of procedure are violated even before a bill is tabled.[477] Therefore, as far as

---

[473]By the abstract review of bills is not meant a matter such as the decision in Hoge Raad, 27 January 1961, *NJ* 1963, 248 (*Van den Bergh*), where the adoption procedure of a law is questioned *after* its adoption. This was clearly review of a legislative enactment, while the focus here rests on review taking place during the legislative process. For a discussion of the *Van den Bergh* case and judicial review of legislative procedure in an *a posteriori* setting, see §§ 245–247.

[474]Ondernemingskamer Hof Amsterdam (Enterprise Division of the Amsterdam Court of Appeal), 18 February 1999; Ondernemingskamer Hof Amsterdam, 22 July 1999; Kortmann, *supra* note 348, at 378–379; C.A.J.M. Kortmann, "Is een wetsvoorstel onschendbaar?", 48 *Ars Aequi* 473 (1999).

[475]Gerechtshof te 's-Gravenhage (The Hague Court of Appeal), 27 September 1990, *AB* 1991, 85.

[476]On the weak review of acts of parliament in the Netherlands, see §§ 40, 93, 311.

[477]Hoge Raad, 19 November 1999, *NJ* 2000, 160; Hoge Raad, 14 April 2000, *NJ* 2000, 713 C.A.J.M. Kortmann, "Nogmaals: Is een wetsvoorstel onschendbaar?", 49 *Ars Aequi* 107 (2000).

enforcing the Constitution is concerned, parliament is dealt a good hand as the courts may at most only exercise weak review over its laws, while having to respect the sanctity of bills from any sort of review. This is not exactly the same as the doctrine of parliamentary sovereignty in the United Kingdom, as the idea of higher law binding on parliament in the form of an entrenched constitution is not controversial in the Netherlands.[478] What is controversial, however, is the judiciary's role in effecting such higher law in the face of parliament's view on it, as expressed through its acts of parliament.

190   The Council of State probably comes closest to some sort of prior non-legislative check on bills.[479] The Council of State is one of the oldest high offices of state in the country and serves a dual function. The body is divided into two chambers, one of which forms the highest court in administrative law matters, while the other exercises an advisory function. This latter chamber's advisory opinions are not binding, but serve as an aid to the government and parliament in evaluating the quality of bills. In drafting such opinions, the Council does not fulfil a judicial function, although it can be of great help to legislators in deciding whether to proceed with or amend pending bills.[480] For example, a controversial bill concerning electoral reform was withdrawn, even before the lower house could vote on it, after a damning opinion by the Council highlighted a number of its shortcomings.[481] The very existence of a special body such as the Council of State also militates against the idea that courts might have a weak power to review the constitutionality of bills, as this would undermine the very purpose of the Council.

191   In addition to the Council of State's opinions, the government can also request the Supreme Court to render advice on matters it deems fit to be put to that Court.[482] This is for example what happened in respect of the Halsema Proposal, where the government requested the Court to give its view on the question of expanding judicial review, as it had done on a number of previous occasions where core constitutional questions were at issue.[483] Important legislative bills can therefore also be put to the Supreme Court for its opinion. Admittedly, this does not happen often and is not

---

[478]P.B. Cliteur, *Constitutionele toetsing* ('s-Gravenhage: Teldersstichting, 1991), at 78–79.

[479]Secs. 73–75 of the Constitution; Wet op de Raad van State, 9 March 1962; C.A.J.M. Kortmann, *supra* note 348, 286–288.

[480]Cf. Hirsch Ballin, *supra* note 374, at 162–163.

[481]*Parliamentary Proceedings II* 2004/2005, 29 986, no. 2; *Parliamentary Proceedings II* 2004/2005, 29 986, no. 5; Leenknegt and Van der Schyff, *supra* note 114, at 1141–1142.

[482]Wet op de rechterlijke organisatie, 18 April 1827, s. 74.

[483]*Parliamentary Proceedings II*, 2002–2003, 28, 331, A.

the same as prior judicial review or as detailed as opinions drafted by the Council of State, but it does show that the legislative process is not an insular world that entirely avoids the judicial branch in contemplating the merits of bills. Furthermore, the legislative process is also aided by reports drafted by the Council for the Judiciary (*Raad voor de Rechtspraak*), which focuses on the impact of draft legislation on the efficacy and good organisation of the bench.[484] In this regard, the constitutional changes intended by the Halsema Proposal were scrutinised to decide their desirability as far as the working of the judiciary was concerned.[485] However, although this amounts to a form of non-legislative scrutiny of bills, it is not the same as checking whether a bill demonstrates an adequate level of fundamental rights protection.

192   The abstract review of bills as it is know in France for example is therefore absent in the Netherlands. In this respect, the Halsema Proposal does not aim to bring about any change. The bill is concerned with granting the courts a binding power to review the constitutionality of *acts of parliament* and does not foresee the strong or weak review of *bills*. The idea is to largely mirror the system of decentralised review of legislation currently used in checking whether national laws accord with international law in terms of section 94 of the Constitution.[486]

The National Convention, which was entrusted with contemplating the constitutional future of the Netherlands also considered the idea of allowing the judicial review of bills. In its final report, published in 2006, the Convention similarly decided against prior judicial review, by emphasising that constitutional review during the legislative process remains the primary duty of the legislature.[487] It argued that other options would distort the desired balance of power between the legislature and the judiciary when it comes to constitutional review. However, the Convention did note that constitutional review during the legislative process had to be enhanced. This could be achieved by relying for example more on the Constitutional Section of the civil service to review all bills on constitutionality and by heeding the opinions of the Council of State more.[488] Opinions, which, the Convention felt, could play an important role in aiding the courts to judge the final product passed by parliament and signed into law.

---

[484]Wet op de rechterlijke organisatie, 18 April 1827, s. 95.

[485]*Parliamentary Proceedings II*, 2002–2003, 28, 331, no. 6.

[486]On review in terms of s. 94 of the Constitution, *see* § 44.

[487]Hoekstra, *supra* note 135, at 46.

[488]*See* generally about the questions and problems related to the legislative process in the Netherlands, P.P.T Bovend'Eert, "De wetgevende macht van het parlement", in J.Th.J. van den Berg, L.F.M. Verhey and J.L.W. Broeksteeg (eds.), *Het parlement* 91 (Nijmegen: Wolf Legal Publishers, 2007).

193 In sum, both the Halsema Proposal and the National Convention's report express a desire that the abstract review of bills should remain in political hands. This is not surprising in a legal system that is used to a relatively strict separation of powers. However, as will be explained below, old suspicions of the judiciary conducting constitutional control of acts of parliament seems to be waning in comparison.

5.3.2 Abstract or Concrete Review of Legislation

194 Judicial review may be exercised in respect of most posited legal norms in the Netherlands. Section 94 of the Constitution, which regulates treaty review, makes this plain by confirming that international norms apply to all "statutory regulations in force". Technically this means that even the Constitution may be reviewed in the light of international law, because international norms are of a higher order than national norms. The only norms immune to being denied application by the courts are international norms themselves, as the bar on review in section 120 of the Constitution extends to testing the constitutionality of treaties.[489] The crux of getting to grips with judicial review is not so much whether most norms of law *may* be reviewed, as treaty review is possible in most instances, as it is what the modalities of such review look like.

195 The Halsema Proposal is silent about the modalities that are to apply to the proposed review under section 120 of the Constitution. In this, it reflects section 94 of the Constitution, which governs treaty review, as this provision does not elaborate on the applicable modalities of review either. This means that the normal practices and procedures of the courts are to apply in carrying out judicial review under these provisions – in a system dedicated to the review of legislation it is not altogether surprising that this implies a focus on the concrete review of higher law.[490] Interestingly though, abstract review is also possible before the country's courts under some circumstances even though there are no special constitutional procedures allowing for such review, as is the case in South Africa by comparison.[491]

---

[489]On this, *consult* Peter Rehorst, "Constitutional Jurisdiction in the Context of State Powers: Types, Contents and Effects of the Decisions on the Constitutionality of Legal Regulations", 9 *Hum. Rights L. J.* 11 (1988), at 13.

[490]E.g. Hoge Raad, 2 February 1982, *NJ* 1982, 424, where the Supreme Court held that the right to equality in art. 26 of the International Covenant on Civil and Political Rights (1966) was directly applicable to disputes before courts in the Netherlands.

[491]Cf. Van Houten, *supra* note 107, at 230.

196   For example, in 2007 the Association of Netherlands Municipalities (*Vereniging van Nederlandse Gemeenten*) brought an action against the state, arguing that changes to immovable property taxes were at odds with article 9 of the European Charter of Local Self-Government of 1985.[492] The court entertained the matter, even though there was not a concrete dispute to be resolved. The court's review was not incidental to the matter, but the object itself, as the Association challenged the law itself without focusing on its application in any particular case. In other words, abstract judicial review. The court, however, found for the state, as it held that the Charter's provisions were not enforceable law, but could be applied by the state as it saw fit without the courts being allowed to question legislative wisdom. Importantly though, the court did not find for the state because of the abstract nature of the Association's claim, this it readily accepted. Similarly, the civil chamber of the Supreme Court allowed human rights organisations to bring a claim against a procedure founded on the Immigration Act, even though the claim did not concern an actual set of facts.[493] The claimants were initially refused standing in administrative law proceedings, because their grievance did not concern a particular asylum seeker's case. But they were able to have the matter heard in accordance with civil law because the administrative law route had been closed to them, thereby denying them an effective legal remedy. Again, abstract judicial review was allowed.

197   It is therefore somewhat puzzling that the preliminary report of the National Convention's working group on the Constitution stated that if acts of parliament were to be constitutionally reviewed by the courts, it would be difficult to contemplate the abstract review of legislative enactments.[494] The preliminary report seems to labour under the impression that the only form of judicial review of legislation currently allowed is concrete review, which it thinks unlikely to change in future. Yet, a measure of abstract review is already a given under the normal rules of procedure, albeit in a minority of cases compared to concrete review. In addition, there seems to be no reason why such review would not be possible if reforms, such as those contemplated by the Halsema Proposal, were to be introduced.

What the report probably meant is that it would be difficult to contemplate giving political organs special standing to initiate abstract review, an idea that was put forward in Jan-Willem Sap's model for a constitutional

---

[492] Rechtbank 's-Gravenhage, 18 April 2007 (*Society of Local Councils*); European Charter of Local Self-Government of 1985, ETS no. 122.

[493] Hoge Raad, 3 September 2004, *RvdW* 2004, 102.

[494] Zoethout et al., *supra* note 136, at 31, 40, Appendix 2, who state that decentralised abstract review of posited norms is difficult to imagine as part of future reforms in the Netherlands. However, it is already a distinct possibility in the current system, as the examples mentioned in the text show.

court in the Netherlands.[495] In this, the report is probably correct, contrary to Sap's views. This is because the Netherlands' tradition of seeking political consensus and coalition government usually means that a host of political views are factored in arriving at legislation, which leaves less room for judicial intervention to ensure that all voices are heard during the legislative process.[496]

198 Concluding, it can be noted that judicial review in the Netherlands does not allow the abstract review of bills in any shape or form. Judicial control of the legislative process in this way would be a bridge too far in a legal system that generally relies on a relatively strict separation of powers. Instead, the gaze of the judiciary centres on the concrete review of legislation and this the Halsema Proposal seeks to continue. As to the abstract review of legislation, the possibility to conduct such review does exist, although special constitutional procedures have not been devised for this form of review yet. However, this form of review seems to be somewhat under-explored in the constitutional field at present.

5.4 South Africa: Protecting Political Minorities

5.4.1 Abstract Review of Bills

199 A dispensation predicated on parliamentary sovereignty is obviously not an ideal candidate for the judicial review of legislation, let alone the abstract review of bills. For much of the country's history, the courts had to make do with common law rights and presumptions in guiding the interpretation of acts of parliament. However, the doctrine of parliamentary sovereignty and an emphasis on the literal or textual interpretation of legislation meant that very little came of these interpretive powers in practice.

200 The transition to constitutional supremacy and justiciable rights brought a radical change in this respect. The interim Constitution stipulated that all legal norms are capable of judicial review.[497] This position was retained under the final Constitution, as section 172(1) states that:

> When deciding a constitutional matter within its power, a court – (a) must declare that any law or conduct that is inconsistent with the Constitution is invalid to the extent of its inconsistency (...).

---

[495] Sap, *supra* note 367, at 599.

[496] *Consider* the observations about the Dutch *poldermodel* democracy in § 42.

[497] S. 98(2), (9) of the interim Constitution.

The point is further driven home in section 8(1), which contains the principle that the Bill of Rights applies to all *law*. This is also reinforced by the duty resting on every court and tribunal to interpret legislation and develop the common law and customary law in line with the Bill of Rights.[498] More particularly, the Constitutional Court has held in relation to acts of parliament that such acts may be judicially reviewed once they have been assented to without being in operation yet, because by that time the legislative process has run its course.[499]

201   The advent of judicial review in the 1990s brought with it not only the judicial control of legislative enactments, but also the judicial control of bills. Importantly, the Constitution of 1996 was itself the product of prior and therefore abstract review. The interim Constitution provided that the final Constitution could only be adopted once the Constitutional Court had certified that the text was in accordance with the set of Constitutional Principles agreed on during the political negotiations. As section 71 of the interim Constitution provided:

> (1)   A new constitutional text shall-
>   (a)   comply with the Constitutional Principles contained in Schedule 4; and
>   (b)   be passed by the Constitutional Assembly in accordance with this Chapter.
> (2)   The new constitutional text passed by the Constitutional Assembly, or any provision thereof, shall not be of any force and effect unless the Constitutional Court has certified that all the provisions of such text comply with the Constitutional Principles referred to in subsection (1)(a).

As mentioned earlier, the Constitutional Court duly discharged its duty by first refusing certification, which meant that the Constitutional Assembly had to pay greater attention to honouring these cardinal principles before the final Constitution came into being.[500]

202   The Constitution itself also makes provision for prior control in a number of instances. For example, if the president or a premier of a province has reservations about the constitutionality of a bill presented for assent and signature, they may refer it back to the relevant legislature for reconsideration.[501] If, after having been reconsidered, the bill is presented anew, but the president or premier still has reservations, they may refer

---

[498]Secs. 167(5), 170, 39(2) of the Constitution.

[499]*Khosa and Others v. Minister of Social Development and Others; Mahlaule and Others v. Minister of Social Development and Others*, 2004 (6) BCLR 569 (CC), 2004 (6) SA 505 (CC), at paras. 90–91; *Doctors for Life International v. Speaker of the National Assembly*, *supra* note 278, at paras. 62, 65.

[500]*See* § 70.

[501]Secs. 79, 121 of the Constitution.

the bill to the Constitutional Court for a definite ruling. In other words, first a legislative route must be followed to reconsider a bill's constitutionality, before the judicial avenue may be explored. But the president, or the premier concerned, must sign a bill into law if the Constitutional Court decides that the bill is constitutional, irrespective of the executive's reservations. Office bearers in South Africa therefore have no similar veto to that of the president of the United States of America, who may refuse to sign legislation into law, thereby forcing the legislature to readopt such legislation with a special majority in order for it to become law.

203 *Ex parte President of the Republic of South Africa In re: Constitutionality of the Liquor Bill* presents an example of the exercise of these powers of prior review.[502] After not being satisfied with a bill's reconsideration by parliament, the president referred the bill to the Constitutional Court for it to decide whether the bill had encroached on an exclusive provincial competence relating to alcohol licences, the Court subsequently held that the bill was indeed unconstitutional. The Constitutional Court went on to clarify prior review in *Doctors for Life International v. Speaker of the National Assembly* where it ruled that *after* a bill has been adopted by both houses of parliament, but not yet signed by the president, the president is the only person who may request that the constitutionality of that bill be judicially reviewed, thereby excluding challenges from anyone else.[503] The Court reasoned that the president was the constitutionally appointed guardian of the public's rights and should not be pre-empted in exercising this duty, although interestingly the Court did leave the question open whether prior review may be sought by other parties *before* a bill has been passed by parliament.[504]

204 Although not of central importance for our focus, it may be noted that the federal character of the country's new constitutional structure

---

[502] *Ex parte President of the Republic of South Africa In re: Constitutionality of the Liquor Bill*, 2000 (1) BCLR 1 (CC), 2000 (1) SA 732 (CC); Rassie Malherbe, "Die drankwetsontwerp: Vooraf kontrole en grondwetlike gesagsverdeling verder omlyn", 63 *Tydskrif vir Hedendaagse Romeins-Hollandse Reg* 321 (2000). *See also In re: Constitutionality of the Mpumalanga Petitions Bill*, 2001 (11) BCLR 1126 (CC), 2002 (1) SA 447 (CC).

[503] *Doctors for Life International v. Speaker of the National Assembly*, *supra* note 278, at par. 54. The Court only made mention of the president in its judgment, but there seems to be no reason why the same should not apply to a provincial premier who requests prior review.

[504] Ibid., at par. 71. Commenting on this, if the Constitution's drafters went to the effort of describing prior review at the behest of the president or a premier in so many words, it is probably reasonable to assume that they meant for prior review to only take place under those circumstances. Prior review significantly transgresses the separation of powers, and this militates against simply deducing the possibility of such review (e.g. before the adoption of a bill by parliament) if the Constitution does not expressly allow it.

means that each of the nine provinces may adopt its own constitution.[505] However, provincial constitutions may only become law once the speaker of the relevant legislature has referred the adopted text to the Constitutional Court for certification that the document is consistent with the national Constitution.[506] This also holds for amendments to provincial constitutions. To date, only two provinces, namely KwaZulu-Natal in 1996 and the Western Cape in 1997, have adopted their own constitutions. Of the two provincial constitutions that of KwaZulu-Natal has not yet come into effect because the Constitutional Court refused it certification, while that of the Western Cape was certified at the second attempt and became law in 1998.[507]

5.4.2 Abstract or Concrete Review of Legislation

205 As to the judicial review of legislative enactments, this can be either abstract or concrete. For the abstract control of an act of parliament at least thirty members of the National Assembly must apply to the Constitutional Court requesting it for an order which declares that all or part of a specific act is unconstitutional.[508] Such an application must be brought within 30 days of the date on which the president assented to and signed the act in question. However, because the norms to be reviewed have already been posited, in other words applicable law, the Constitutional Court may order that the act has no force until it has finally decided the matter, provided that this is in the interests of justice and the application has a reasonable chance of success.[509] This is evidently a form of abstract review, as the applicants do not call on the court to resolve a particular dispute by applying an act of parliament to it, but request the court to test whether such an act is compatible with the constitutional hierarchy of norms in South Africa.

---

[505] Secs. 104(1)(a), 142 of the Constitution.

[506] Secs. 143, 144 of the Constitution. Cf. Stuart Woolman, "Provincial Constitutions", in Stuart Woolman and Theunis Roux (eds.), *Constitutional Law of South Africa* 21i (Cape Town: Juta, 2nd ed., 2006); Rassie Malherbe, "The Role of the Constitutional Court in the Development of Provincial Autonomy", *SA Pub. L.* 255 (2001).

[507] *In re: Certification of the Constitution of the Province of KwaZulu-Natal 1996*, 1996 (11) BCLR 1419 (CC), 1996 (4) SA 1098 (CC). This province's constitution usurped too much power, leaving the Constitutional Court to hold, at par. 47, that it was "fatally flawed". And regarding the Western Cape: *In re: Certification of the Constitution of the Western Cape, 1997*, 1997 (9) BCLR 1167 (CC), 1997 (4) SA 795 (CC); *In re: Certification of the Amended Text of the Constitution of the Western Cape, 1997*, 1997 (12) BCLR 1653, 1998 (1) SA 655 (CC). Cf. E.F.J. Malherbe, "Provinsiale grondwette: 'n Barometer van provinsiale outonomie?", *J. S. Afr. L.* 344 (1998).

[508] S. 80 of the Constitution.

[509] S. 80(3) of the Constitution.

Abstract review of legislation is not only possible in respect of acts of parliament, but can also be requested in the case of laws passed by each of the nine provincial legislatures.[510] One fifth of the members of a provincial legislature can request the Constitutional Court to carry out abstract review within 30 days of the provincial premier having assented to and signed the contested piece of legislation.

206 This stands in contrast to the interim Constitution. The interim Constitution did not allow the abstract review of *legislation*, but only of *bills*, on request of one third of the members of either the National Assembly, Senate or the relevant provincial legislature.[511] In other words, the abstract review of bills instead of the review of enactments was allowed. This change was probably decided, as the Constitutional Court was uncertain as to when during the legislative process a bill had to be referred to it, and what would happen if a bill became law before the Court ruled on its constitutionality.[512] Another change relates to the fact that the upper house of parliament, the National Council of Provinces, is not empowered to lodge an application for abstract review, as its predecessor the Senate was able to do. It has become easier though for the members of the provincial legislatures to request abstract review, as at present only one fifth of their members are required to petition the Court and no longer at least one third as had been the case under the interim Constitution.[513]

207 However interesting the *abstract* review of legislation may be in South Africa, the most common form of control over legislation is of a *concrete* nature.[514] Without specific jurisdiction to conduct abstract review, courts are hesitant to stray from deciding the facts presented them. In making

---

[510]S. 122 of the Constitution.

[511]Secs. 98(2)(d), 106(4)-(5) of the interim Constitution. E.g. concerning provincial bills *In re: The School Education Bill of 1995 (Gauteng)*, 1996 (4) BCLR 537 (CC), 1996 (3) SA 165 (CC); *In re: KwaZulu-Natal Amakhosi and Iziphankanyiswa Amendment Bill of 1995; In re: Payment of Salaries, Allowances and Other Privileges to the Ingoyama Bill of 1995*, 1996 (7) BCLR 903 (CC), 1996 (4) SA 653 (CC), and regarding a national bill *In re: The National Education Policy Bill No. 83 of 1995*, 1996 (4) BCLR 518 (CC), 1996 (3) SA 289 (CC).

[512]Cf. *In re: The School Education Bill of 1995 (Gauteng)*, ibid., at par. 2.

[513]S. 122 of the Constitution.

[514]As the Constitutional Court stressed in *Zantsi v. Council of State, Ciskei*, 1995 (10) BCLR 1424 (CC), 1995 (4) SA 615 (CC), at par. 7: "It is not ordinarily desirable for a court to give rulings in the abstract on issues which are not the subject of controversy and are only of academic interest (...)." As examples of concrete review can be mentioned: *S. v. Makwanyane, supra* note 32, where the death sentences of the applicants were commuted to life imprisonment, and *S. v. Lawrence; S. v. Negal; S. v. Solberg*, 1997 (10) BCLR 1348 (CC), 1997 (4) SA 1176 (SA), where the applicants unsuccessfully sought the quashing of their convictions for trading on Sunday because their convictions did not violate the right to freedom of religion and conscience guaranteed in the Bill of Rights.

the point, the Constitutional Court pointed out by reference to the United States doctrine of "case and controversy" that constitutional questions are not to be anticipated or decided where a matter can be resolved by simply applying civil or criminal law as it stands.[515] Similarly, the Court decided not to make an order in *JT Publishing (Pty) Ltd v. Minister of Safety and Security* because during the course of the trial the situation had changed so as to render the matter moot and only of theoretical interest:

> The current state of affairs differs significantly from the situation that existed at the time when Daniels J. heard the application for a referral. (...) For Parliament has now achieved the purpose that the suspension was meant to serve by passing in the meantime the Films and Publications Act (65 of 1996), which repeals entirely both the Publications Act and the Indecent or Obscene Photographic Matter Act, replacing the pair with a substantially different scheme. The new statute was enacted very recently, and it has not yet been brought into operation. But that will no doubt happen soon (...). The old statutes which are already obsolete, will both then terminate. Neither of the applicants, nor for that matter anyone else, stands to gain the slightest advantage today from an order dealing with their moribund and futureless provisions. No wrong which we can still right was done to either applicant on the strength of them. Nor is anything that should be stopped likely to occur under their rapidly waning authority.[516]

What is conceivable though is that an abstract element may be introduced where a claim is brought in the "public interest", as provided for in section 38(d) of the Constitution. Although the Constitutional Court has been careful to stress that this provision covers concrete and not abstract review because it only applies where rights are infringed, it cannot be denied that a generous approach as proposed by some judges on what constitutes an infringement could dilute the concrete nature of review somewhat.[517] Yet, this does not take away that review is primarily geared towards concrete matters and not abstract questions, bar the constitutional provisions especially designed for abstract review.

208   Overall, the modalities of review possible under the South African Constitution attest to a pronounced counter-majoritarian streak. Not only was the Constitution itself subject to prior abstract review, but it includes the possibility for such review to be conducted of national and provincial bills at the request of the respective executive, while legislative minorities may initiate the abstract review of legislative enactments within 30 days of executive assent. The purpose is clearly to allow political minorities to conduct their case in court, as compensation for their failure to block bills

---

[515]*Zantsi v. Council of State, Ciskei, supra* note 514, at paras. 2–3.

[516]*JT Publishing (Pty) Ltd v. Minister of Safety and Security*, 1996 (12) BCLR 1599 (CC), 1997 (3) SA 514 (CC), at par. 16.

[517]*Fereirra v. Levin; Vryenhoek v. Powell*, 1996 (1) BCLR 1 (CC), 1996 (1) SA 984 (CC), at par. 35. *See also* §§ 165, 235; *Zantsi v. Council of State, supra* note 514, at par. 7.

from passing into law. If abstract review is not initiated or unsuccessful, litigants are still free to evoke higher law in concrete matters to be decided by the courts.

5.5 Concluding Remarks

209 It goes without saying that by narrowing the range of legal norms whose compatibility with higher law a court may review, the influence of the bench can be restricted quite severely. This is something that would obviously benefit the legislature, which sees some of its decisions shielded from the courts as a consequence. One should be careful not to traverse this sort of ground too often, as it could easily lead to the judicial function being negated, albeit not in so many words. Such near limitless faith in the democratic legitimacy of acts of parliament has proved to be exaggerated, thereby requiring a judicial counter-balance.[518]

210 In this respect, the countries under study do not disappoint. All three of their legal systems have the review of a wide range of posited norms in common, more particularly the concrete review of such norms. Litigants may call on a court to give priority to higher norms in judging everyday laws that apply to their case. The HRA applies to all legislation, not to mention the common law and actions undertaken by public authorities, which is similar to the South African Constitution that applies to the whole body of law and all conduct. Treaty review in the Netherlands also affects all legal regulations, making judicial review possible in every setting where applicable international law can be identified. The effect of this concrete review of legislation is that higher law becomes part of a court's tools in settling a matter. This goes some way towards satisfying ideals such as "bringing rights home" by incorporating the European Convention on Human Rights in the United Kingdom and creating a new rights-based culture in South Africa. Rights are in this way made tangible in actual disputes and are not just treated as lofty and faraway ideals. In this regard, the Halsema Proposal would not herald any real change to the state of play in the Netherlands, as a wide range of legal norms are already capable of being reviewed against the background of international law. Instead, it will add to the courts' arsenal of higher norms by freeing some fundamental rights from the bar on binding review in section 120 of the Constitution. On account of the above it would be correct to observe that the concrete review of legislative enactments is uncontroversial in the United Kingdom, the Netherlands and South Africa, even to the extent of forming the mainstay of judicial review in these legal systems.

---

[518]*See* again §§ 86–89.

211 While the *concrete* review of legislation may not be controversial, the same cannot be said of the *abstract* review of legislation, and even less so of legislative bills. First though attention is paid to the abstract review of legislation.

The discussion of the United Kingdom revealed a very strong emphasis on solving disputes through the application of law, a consequence of which is to sideline the abstract review of posited norms. The British judiciary has proved itself reluctant to entertain hypothetical and abstract questions that will not serve the end of concrete review, as the House of Lords has made it plain that a court must be led by a particular set of facts and not attempt any legislative spring-cleaning.[519]

While a distinct possibility in the Netherlands in some proceedings, the question of the abstract review of legislation does not warrant enough importance in that country for special constitutional procedures to be devised with which to claim such review, as the National Convention's preliminary report evidences.[520] This stands in clear contrast to South Africa. There political minorities in the National Assembly and the provincial legislatures may request the Constitutional Court to conduct abstract review of legislative acts provided that certain constitutional requirements are met. In South Africa the need was clearly felt to add another dimension to the review of legislation by specially designed procedures for initiating abstract review, whereas in the United Kingdom and the Netherlands no such exigency was identified for similar measures to modify or enhance the modalities of review already available to litigants.

212 Moreover, South Africa also allows the abstract review of bills referred to the Constitutional Court by the president or a provincial premier and of provincial constitutions that must be certified before they may come into operation.[521] The legal orders of the Netherlands and the United Kingdom make prior review impossible, apart from Scottish bills that may be reviewed by the United Kingdom's new Supreme Court.[522] However, far from limiting Westminster's power, this provision is actually designed to protect its sovereignty by preventing a lesser legislature from contradicting it. Whereas the referral of provincial constitutions in South Africa can be explained as a necessary consequence of the country's federal-like structure that requires each of the various legislatures to keep to their constitutional boundaries without giving any of them the ultimate word over the other. By

---

[519]*R. v. Her Majesty's Attorney General (Appellant) Ex parte Rusbridger (Respondent)*, *supra* note 323, at par. 36 (*per* Lord Hutton).

[520]*See* §§ 192, 196.

[521]*See* §§ 201–203.

[522]*See* §§ 178–179 on the United Kingdom and §§188–193 on the Netherlands.

comparison, this situation is less likely to arise in unitary states such as the United Kingdom and the Netherlands.[523]

213 More complicated to explain in comparative perspective is the *executive* power to request abstract review of legislation in South Africa. This power might not be as strong as one might suspect at first glance, though. In South Africa, a bill may only be referred for judicial review after it has been sent back to the responsible legislature for fresh consideration and still found wanting by the executive. The fact that a particular executive will also nearly always reflect a legislature's political majority, places the actual worth of this power further in perspective. It is not an instrument for the use of political minorities, as it is in France. In addition it emphasises the political process over and above judicial recourse. The abstract review of bills is thus constitutionally quite limited in South Africa and its use reduced given the political context. Nonetheless, its presence testifies to a willingness to transcend the traditional boundaries that exist between the legislature and the judiciary, which is unparalleled both in the United Kingdom with its insistence on parliamentary sovereignty and in the Netherlands' with its traditional adherence to a strict separation of powers. This willingness is reinforced by the fact that the Constitutional Court has left undecided the question whether bills may be reviewed *before* they have been adopted by parliament and the president, must decide whether to assent to it or not – or the premier as the case may be.[524]

214 This difference is accentuated when South Africa's constitution-making process is brought into the equation. While the British and Dutch constitutional orders essentially evolve through incremental reform carried through by successive generations of politicians, the entire South African dispensation was made dependent on the Constitutional Court giving its fiat after a negotiation process lasting only a few years.[525] Had the Constitutional Court not certified the final text adopted by the Constitutional Assembly, the new order could not have materialised. Prior review was used as a screening method to ensure that the constitutional drafters respected the pact of core principles agreed on during the preceding political negotiations. Not simply content with the judicial review of whether the final text had come about according to a "legitimate process", as proceduralists such as John Ely might advocate, the Court's duty was very much that of judging whether the constitution-making process also

---

[523]Moreover, the Constitutional Court has only been called upon twice to certify such texts, *see* § 203.
[524]*Doctors for Life International v. Speaker of the National Assembly, supra* note 278, at par. 71. *See* again par. 71.
[525]On the certification of the Constitution, *see* § 201 and also §§ 68, 70.

achieved a "legitimate outcome".[526] Increasing the scope of judicial review in such a manner clearly came at the expense of the political process, whose room to manoeuvre was restricted quite substantially. This presents a vivid example of constitutionalism where a political majority is not simply "the rule of the people, but the rule of the people within certain predetermined channels, according to certain prearranged procedures".[527]

215 This brief survey of the three countries' modalities of review leads essentially to the following question. What lies behind the preference for the concrete review of legislation, as opposed to the abstract review of bills and legislation? Put differently, why does is seem that judicial review in the three systems turns more controversial the less concrete it becomes and especially when it allows for the review of bills and not only posited norms?

216 As explained above, concrete review satisfies the demand in each of the three systems to make fundamental rights tangible to all. For the legislature, the benefit lies in the fact that a court must restrict itself as much as possible to the case at hand. This means that legislative wisdom is not questioned more than is necessary, something which is the case the greater the focus on abstract review is, as the more susceptible a system as a whole becomes to speculation and judicial scrutiny. The judiciary's principle concern in such a matter relates to the integrity of a contested norm in the greater constitutional scheme of things, and is not restricted by an actual set of facts calling for resolution.[528] Putting an entire act of parliament before a court to be tested *in abstracto*, is very different from contesting a particular section in it and then only to the extent that its application is unfavourable for the applicant's case.[529] Abstract review therefore adds another dimension to the judiciary's powers, as it no longer has to concentrate simply on resolving a dispute with an injection of higher norms of law, but can widen its gaze somewhat. This is especially true where a court may

---

[526]Cf. John Hart Ely, *Democracy and Distrust: A Theory of Judicial Review* (Cambridge, MA: Harvard University Press, 1980).

[527]As S. Holmes, "Precommitment and the Paradox of Democracy", in Jon Elster and Rune Slagstad (eds.), *Constitutionalism and Democracy* 231 (Cambridge: Cambridge University Press, 1988), defined the relationship between democracy and constitutionalism.

[528]Brewer-Carías, *supra* note 429, at 209, explains that under such circumstances the only purpose is to maintain the hierarchy of legal norms and protect the constitution.

[529]E.g. the South African Constitutional Court had to consider a bill quite exhaustively *In re: The School Education Bill of 1995 (Gauteng)*, *supra* note 511, while in *Christian Education South Africa v. Minister of Education*, 2000 (10) BCLR 1051 (CC), 2000 (4) SA 757 (CC), it had to confine itself to the question whether the prohibition on capital punishment in independent schools on the basis of s. 10 of the Schools Act, no. 84 of 1996, was constitutional.

review *bills* and not only *legislation* in this manner. Sidestepping the traditional separation of powers in such a way strengthens the judicial hand
even more by allowing it a say in what may become law, and not only over
matters that have passed into law.

217 This explains why the constitutional drafters in South Africa found
the idea of prior review so appealing. By placing a judicial check on the
country's constitution-making, and later its legislative process, they guaranteed political minorities that they would not be left out in the cold.[530] The
white minority who had benefited from the country's democratic deficit in
the past needed to be convinced that the advent of multiracial democracy
would not harm them, as Ran Hirschl has also argued.[531] This particular explanation for prior review was captured quite accurately by Tom
Ginsburg.[532] He explains that its agreement brings otherwise unobtainable
constitutional bargains within reach, as the reassurance of such review low-
ers the cost of constitution-making and encourages minorities to participate
in the process. Viewed more from a substantive and less of a political or bar-
gaining angle, the judicial curbs on the Constitutional Assembly can also be
understood as "possibility-generating restraints" because the blocks necessary to build a successful democracy were guaranteed for the future by
putting safe core principles such as the separation of powers from possible
majoritarian intrusion.[533] In a country where the past haunts the present
the argument won ground that just as a minority had abused the legislative process a majority had to be shielded from the temptation of maybe
doing the same and thereby repeating an unhappy history. The purpose of
prior judicial review was therefore to create an avenue through which a
democratic majority could be curtailed if it was called for by the situation.
Such a judicial "deterrent" rang true not only during the drafting of the
Constitution, but still holds some currency in a country where legislative
power has been resting in the hands of one political party since the new
order's inception.

218 While South Africa might have been justified in adopting the fairly
drastic measure of prior review as part of its constitution-making process

---

[530]Klug, *supra* note 172, at 52, explains how the white-dominated National Party insisted
on this process as it realised that if left to the will of the majority only, the Party would
have little influence over the constitution-making process.

[531]Hirschl, *supra* note 6, at 50–99, 216–218. As Pedro Magalhaes, *The Limits to
Judicialization: Legislative Politics and Constitutional Review in Iberian Democracies*
(Doctoral dissertation, Ohio State University, 2002), at 21 notes: "When the political
actors that dominate the constitution-making process expect to lack control over legislatures in the future, judicial review of legislation may emerge as an institution designed
to protect their interests." (Quoted in Hirschl, at 41.)

[532]Ginsburg, *supra* note 5, at 33.

[533]Holmes, *supra* note 527, at 235.

and ultimately as part of its legislative process, the device of prior review would conceivably be superfluous in consolidated democracies such as the United Kingdom and the Netherlands. The fact that parliamentary democracy in these two countries is very much a reliable vehicle by which people's rights have for the most part been protected throughout the years has warranted less of an intrusion on the balance of institutional power between the legislature and the judiciary. This becomes all the more plausible when one considers that South Africa saw the construction of a completely new parliamentary democracy which still has to cut its teeth as well as contend with a powerful minority fearing the loss of its traditional influence.[534] This difference in context naturally means that while radical measures were appropriate for South Africa the same cannot be said of the United Kingdom and the Netherlands. The purpose of judicial review would have been overshot and the intended relationship between the legislature and the judiciary disturbed too much had the HRA included provisions on the abstract control of bills or legislation, just as the Halsema Proposal might have found it difficult to justify the introduction of similar mechanisms in the Netherlands. Concentrating resources in order to resolve concrete disputes clearly proved more important than the desire to create special constitutional mechanisms with which to conduct prior review.

219 In essence, democratisation in South Africa brought political uncertainty with it, which raised the demand for judicial insurance.[535] Judicial insurance which came partly in the form of modalities allowing prior review of the constitution-making process and the abstract review of legislation. Conversely, the absence of comparable uncertainty in the United Kingdom and the Netherlands lessened the need to respectively restrict parliamentary sovereignty and transcend the separation of powers in the same manner. Based on the countries' compared experience, one could say that the South African experience strengthens the argument that the greater a society's faith in its democratic institutions and processes in factoring fundamental rights, the smaller the need will be for judicial checks of its political and constitutional choices. Such faith, however, does not jeopardise the principle of, or the need for judicial review, as no democracy is perfect. Instead, gauging the limits of *reasonable* faith in electoral democracy helps to decide the acceptable modalities of review for a particular society.

---

[534]Cf. Erhard Blankenburg, "'Warum brauchen wir kein Verfassungsgericht?': Die niederländische Diskussion im Licht der deutschen Erfahrung", in Anita Böcker et al., *Migratierecht en rechtssociologie, gebundeld in Kees' studies* (Nijmegen: Wolf Legal Publishers, 2008), at 303, 310, who explains that the Dutch parliament has been a source of protection for rights, thereby minimising the need for judicial review.

[535]To paraphrase Ginsburg, *supra* note 5, at 33.

Chapter 6
Content of Review

6.1 Introduction

220 The third element of review to be discussed – in addition to its judicial fora and modalities, which were addressed in the previous chapters – is that of its content. What is it that is actually scrutinised when a court tests the quality of legislation? This question is left unaddressed by the fora of review that provide insight into the judicial actors, and the modalities of review that draw attention to the context of review.

Taken at its broadest, the content of review can pertain to the legality and legitimacy of a norm.[536] Legality, simply put, involves the technical issue whether the norm in question is a legal one, while legitimacy concerns its material value as measured against fundamental rights. A court must always decide if what it is presented is actually a law, otherwise any norm can be pleaded before judges without them having the ability to establish if it really is a law. The greater the bench's powers to analyse a norm's legal pedigree, the more the judiciary ventures onto the middle ground between it and the legislature.

221 The purpose of the legality requirement is to check whether a norm that purports to be law was in fact properly adopted. In the case of legislation, this not only presupposes a legislature, but it also brings with it that the proper legislative procedure was followed.[537] This procedure usually entails that a legislature must pass a bill after which it is signed by the head of state and published. By recognising the legislative procedure, courts know whether they are dealing with an act of parliament properly constituted or not. In systems that recognise judicially enforced constitutional supremacy, courts are sometimes also empowered to test the formal qualities of acts of parliament before applying their

---

[536]Van der Schyff, *supra* note 18, at 132–167.

[537]M.C.B. Burkens, *Beperking van grondrechten* (Deventer: Kluwer, 1971), at 93; Van der Schyff, *supra* note 18, at 136–137.

provisions. The idea is that the courts must exercise control over the legislature to ensure that only laws dutifully enacted are recognised as law. The Namibian Constitution of 1990 is a good example, as it not only details the legislative process but also empowers the courts to decide any matter relating to the interpretation and implementation of the Constitution.[538] In other words, the courts are designated as organs that must protect the document's provisions in matters before them to ensure the Constitution prevails over all other laws and actions. This includes not only constitutional provisions guaranteeing fundamental rights, but also those provisions dictating the legislative process and parliament's composition among others. The situation is quite different in jurisdictions that prescribe to undiluted parliamentary sovereignty, as the courts there are prevented from testing if the required legislative procedure was indeed followed when an act of parliament was adopted. The effect is obviously to divide the middle ground in favour of the legislature over the judiciary, as courts have to take the legislature at its word that what it claims to be a law did actually ensue from the legislative process.[539]

222   The legality requirement has further been given flesh by declarations of rights. Such bills often stipulate that their guarantees may only be limited by a "law". This not only asks of a court to establish the legal pedigree of a contested law by checking if it was passed by a competent body following the required procedure, but it also concerns its general applicability, accessibility and clarity. The German Constitution of 1949, for instance, states in section 19(1) that rights may not be limited by a law designed for a particular case, but that laws must apply equally to everyone to ensure that no one may be singled out for discrimination or punishment.[540] As to the other aspects of legality, the European Court of Human Rights has emphasised that a "law" must be accessible, as it would otherwise make little sense to enact laws while keeping their content secret so that people do not know what binds them.[541] Lastly, a law must be clear, which is another way of putting that a law must be

---

[538]Namibian Constitution (1990), at secs. 44, 67, 77, 79(2), 80(2).

[539]For delegated legislation the situation is different. Most jurisdictions, be they inspired by parliamentary sovereignty or judicially enforced constitutional supremacy, allow the courts to test whether such legislation is in accordance with the enabling act of parliament. One only has to recall the case already discussed of *R. v. Lord Chancellor, Ex parte Witham, supra* note 62, where a court in the United Kingdom reviewed delegated legislation to test if it met the requirements of its parent statute.

[540]Cf. *United States v. Lovett*, 328 US 303 (1946), at 428; Rautenbach and Malherbe, *supra* note 22, at 345–346.

[541]*Sunday Times v. The United Kingdom* of 26 April 1979, *Publ. Eur. Court H.R.*, Series A, no. 30, at par. 271: "First, the law must be adequately accessible: the citizen must be able to have an indication that is adequate in the circumstances of the legal rules applicable to a given case."

reasonably intelligible so as to be predictable in practice.[542] The question here is not whether one agrees with the law, or whether it is justified, but simply whether a law is understandable for people to be able to act in accordance with its provisions.

223 Whereas legality is concerned with recognising a law, legitimacy concerns itself with the value system underlying that law. In other words, having passed a law, was parliament justified in passing that law? The function of higher law is then not as a tool with which to investigate the technical features of a norm, but the quality of its logic. Herein resides the crux of the judicial review of legislation. The act of judicial review would ring very hollow indeed were the courts not allowed to review the legitimacy of a law. Theodor Maunz and Reinhold Zippelius captured the importance of legitimacy review by explaining that trying to protect rights without this possibility is not of much use, as everything again depends on the will of the legislature.[543] This leads to the protection of rights becoming a political project while any meaningful judicial input and oversight is sidelined.

224 In structuring review some systems choose to allow legislation to be tested only for its compatibility with civil and political rights, as opposed to other systems that are more open to such review also being conducted in the light of socio-economic rights.[544] While the traditional dichotomy between civil and political rights and socio-economic rights evaporates for some, for others it is still a clear division to be maintained in deciding which forms of higher law to apply and which not. This will also become clear upon taking a closer look at the systems under study. Systems not only differ as to the range of rights according to which review must be carried out, but importantly also as to how such review is to be conducted. Obviously, where no conflict arises between legislation and a particular right the matter comes to an end.[545] On the other hand, where there is

---

[542] The standard formulation being that of the European Court of Human Rights in *Sunday Times v. The United Kingdom, supra* note 541, at par. 271: "Secondly, a norm cannot be regarded as 'law' unless it is formulated with sufficient precision to enable the citizen to regulate his conduct: he must be able – if need be with appropriate advice – to foresee to a degree that is reasonable in the circumstances, the consequences which a given action may entail."

[543] Theodor Maunz and Reinhold Zippelius, *Deutsches Staatsrecht* (München: Beck, 28th ed., 1991), at 158.

[544] Tushnet, *supra* note 284, at 178–180; Daphne Barak-Erez and Aeyal M. Gross, "Introduction: Do We Need Social Rights?: Questions in the Era of Globalisation, Privatisation, and the Diminished Welfare State", in Daphne Barak-Erez and Aeyal M. Gross (eds.), *Exploring Social Rights: Between Theory and Practice* 1 (Oxford: Hart Publishing, 2007) who speak of socio-economic rights as being relegated to a second-class status.

[545] There need not necessarily be a conflict between *legislation* and higher law. One can think of an *action* based on legislation also constituting an interference with higher law. However, this study restricts itself primarily to legislation, as explained earlier in § 11.

conflict courts usually test the legitimacy of the contested law's purpose and decide whether it was reasonable or really necessary for the law to read as it does. This is usually done in the context of a limitation provision, whose requirements must be met in order for a law to intrude on the protection of a particular right.[546] Article 10(2) of the European Convention on Human Rights illustrates this as it not only regulates the legality of a norm by requiring that an interference must be "prescribed by law", but also its legitimacy by stating that it must be "necessary in a democratic society".[547] The values and aspirations of such a society function as the backdrop against which a contested law is to be measured to decide whether its need may trump the imperative of higher law.[548]

225   During this stage of the evaluation courts usually enquire as to the proportionality of a law through a balancing exercise.[549] Once its purpose has been determined as being legitimate, does the law strive to meet that purpose in a legitimate way? Or, does the law overshoot its purpose by limiting higher law too much which means that higher law was violated? A court has to decide if the legislature struck a correct balance in making the law.[550] It goes without saying that this is sensitive territory, as the bench can easily be accused of being overzealous in usurping the legislature or too timid by not paying enough attention to the dictates of higher law. This is a problem that not only arises during limitation analysis, but obviously also when judges interpret a law and any applicable higher law to determine if there is conflict between them before considering whether an interference is justified.[551]

---

[546]Limitation provisions need not only be written, but can also be unwritten. That is, implied by the courts, as in the case *Relating to Certain Aspects of the Laws on the Use of Languages in Education in Belgium v. Belgium* of 23 July 1968, *Publ. Eur. Court H.R.*, Series A, no. 6, at par. B 5 of the Law, regarding the right to education in art. 2 of the Protocol no. 1 to the European Convention. *See* Van der Schyff, *supra* note 18, at 16, 127.

[547]Art. 10(2) reads: "The exercise of these freedoms, since it carries with it duties and responsibilities, may be subject to such formalities, conditions, restrictions or penalties as are *prescribed by law* and are *necessary in a democratic society*, in the interests of national security, territorial integrity or public safety, for the prevention of disorder or crime, for the protection of health or morals, for the protection of the reputation of others, for preventing the disclosure of information received in confidence, or for maintaining the authority and impartiality of the judiciary." (Emphasis added.)

[548]Cf. Susan Marks, "The European Convention on Human Rights and its 'Democratic Society'", 66 *Br. Yearb. Int. L.* 209 (1995).

[549]Van der Schyff, *supra* note 18, at 152–154; the Canadian decision in *The Queen v. Oakes*, (1986) 26 DLR (4th) 200 (SCC), at 225.

[550]Karen Reid, *A Practitioner's Guide to the European Convention on Human Rights* (London: Sweet & Maxwell, 1998), at 37.

[551]Tushnet, *supra* note 284, at 170–171.

Judicial review is not always a matter of applying limitation provisions though, as some rights hold that their protection may never be intruded upon. Again the European Convention provides a good example, as article 3 contains an absolute prohibition on torture. Whereas speech may be limited, torture may never be allowed.[552] The nature of the "absolute" protection seats in the variableness of the interpretation of what amounts to torture.[553] These views and understandings of the right's meaning may come to change over time, which can lead to disagreement about the limits of interpretation.

226 This introduction has shown the possible elements at work in understanding the content of review and also points to the underlying interplay between the legislature and judiciary in dividing the middle ground between them. But what does legality and legitimacy review look like in each of the systems being studied? This question will be addressed below after which the systems are compared. Each evaluation will begin with an explanation of what amounts to higher law in that particular system, as it would otherwise make little sense to investigate legality and legitimacy review without knowing the benchmark of review.

6.2 United Kingdom: Discovering Proportionality

227 Accepting the idea of higher law is still somewhat controversial in the United Kingdom.[554] However, the HRA will be treated as higher law for current purposes as it fulfils the same function as recognised sources of higher law in other systems, namely that of an instrument with which to gauge and measure the quality of other laws.

Higher law for the purpose of the HRA consists of what the Act terms in section 1 as "Convention rights". By this is meant the rights to be found in the European Convention on Human Rights that parliament decided to

---

[552]For example, *Chahal v. The United Kingdom* of 15 November 1996, *Reports*, 1996-V, at par. 80.

[553]In *Selmouni v. France* of 28 July 1999, *Reports and Judgments and Decisions*, 1999-V, at par. 101, the European Court of Human Rights explained that as times change, so do interpretations, which could mean that actions which did not previously qualify as torture, may come to be qualified as such at a later stage. Cf. Michael K. Addo and Nicholas Grief, "Does Article 3 of the European Convention on Human Rights Enshrine Absolute Rights?", 9 *Eur. J. Int. L.* 510 (1998).

[554]Traditionally acts of parliament are viewed as the highest form of law without being subject to higher law, in order to respect parliament's sovereignty; parliament can theoretically not be bound by any source of law apart from its own political will. Cf. Anthony Bradley, "The Sovereignty of Parliament – Form or Substance?", in Jeffrey Jowell and Dawn Oliver (eds.), *The Changing Constitution* 26 (Oxford: Oxford University Press, 5th ed., 2004), at 28–29.

incorporate. These are articles 2–12 and 14 of the Convention, as well as articles 1–3 of its First Protocol and article 1 of the Thirteenth Protocol. Each of these provisions is set out in Schedule 1 to the HRA, and are referred to in the HRA as if one is referring to a right in the Convention. For example, article 10, the right to freedom of expression in the Convention, is also referred to as article 10 by the Act, thereby easing comparison with the jurisprudence of the Strasbourg Court and literature regarding the Convention. Incorporation was not complete though, as a number of provisions were not adopted as domestic legislation, such as article 13 which guarantees everyone an effective remedy before a national authority against the violation of their rights.

Yet, aside from a number of gaps, the Act translates a wide range of the European Convention's provisions into domestic law to be used in judging both the legality and legitimacy of interferences with any of the incorporated rights.[555]

6.2.1 Legality

228 The principle of parliamentary sovereignty can only be respected by the United Kingdom's courts once they know what an act of parliament is. Otherwise, how else can the bench apply the legislature's will without simply guessing? In recognising the legality of an act of parliament, the courts follow the "enrolled rule". According to the classic statement by the House of Lords this means that:

> All that the Court of Justice can do is to look to the Parliament roll: if from that it should appear that a Bill has passed both Houses and received Royal Assent, no Court of Justice can inquire into the mode in which it was introduced into Parliament, or into what was done previous to its introduction, or what passed in Parliament during its progress in its various stages through both Houses.[556]

Apart from affirming that the abstract review of bills is not possible, as already discussed, the quote also points to what a court must take note of in recognising an act of parliament. Namely, once it is clear to a court that a bill was passed by both houses of parliament and received royal assent it is obliged to apply the provisions of that act.[557]

---

[555]Wadham et al., *supra* note 57, at 17–18, list a number of protection gaps in the HRA, arguing that the right to an effective remedy, article 13 of the European Convention on Human Rights, had to be incorporated as well, instead of assuming that adopting the HRA is sufficient in providing such a remedy.

[556]*Edinburgh and Dalkeith Railway Co v. Wauchope*, (1842) 8 Cl and F 710, at 725. Confirmed by Lord Bingham of Cornhill in *Jackson v. Her Majesty's Attorney General*, *supra* note 93, at par. 27.

[557]Bradley, *supra* note 554, at 35–37; Feldman, *supra* note 37, at 32.

229 Another implication of the quote is that once it has recognised an act of parliament as correctly enrolled, a court may not review the parliamentary procedure followed in adopting that law. This was confirmed in *British Railways Board v. Pickin* where it was claimed by one of the parties that parliament was misled in passing the legislation, but where it was held that courts had "no concern with the manner in which parliament or its officers" discharge their duties.[558] Consequently the act that came about was valid and had to be given effect. In practice courts look at the "enactment formula" to see how and by who a law was passed. Acts of parliament state in their preamble that they were:

> [E]nacted by the Queen's most Excellent Majesty, by and with the advice and consent of the Lords Spiritual and Temporal, and Commons, in this present Parliament assembled, and by the authority of the same.

Reading this it is clear that a bill becomes a law when the head of state and both houses of parliament resolve to enact it.

230 An exception to this rule of recognition was created by the Parliament Acts of 1911 and 1949.[559] A political deadlock between the House of Commons, dominated by the Liberals, and the House of Lords, dominated by the Conservatives, led to the upper house voting down legislation accepted by the Commons. This meant that a house lacking a democratic base vetoed important pieces of legislation such as the budget of 1909, although the bill had the support of the democratically-elected lower house. The Liberal government threatened to create a sympathetic majority in the House of Lords through new appointments, something which the Conservatives wanted to stave off by agreeing to the Parliament Act of 1911. The purpose of the 1911 Act, later amended by the 1949 Act, is to allow the House of Commons to present a bill for royal assent without the House of Lords' consent, thereby in effect bypassing the second chamber.[560] However, the exception to the normal procedure is very rarely used and does not apply to bills aiming to extend the life of parliament beyond 5 years.[561] The House of Lords, sitting judicially in *Jackson v. Her Majesty's*

---

[558]*Pickin v. British Railways Board*, [1974] AC 765. Confirmed in *Jackson v. Her Majesty's Attorney General*, *supra* note 93, at par. 27 (*per* Lord Bingham of Cornhill), at par. 49 (*per* Lord Nicholls of Birkenhead).

[559]*Jackson v. Her Majesty's Attorney General*, *supra* note 93, at paras. 9–21; Feldman, *supra* note 37, at 113; Parpworth, *supra* note 31, at 87–91; Richard Ekins, "Acts of Parliament and Parliament Acts", 123 *L. Quart. Rev.* 91 (2007).

[560]The effect of the Parliament Acts is that the House of Lords may not delay money bills for more than a month. All other public bills (save those wanting to extend the life of parliament beyond five years) may be passed by the Commons alone after two successive sessions and a year has passed between the first reading and the bill's acceptance in the second session.

[561]The Acts have only been used the pass the Government of Ireland Act (1914); Welsh Church Disestablishment Act (1915); Parliament Act (1949); War Crimes Act

Attorney General, recently affirmed that laws passed according to these acts are properly enacted acts of parliament.[562]

231 But what is the impact of the HRA on the traditional conception of legality as embodied in the "enrolled rule"? The European Court of Human Rights makes it clear that any interference with a right must have a legal basis, but leaves the question as to whether there is such a basis very much to a member state's domestic law.[563] Interpreting the HRA against this background makes it clear that the Act was not intended to import any new requirements into United Kingdom law with which to judge when the legal pedigree of a law. This leaves the "enrolled rule" very much intact, together with the insularity of the legislative process from judicial scrutiny it implies, as Lord Bingham of Cornhill confirmed in *Jackson v. Her Majesty's Attorney General*.[564]

232 However, this is not all there is to be said about legality under the HRA. Where a Convention right requires that an interference be "in accordance with the law" or "prescribed by the law" it not only means that a limitation must have a legal pedigree, but also that it must be accessible and clear enough to be predictable according to the European Court of Human Rights, as explained in the introduction to this chapter. These three requirements are not entirely novel to British law, as they repeat similar requirements found at common law. For instance, Blackstone's *Commentaries on the Laws of England* argued that:

> [A] bare resolution, continued in the breast of the legislator, without manifesting itself by some external sign, can never be properly a law. It is requisite that this resolution be notified to the people who are to obey it.[565]

The importance of the HRA is to place legality on a firmer footing and to enable courts to take greater note of Strasbourg decisions regarding legality. Doing exactly this, in *R. v. Shayler*, Lord Hope of Craighead enunciated principles similar to those developed by the European Court of Human Rights to evaluate the legality of an interference with a Convention right.[566]

(1991); European Parliamentary Elections Act (1999); Sexual Offences (Amendment) Act (2000); Hunting Act (2004).

[562] *Jackson v. Her Majesty's Attorney General*, *supra* note 93, at paras. 39–41, 68–70, 128. In this matter the Hunting Act (2004) was challenged. The Act was passed under the 1911 and 1949 Parliament Acts. It was argued that the 1949 Act, which amended the 1911 Act, had to have been adopted by both legislative chambers, as it wished to amend the 1911 Act which was passed by both chambers. The House of Lords rejected the argument; the 1911 Act was itself not immune from the qualified procedure it created.

[563] *Silver v. The United Kingdom* of 25 March 1983, *Publ. Eur. Court H.R.*, Series A, no. 61, at par. 86.

[564] *Jackson v. Her Majesty's Attorney General*, *supra* note 93, at par. 27.

[565] Blackstone's *Commentaries on the Laws of England*, vol. I (1765), at 45–46.

[566] *R. v. Shayler*, [2002] UKHL 11.

In sum, incorporating the European Convention on Human Rights has not meant any radical changes to constitutional pillars such as the "enrolled rule", but may very well encourage the courts to take a closer and more stringent look at the accessibility and clarity of legislation.[567]

6.2.2 Legitimacy

233 The real impact of the HRA seats in the legitimacy review it requires. Whenever dealing with the law, a court must logically first distil its meaning before the law can be applied. This is precisely where the HRA comes into play, as it hands a judge a normative set of principles to follow when interpreting a piece of legislation. Where a Convention right cannot be reconciled with legislation, the tested norm can be said to be want for legitimacy, as it should have reflected the substantive interests protected by the applicable Convention right. However, courts in the United Kingdom may not strike down legislation because of such illegitimacy. At most, certain courts may issue a declaration of incompatibility leaving the problem to be corrected by the legislative process. Still, even though a law may not be declared invalid, a court must go through a similar process in deciding whether a law is compatible with higher law as any other court with the power to strike down laws would have to do. The difference seats not so much in how a court arrives at a particular conclusion, but ultimately in what happens to that conclusion. This issue will be discussed in the following chapter. The emphasis here rests on how a court arrives at its conclusion.

In this regard, a proper understanding of the scope of legitimacy review under the HRA invites two questions. The first relates to the instances in which the HRA can be applied, and the second pursues the manner in which the Act is to be applied in such instances.

234 Firstly, under which circumstances must the HRA be applied? The European Convention on Human Rights as the Act's ultimate source reveals something about when it may be relied on. The European Convention is first and foremost a treaty concerned with civil and political rights. One

---

[567] As to executive power, Helen Mountfield, "The Concept of a Lawful Interference with Fundamental Rights", in Jeffrey Jowell and Jonathan Cooper (eds.), *Understanding Human Rights Principles* 5 (Oxford: Hart Publishing, 2001), at 19–21, argues that the HRA's legality requirements will mean that the Crown is no longer able to do everything which is not forbidden (a negative conception), but that the exercise of executive power must be based on a positive basis in law (only that which is allowed). This is undoubtedly correct. Yet, issue can be taken with Mountfield's overreliance on the "predictability" requirement to fetter discretion (at 23–24). This reading is contestable, as it runs the risk of stealing the wind from legitimacy review by asking too many substantive questions under legality review. Cf. Van der Schyff, *supra* note 18, at 180–183.

only has to cast an eye over which rights are protected in the document. A clear example being the right to a fair trial in article 6 and the right to freedom of expression in article 10, both of which have been incorporated in British law. It then requires no stretch of the imagination to identify the purpose of the HRA as primarily a law concerned with warding off the state from the individual and society, as this is the chief function of civil and political rights.[568] Simply put, the state has to be restricted from overly limiting people's freedoms. Had the purpose been that of primarily advancing the cause of socio-economic rights, such as that to work and housing, incorporation of the Convention's sister treaty, the European Social Charter, would have been more desirable instead, something which did not happen.

While it is safe to say that the HRA is an instrument in defence of people's civil and political freedoms against the state, leaving the argument at that would be too hasty.

235 Caution is advisable, in view of rights, such as those to property and to education in the First Protocol to the Convention, being protected as socio-economic interests. Courts will then inevitably be drawn to consider socio-economic issues when applying these rights. Moreover, the usual distinction between civil and political rights on the one hand and socio-economic rights on the other depends on a questionable division between state inaction and action respectively. This distinction is not as clear-cut as may be thought at first glance. Courts, and not least the European Court of Human Rights, have increasingly started to require positive state action in the context of civil and political rights. This discredits the idea that such rights centre nearly exclusively on stopping the state from acting, but highlights that the state may also be compelled to act.[569] The effect of this is obviously to weaken the idea that socio-economic rights cannot be protected by the judiciary as these rights may lead to the state being ordered to act in upholding such rights. This weakness is accentuated by the fact that courts, and again the Strasbourg Court is a prime example, have come to protect socio-economic interests through the vehicle of civil and political rights.[570] Strikingly, in *Cyprus v. Turkey* the Court held that an issue:

---

[568]For example, *A. and Others v. Secretary of State for the Home Department (no. 2)*, [2005] UKHL, 71[2006] 2 AC 221, where the use of evidence in British courts that was obtained under torture was discussed. On the function of civil and political versus social rights, see Barak-Erez and Gross, *supra* note 544, at 1–2.

[569]Cf. Alastair Mowbray, *The Development of Positive Obligations Under the European Convention on Human Rights by the European Court of Human Rights* (Oxford: Hart Publishing, 2004).

[570]Cf. Eva Brems, "Indirect Protection of Social Rights by the European Court of Human Rights", in Daphne Barak-Erez and Aeyal M. Gross (eds.), *Exploring Social Rights: Between Theory and Practice* 135 (Oxford: Hart Publishing, 2007); Ana Gomez

[M]ay arise under Article 2 of the Convention [the right to life] where it is shown that the authorities of a Contracting State put an individual's life at risk through the denial of health care which they have undertaken to make available to the population.[571]

A strict civil and political reading devoid of social concern would probably not have been so keen to acknowledge that the state's omission could provide sufficient cause for legal action in achieving equal treatment in relation to the right to life.

236 In practice this has translated to the HRA becoming an instrument with which socio-economic issues are protected in the United Kingdom next to its more classic function of ensuring that civil and political rights are respected. For instance, in *Bernard and Another v. Enfield LBC* Haringey Council was held to be not only in breach of its statutory duty in terms of section 21 of the National Assistance Act of 1948, when it refused to provide suitable accommodation to a severely disabled and impecunious woman, but also in violation of her article 8 Convention right to private and family life.[572] Although this matter related to executive action and not legislation as such being tested, it proves the range of instances to which the HRA can be applied.[573] Constitutionalism under the HRA then is not only a matter of restraining the state, but also a question of requiring the state to act where appropriate.

237 The range of review now having been established, the second question may be recalled, namely the manner of review. In applying the HRA to matters before them, courts and tribunals must endeavour to follow interpretations that do not conflict with the Act. This duty, as provided for in section 3 of the HRA, is particularly strong as explained by Lord Steyn in *Ghaidan v. Godin-Mendoza*.[574] The idea is obviously that judges must actively seek to interpret legislation in light of the Act instead of simply opting for a declaration of incompatibility where the going gets a bit tough. In discharging their duties under the Act, courts should consequently be careful not to concentrate excessively on the linguistic features of a statute. His Lordship drove the point home by also noting that:

Nowhere in our legal system is a literalistic approach more inappropriate than when considering whether a breach of a Convention right may be removed by

---

Heredero, *Social Security as a Human Right: The Protection Afforded by the European Convention on Human Rights* (Strasbourg: Council of Europe, 2007).

[571]*Cyprus v. Turkey* of 10 May 2001, *Reports of Judgments and Decisions*, 2001-IV, at par. 219.

[572]*Bernard and Another v. Enfield LBC*, [2002] EWHC 2282, [2003] 2 HRLR 4.

[573]Cf. Ellie Palmer, *Judicial Review, Socio-economic Rights and the Human Rights Act* (Oxford: Hart Publishing, 2007).

[574]*Ghaidan v. Godin-Mendoza, supra* note 220, at par. 46.

interpretation under section 3. Section 3 requires a broad approach concentrating, amongst other things, in a purposive way on the importance of the fundamental right involved.[575]

The provisions of the HRA cannot simply be brushed aside, but the importance of its rights must be factored in constructing legislative meaning.

238 In practice a court's exact approach depends on whether it deals with Convention rights that recognise external interferences so long as these are justified, or rights that prohibit any external interference with a right's protection whatsoever. Most challenges under the HRA relate to rights that allow justified interferences with their protection.[576] When reviewing the justification of such interferences, courts usually follow the Strasbourg Court's lead by conducting proportionality exercises to test the legitimacy of an interference. Lord Nicholls of Birkenhead summarised the position quite succinctly in *Ghaidan v. Godin-Mendoza* with reference to the article 8 Convention right to private and family life where the Rent Act of 1977 differentiated between heterosexual and homosexual couples:

> Such a difference in treatment can be justified only if it pursues a legitimate aim and there is a reasonable relationship of proportionality between the means employed and the aim sought to be realised.[577]

239 The quote clearly shows the ascent of the principle of proportionality as a novel ground for review, something which was not possible before the European Convention's incorporation through the HRA.[578] The effect is that when judging if an interference with a right is necessary in a democratic society, courts must review whether that interference went too far in limiting a right, provided they first checked for a legitimate aim. Proportionality is often likened to asking whether the proverbial sledgehammer was used to crack a nut. Proportionality review allows the courts increased powers of review that were unavailable to them using traditional grounds of review, such as *Wednesbury* reasonableness when reviewing executive action.[579] Lord Steyn explained in *R. v. Secretary of State for*

---

[575]Ibid., at par. 41.

[576]For example, *A. and Others v. Secretary of State for the Home Department (no. 2)*, *supra* note 568, at par. 53.

[577]*Ghaidan v. Godin-Mendoza*, *supra* note 220, at par. 18.

[578]*R. v. Secretary of State for the Home Department, Ex parte Brind*, *supra* note 66; Parpworth, *supra* note 31, at 310; Sir Stephen Sedley, "The Rocks or the Open Sea: Where Is the Human Rights Act Heading?", 32 *J. L. Soc.* 3 (2005), at 9.

[579]Cf. Lord Irvine of Lairg, "Judges and Decision-makers: The Theory and Practice of Wednesbury Review", *Pub. L.* 59 (1996); Paul Kearnes, "United Kingdom Judges and Human Rights Cases", in Esin Örücü (ed.), *Judicial Comparativism in Human Rights Cases* 63 (London: British Institute of International and Comparative Law, 2003), at 73; Ian Leigh and Laurence Lustgarten, "Making Rights Real: The Courts, Remedies, and the Human Rights Act", 58 *Camb. L. J.* 509 (1999), at 522.

the Home Department, Ex parte Daly that the intensity of a court's gaze is higher under proportionality review, than review on traditional grounds.[580] This is because proportionality analysis may require courts to assess the balance struck by the decision-maker and not just decide whether it was within the range of rational or reasonable decisions. His Lordship also pointed out that proportionality goes further than traditional grounds of review inasmuch as it requires attention to be paid to the relative weight of relevant interests and factors. The judge concluded by noting that even the "heightened scrutiny" test developed prior to the HRA in *R. v. Ministry of Defence, Ex parte Smith* may be inadequate to protect people's rights when compared to proportionality.[581] However, allowing proportionality review brings not only with it the benefit of increased scrutiny, but it raises the problem of the extent to which courts may scrutinise the law using this device.

240 Addressing this very question, the European Court of Human Rights recognises that a certain "margin of appreciation" accords to member states of the Council of Europe.[582] Due to its international character, the Court realises that national authorities must enjoy some discretion in how they choose to uphold the Convention given their direct and immediate contact with the situation. Must national courts then also grant the legislature and executive a margin of appreciation in the same vein as the Strasbourg Court does? The answer seems to be no, as these are not international courts having to judge national issues under the HRA, but national courts judging national issues, as Lord Hope of Craighead noticed.[583] Rejecting the doctrine of a margin of appreciation as such, does not deny that some other discretionary area of judgment may need to be left to government when a situation calls for it.[584] While, it cannot be denied that courts must allow parliament some discretion in enacting legislation, the contours of

---

[580]*R. v. Secretary of State for the Home Department, Ex parte Daly*, [2001] UKHL 26, at par. 27.

[581]*R. v. Ministry of Defence, Ex parte Smith*, [1996] QB 517, CA, at 554.

[582]Howard Charles Yourow, *The Margin of Appreciation Doctrine in the Dynamics of the European Human Rights Jurisprudence* (The Hague: Kluwer, 1996); Yutaka Arai-Takahashi, *The Margin of Appreciation Doctrine in the Jurisprudence of the ECHR* (Antwerp: Intersentia, 2002), at 300; Stefan Sottiaux and Gerhard van der Schyff, "Methods of International Human Rights Adjudication: Towards a More Structured Decision-making Process for the European Court of Human Rights", 31 *Hastings Int. Comp. L. Rev.* 115 (2008), at 134–136.

[583]*R. v. Director of Public Prosecutions, Ex parte Kebilene*, [1999] UKHL 43; Wadham et al., *supra* note 57, at 48–49. However, the doctrine keeps rearing its head from time to time. For example, in *A. and Others v. Secretary of State for the Home Department*, *supra* note 230, at par. 37, where the Attorney General referred to the doctrine and argued that British courts should afford the same discretion in issues of national security afforded national authorities by the European Court of Human Rights.

[584]Cf. Lord Lester of Herne Hill and David Pannick, *Human Rights Law and Practice* (London: Butterworths, 1999, first supplement 2000), at par. 3.21.

this desired discretion are murky at best and cannot simply be transplanted from the European level.[585] Unfortunately, this realisation that a court is not judge, jury and executioner when it comes to the HRA is described as "deference" in some quarters.[586] As already argued, this choice of word is unfortunate given the negative connotation it attaches to the courts' role vis-à-vis the legislature and executive, while it might be added that soothing the problem by speaking of "inappropriate deference" as opposed to "appropriate deference" is not very helpful either.[587]

241 The problem is essentially one of deciding to which extent the courts may decide what a democratic society should look like, not only when applying limitation provisions but also when interpreting the protection afforded by rights. When is it appropriate for a court to tell parliament what such an ideal society dictates and when not? In dividing the middle ground between the legislature and the judiciary, Lord Hope of Craighead reasoned as follows in *R. v. Director of Public Prosecutions, Ex parte Kebilene*:

> It will be easier for such an area of judgment to be recognised where the Convention itself requires a balance to be struck, much less so where the right is stated in terms which are unqualified. It will be easier for it to be recognised where the issues involve questions of social or economic policy, much less so where the rights are of high constitutional importance or are of a kind where the courts are especially well placed to assess the need for protection.[588]

Courts will also be more willing to recognise a discretionary area of judgment where it concerns an act of parliament as opposed to executive action, thereby taking note of parliament's democratic legitimacy.[589]

242 However, recognising a measure of discretion will not be done at the expense of people's freedom. This was illustrated in *A. and Others v. Secretary of State for the Home Department*, where the House of Lords jealously guarded the liberty of the individual against the state, even where

---

[585] Lord Nicholls of Birkenhead reasoned in *A. and Others v. Secretary of State for the Home Department*, *supra* note 230, at par. 80, that parliament and the executive deserved "an appropriate degree of latitude" because they were "primary decision-makers" – the courts' role being to check their decisions.

[586] For example, Feldman, *supra* note 37, at 387; Sir David Keene, "Principles of Deference under the Human Rights Act", in Helen Fenwick, Gavin Phillipson and Roger Masterman (eds.), *Judicial Reasoning under the Human Rights Act* 206 (Cambridge: Cambridge University Press, 2007).

[587] *See* again § 113. For example, Aileen Kavanagh, "Deference or Defiance? The Limits of the Judicial Role in Constitutional Adjudication", in Grant Huscroft (ed.), *Expounding the Constitution: Essays in Constitutional Theory* 184 (Cambridge: Cambridge University Press, 2008), at 189–190, argues that showing "deference" is not by definition pejorative, but only when it is taken too far.

[588] *R. v. Director of Public Prosecutions, Ex parte Kebilene*, *supra* note 583.

[589] Helen Fenwick, *Civil Liberties and Human Rights* (London: Cavendish Publishing, 3rd ed., 2007), at 189–190.

that liberty was encroached upon by reason of combating terrorism.[590] In the matter a declaration of incompatibility was issued regarding section 23 of the Anti-Terrorism, Crime and Security Act of 2001. This provision allowed for suspected international terrorists to be detained without charge for indefinite periods of time despite the fact that their removal from the United Kingdom was prevented either temporarily or even indefinitely.[591] This possibility of detention without trial did not apply to British nationals, which led the House of Lords to rule that section 23 was disproportional in its effect and therefore a violation of the applicants' article 14 Convention right to be treated equally. Lord Bingham of Cornhill noted that it did not matter that the provision only affected a small group of people, as any interference with their rights still needed to be justified convincingly.[592] In other words, rights are not to be decided by majority vote or interferences judged justifiable simply because of the number of people affected. Even though terrorism had to be countered, parliament could not simply be dealt a free hand in respect of important rights. In explaining the judiciary's adjudicative role, his Lordship noted that although courts must respect democratic decisions this does not preclude that people's rights must made be effective, adding that the HRA itself confers a democratic mandate on the courts to decide whether the law complies with Convention rights.[593] Lord Nicholls of Birkenhead made a similar point by explaining that although a certain degree of latitude is left to parliament, the courts must still decide whether people's rights were factored properly.[594]

243   What constitutes good practice in the field of people's rights in a democratic society is a matter of debate and not always clear. What is clear, though, is that British courts have received a mandate through the HRA to check whether parliament and the executive gave appropriate weight to fundamental rights in exercising their powers. Courts cannot follow a "hands-off" approach when it comes to judging legislation, as this would mean an abdication of their new powers. As Conor Gearty explains, since the coming into force of the HRA "the issue of judicial competence can no longer be avoided", or brushed aside by "glib assumptions" about judicial deference to the legislature.[595] While courts, especially in the 1990s, may

---

[590]*A. and Others v. Secretary of State for the Home Department*, *supra* note 230. See generally, Aileen Kavanagh, "Judging the Judges under the Human Rights Act: Deference, Disillusionment and the 'War on Terror'", *Pub. L.* 287 (2009).

[591]This because of international law or "practical considerations" according to the act.

[592]*A. and Others v. Secretary of State for the Home Department*, *supra* note 230, at par. 68.

[593]Ibid., at paras. 39, 40, 42.

[594]Ibid., at paras. 80–81.

[595]Gearty, *supra* note 84, at 121.

have gone some way towards protecting liberty through the vehicle of common law rights and maxims, they now have to go a step further down that path of judicial vigilance.[596]

6.3 The Netherlands: Which Way Forward?

244 While the idea of higher law is to some degree contentious in the United Kingdom, the Netherlands on the other hand is characterised by a wealth of higher law. The Charter of the Kingdom, the Constitution, international law and unwritten principles of law which are deemed fundamental, such as legal certainty, can all be identified as sources of higher law.[597] The question faced by the Dutch legal order is not so much if higher law exists, but centres instead on what the role of the judiciary vis-à-vis such law should be. This becomes clear when the *bar* on strong constitutional review in section 120 of the Constitution, which is interpreted as also extending to the Charter and fundamental legal principles, is compared with the courts' *duty* based on section 94 to enforce binding provisions of treaties and decisions of international organisations.[598] As explained when the legal order of the Netherlands was discussed, it is this dichotomy that the Halsema Proposal seeks to iron out, at least to a certain extent, by allowing the courts to enforce selected rights in the Constitution against acts of parliament.[599] The Proposal, were it to be successful, will have consequences for reviewing both an act of parliament's legality as well as its legitimacy.

6.3.1 Legality

245 In the discussion of the modalities that apply to the judicial review of legislation in the Netherlands it became clear that courts may neither correct mistakes made in the legislative procedure before a bill is submitted to parliament nor during its consideration by that body.[600] But what about the finished product? May courts test whether an act of parliament

---

[596]Cf. Fenwick, *supra* note 589, at 195, who warns that neglecting the HRA might be more damaging to people's rights than the constitutional position prior to the HRA had been.

[597]On these sources, *see* Kortmann, *supra* note 348, at 90 (Constitution), 106 (Charter), 131 (international law), 135 (fundamental principles), and 113 (on EU law in particular).

[598]On constitutional review, *see* § 39 and on treaty review, §§ 43–44.

[599]*Parliamentary Proceedings II*, 2002–2003, 28, 331, no. 9, at 11. *See also* § 51.

[600]*See* the discussion of the abstract review of bills in §§ 188–193.

was properly passed before applying it to cases before them? In answering this question, attention needs to be paid to the Supreme Court's classic decision of 1961 in the matter of *Van den Bergh*.[601] The applicant was a professor of law, but also a member of the lower house of parliament. By virtue of his membership of the house he became entitled to a pension for the time he served as an elected member. However, the amount of his pension was reduced, the reason for this was the introduction of a general state pension for everyone who reached the age of 65. The decision to reduce pension rights in this way was clothed in an act of parliament, because the Constitution stated then, as it does now, that the remuneration of sitting and past members of parliament had to be regulated in an act of parliament that had been adopted by a two-thirds majority.[602] The applicant complained that the bill used to limit his pension rights had not been voted on at all in the lower house as no member had requested a vote.[603] He further doubted whether two-thirds of that house's members were even present when the bill was passed. This he claimed, was evidence that the bill passed in contravention of constitutional requirements, thereby making its enactment void.

246 The Supreme Court heard the matter and decided against the applicant. It held that a court may not pose the question whether a particular text is a properly constituted act of parliament according to the legislative procedure set out in the Constitution, so long as it can be determined that the text was adopted by both houses of parliament and signed by the sovereign.[604] The Court, interestingly, did not limit itself to the manner of promulgation in identifying if it was dealing with a real act of parliament. It did not identify the act based solely on its publication in the Official Gazette, but the Court also studied reports of the relevant parliamentary proceedings to determine if the bill had indeed passed both houses.[605] This, however, was merely a factual exercise, as the Court did not enquire if each house had followed the proper procedure in adopting the bill, but simply whether a house had adopted it at all. While showing similarities with the "enrolled rule" in the United Kingdom, courts in the Netherlands permit themselves to go a bit further by checking whether a bill did really pass parliament instead of simply relying on the manner and wording of

---

[601] Hoge Raad, 27 January 1961, *NJ* 1963, 248; Van Houten, *supra* note 107, at 41–46; Kortmann, *supra* note 348, at 376–377; Leonard F.M. Besselink, *Constitutional Law of the Netherlands: An Introduction with Texts, Cases and Materials* (Nijmegen: Ars Aequi Libri, 2004), at 91–94.

[602] Currently s. 63 of the Constitution.

[603] *Van den Bergh* judgment, *supra* note 473, 31.

[604] Ibid., at 33.

[605] Ibid.

its promulgation, such as in the United Kingdom.[606] In the *Van den Bergh* case the Supreme Court effectively rejected the views of authors such as R. Kranenburg and C.W. van der Pot who argued that a court must determine whether it is dealing with an act of parliament by looking solely at how it was promulgated without looking at whether parliament in fact adopted the bill.[607]

247 In support of its position the Supreme Court referred to the bar on constitutional review in the Constitution, thereby confirming one of its earlier judgments from 1912 in which it used the same argument.[608] Although the wording of the constitutional provision has changed over the years, from stating that acts of parliament are "inviolable" to barring courts from reviewing "the constitutionality of acts of parliament" after 1983, the provision's effect has been the same. This means that the Supreme Court's jurisprudence of 1912 and 1961 is still relevant today. The deeper justification of the courts' reticence in reviewing legality is clearly a relatively strict conception of the separation of powers, one which sees the legislature enacting a law while leaving the courts to only recognise it in order for it to be applied. In this regard one could argue that section 87(1) of the Constitution has a positive working in that it provides the correct legislative procedure in adopting an act of parliament, while section 120 has a negative function by restricting the courts' powers in checking if the prescribed procedure was indeed followed, thereby emphasising parliament's primacy in legislative affairs.[609]

Although the courts must *enforce* something as an act of parliament once it becomes clear that the legislature has acted, it could be argued that the courts might still be able to conduct *weak* review of any compliance, or lack thereof, with the required legislative procedure. Nothing stands in the way of the Supreme Court's non-binding review in the *Harmonisation Act* case being repeated, but then in the context of legality review.[610] The case for weak review is also strengthened by the fact that a court reviews the finished product while not intervening before the legislative process has run its course, something which would probably stretch the meaning of section 120 too far.[611]

---

[606]On the enrolled rule in the United Kingdom, *see* §§ 228–229.

[607]R. Kranenburg, *Het Nederlands staatsrecht* (Haarlem: H.D. Tjeenk Willink, 8th ed., 1958), at 289; C.W. van der Pot, *Handboek van het Nederlandse staatsrecht* (Zwolle: W.E.J. Tjeenk Willink, 6th ed., 1957), at 111.

[608]Hoge Raad, 25 November 1912, W. 9419.

[609]S. 87(1) of the Constitution provides: "A Bill shall become an Act of Parliament once it has been passed by the Parliament and ratified by the King."

[610]On non-binding review, *see* Van Houten, *supra* note 107, at 8–11, as well as §§ 40, 93 and § 311.

[611]*See* the opinion expressed in § 188.

248   Having stated the current position of legality under the Constitution, the question can be posed how this may come to change were the Halsema Proposal to be adopted and section 120 amended. The proposed exception to be included in section 120 would enable courts to pass a binding judgment on whether an act of parliament must be applied or not. What the Proposal would not bring about is a similar review of any operative or procedural provisions in the Constitution, such as the legislative procedure set out in sections 81–88 for example. The bar on binding review will only be lifted in respect of selected fundamental rights. Yet, it would be premature to deduce that this leaves the orthodox position on legality entirely intact. The Constitution's provisions which guarantee people's fundamental rights emphasise the legality of any interferences with protected conduct. For example, section 6 states that:

(1) Everyone shall have the right to manifest freely his religion or belief, either individually or in community with others, without prejudice to his responsibility *under the law*.
(2) Rules concerning the exercise of this right other than in buildings and enclosed places may be *laid down by Act of Parliament* for the protection of health, in the interest of traffic and to combat or prevent disorders. (Emphasis added)[612]

The phrase "under the law" indicates that parliament has to decide any limit to the right to freedom of religion as guaranteed in subsection 1, while subsection 2 allows parliament to delegate the responsibility of setting a limit to the right by using the words "laid down by Act of Parliament". The effect is to regulate the limitation of the right more closely as far as the interests protected in subsection 1 are concerned, while granting parliament greater freedom in subsection 2 to appoint a different body to limit that aspect of the right.

249   The Halsema Proposal will thus allow courts the binding power to test whether parliament respected the numerous provisions regulating the extent to which the limitation of a right may be delegated, but it will still leave the legislative process from view. However, in allowing the Constitution to be used in examining aspects of a law's legality in this way, the Proposal will not so much introduce legality review for the first time, as it will extend existing powers of review already enjoyed by the courts. This is because courts must conduct binding legality review in respect of

---

[612]In Dutch: "(1) Ieder heeft het recht zijn godsdienst of levensovertuiging, individueel of in gemeenschap met anderen, vrij te belijden, behoudens ieders verantwoordelijkheid volgens de wet. (2) De wet kan ter zake van de uitoefening van dit recht buiten gebouwen en besloten plaatsen regels stellen ter bescherming van de gezondheid, in het belang van het verkeer en ter bestrijding of voorkoming van wanordelijkheden."

the Netherlands' binding treaty obligations, as already explained above and elaborated on below.[613] In practice this means that courts must review whether an interference with a fundamental right, such as the right to freedom of assembly in article 11 of the European Convention on Human Rights, has a legal basis and whether the norm containing the limitation is readily accessible and clear enough to be applied.[614] Against this background the Halsema Proposal will allow courts to use the Constitution to come to a binding decision as to whether the power to limit a right was properly delegated or not. This is something which is not emphasised in treaties, where the focus rests mostly on simply identifying a legal basis as such.[615]

6.3.2 Legitimacy

250   Just as legality review is not new to the Dutch legal order, so too is legitimacy review a familiar face. The Netherlands' monist system of giving effect to international law means that such norms are treated as part of the law to be applied in the country's courts, not to mention that international law is hierarchically superior to national norms, which even include the Constitution. This monist tradition combined with the duty of the courts to apply lower law in conformity with higher law means that legislation must be judicially reviewed for compatibility with the country's treaty obligations. The Constitution places no bar on what may be termed treaty review, as it does on constitutional review in section 120, but it simply refines international law's application by providing in section 94 that in order to be applied by the judiciary such law must be "binding on all persons".

251   As international law has grown both in importance and scope since the Second World War, so has the range of international norms to be applied in Dutch courts increased as well. Section 94 of the Constitution implies that for a norm to be binding, and thus applicable law, it must be directly enforceable by a court without having to be worked out in more detail by the legislature. In addition an international norm must be directed at the people and not only be intended to bind the state. In practice these

---

[613] On treaty review in terms of s. 94 of the Constitution, see §§ 43–44 and § 308.

[614] On these legality requirements, see § 222.

[615] For example, art. 18(3) of the International Covenant on Civil and Political Rights (1966) stipulates that interferences with the right to freedom of religion must be "prescribed by law", without including any instructions on whether the power to limit the right may be delegated or not – a simple legal basis suffices. *Compare* s. 7 of the Dutch Constitution, which sets out how different forms of media may be limited – some may only be limited by an act of parliament, others through delegated legislation.

requirements are understood to allow the judicial application of typical civil and political rights, such as the right to freedom of expression; while barring the courts from reviewing whether legislation conforms to rights which protect socio-economic interests.[616] So while all international law applies directly to the Dutch legal order without requiring any incorporation into national law, as was the case with the HRA in giving effect to the European Convention on Human Rights, not all international norms are directly applicable in Dutch courts. Courts may only apply such law when the requirements of section 94 have been satisfied.

252 Some of the most common treaties applied by courts include the European Convention on Human Rights and the International Covenant on Civil and Political Rights. This brings with it that courts in the Netherlands must, for example, check whether an interference with the protection of a right pursues a legitimate aim, while also enquiring as to whether the aim is pursued proportionally for the interference to be necessary in a democratic society. A case in point is the decision of the Supreme Court in 1996 that journalists may refuse to reveal their sources by reason of the right to freedom of expression in article 10(1) of the European Convention, but that this right may be limited where a court judges that a source's identity is necessary to be revealed in a democratic society in accordance with the limitation provision in article 10(2).[617] The Supreme Court followed the precedent set by the European Court of Human Rights in *Goodwin v. The United Kingdom* in arriving at its decision which saw the Supreme Court overturning its original position, dating from 1977, that journalists must reveal their sources unless the contrary is proved.[618] Although following the Strasbourg Court's lead, courts in the Netherlands, just as those in the United Kingdom, cannot grant national authorities a "margin of appreciation" in holding them to account, as this would deny the fact that national courts are better placed than international benches to evaluate local situations.[619]

253 National courts have not only tried their hand at enforcing international civil and political rights, they have also ventured onto the domain of socio-economic matters on occasion. The right to strike is a good example. This right has long been contentious in the Dutch political landscape, so

---

[616]Burkens et al., *supra* note 13, at 337–341.

[617]Hoge Raad, 10 May 1996, *NJ* 1996, 578.

[618]*Goodwin v. The United Kingdom* of 27 March 1996, *Reports*, 1996-II.

[619]Cf. A.J. Nieuwenhuis, "Van proportionaliteit tot appreciatiemarge: De noodzakelijkheidstoets in de jurisprudentie van het EHRM", in Aernout J. Nieuwenhuis, Ben J. Schueler and Carla M. Zoethout (eds.), *Proportionaliteit in het publiekrecht* 37 (Deventer: Kluwer, 2005), at 56–59.

much so that the matter is not expressly regulated in the Constitution.[620] The effect of this was the courts had to decide issues relating to strike action on the basis of tort law. This presented very much an indirect solution to a question that is expressly dealt with in a number of other national constitutions. The matter was still not resolved at the time of the Constitution's grand revision in 1983, which meant that the right to strike was again not codified even though the constitutional legislature found it fit to include a host of other socio-economic rights in the first chapter of the Constitution.

254 The problem of constitutionalising the right to strike had been avoided, but this did not mean to say that the question had been resolved or that continuing to address it through the law of torts sufficed in any meaningful way. In the end it fell to the Supreme Court to address the matter and place it on a more secure footing in response to the lack of political consensus in this field. In a landmark decision in 1986, the Supreme Court held that the right to strike as contained in article 6(4) of the European Social Charter was directly enforceable, which meant that litigants could rely on the right in judicial proceedings.[621] No longer was the right to strike in article 6(4) of the Charter deemed to only concern the state, but the courts could also take note of it in resolving issues before them. This decision was quite radical as it concerns a socio-economic right, and what is more, a socio-economic right whose text and drafting history contradicted the idea that it should be directly applicable in domestic legal orders – something which the Supreme Court disputed in an unconvincing way.[622]

255 Evert Alkema has shown that in general courts in the Netherlands have over the last three decades not only become more comfortable with the idea of applying international higher law when reviewing national norms, they have also shown bursts of activism by from time to time venturing onto uncharted territory.[623] The right to strike confirms this. Although a dichotomy exists in theory between the application of rights that protect civil and political interests as opposed to socio-economic interests, cases such as the right to strike have shown that this division is not always followed by the country's courts.

The Supreme Court also took large swathes family law to task over the years by twisting the law's literal meaning on a number of important points

---

[620]Cf. Besselink, *supra* note 601, at 154.

[621]Hoge Raad, 30 May 1986, *NJ* 688.

[622]Cf. Wilhelm Wengler, *Die Unanwendbarkeit der Europäischen Sozialcharta im Staat* (Bad Homburg: Gehlen, 1969).

[623]Evert Alkema, "The Effects of the European Convention on Human Rights and Other International Human Rights Instruments on the Netherlands Legal Order", in Rick Lawson and Matthijs de Blois (eds.), *The Dynamics of the Protection of Human Rights in Europe: Essays in Honour of Henry G. Schermers*, vol. III, 1 (Dordrecht: Martinus Nijhoff, 1994), at 13–14.

to conform to the European Convention on Human Rights, thereby proving parliament wrong when it predicted earlier that the Convention would have a negligible effect on Dutch law as it already conformed to the treaty.[624]

256 Even so, as Alkema's survey also shows, it is not always easy to predict where bursts of activism will occur. This has led Henry Schermers to lament that legal certainty may not always be served by such judicial forays.[625] What is clear though, is that courts are becoming less timid in their dealings with higher law, being emboldened to apply treaties whose judicial treatment is uncontroversial, such as the European Convention on Human Rights and the International Covenant on Civil and Political Rights, but also the odd provision from treaties such as the European Social Charter. Long gone are the days when the courts moulded their interpretations of international law to suit acts of parliament and not the other way round.[626] While not so much displacing the relatively strict conception of the separation of powers that exists in the country, as espoused by the formidable likeness of G.J. Wiarda and C.A.J.M. Kortmann, the increased judicial application of international higher law evidences changing attitudes about the role of the courts and may even point to things to come.[627]

257 In studying the effect of international higher law on the Dutch national legal order, one has to be careful not to lose sight of national higher law. While the importance of international law has increased gradually over time, the role of the Constitution as an instrument with which to scrutinise the legitimacy of acts of parliament in many ways harks back to 1848, the date when the bar on constitutional review was first adopted. The Supreme Court in the *Van den Bergh* case confirmed that the bar, currently in section 120 of the Constitution, not only extended to reviewing the legality of

---

[624]For example, Hoge Raad, 18 January 1980, *NJ* 1980, 463; Hoge Raad, 4 June 1982, *NJ* 1983, 32; Hoge Raad, 21 March 1986, *NJ* 1986, 585; Hoge Raad, 10 November 1989, *NJ* 1990, 628; Alkema, *supra* note 623, at 4–6.

[625]Henry G. Schermers, "Some Recent Cases Delaying the Direct Effect of International Treaties in Dutch law", 10 *Mich. J. Int. L.* 266 (1989), at 275. Exploring judicial activism, *see* Marc de Werd and Reiner de Winter, "Judicial Activism in the Netherlands: Who Cares?", in Rob Bakker, Aalt Willem Heringa and Frits Stroink (eds.), *Judicial Control: Comparative Essays on Judicial Review* 101 (Antwerp: Maklu, 1995).

[626]Cf. Alkema, *supra* note 623, at 5.

[627]Wiarda, *supra* note 250, at 97–104, argued that although the separation of powers in the Netherlands was not absolute, it did not mean that judges could be allowed to act as arbiters distinguishing the reasonable from the unreasonable. He lamented the tendency of calling on judges to enforce principles of good governance, instead of simply applying the objective law as presented them. To him, the solution in keeping the judiciary strictly separate from the legislature and executive when it comes to law-making lies in enacting clear norms that will leave little or no room for judicial creativity (at 105–107). Similarly C.A.J.M. Kortmann, *Staatsrecht en raison d'Etat* (Deventer: Kluwer, 2009), at 11–12, criticises the Supreme Court's "law-making" as overstepping its powers resulting in more confusion than good.

an act of parliament, but that the courts had to apply the law irrespective of its material constitutionality.[628] Constitutional guarantees can therefore not be used by the courts as a ground for not applying an act of parliament where such a law contradicts the higher law contained in the Constitution.

258 Courts do though have a duty to interpret legislation in a manner that is consistent with the Constitution. However, this duty has been rather neglected in practice as many of the best examples of such interpretation date from decades ago, whereas more recent examples are far and few between.[629] This is somewhat remarkable, as courts in the United Kingdom have seized the opportunity to interpret the law in conformity with the HRA, while a similar awareness has not caught on in the Netherlands, even though the comparable duty there is a much older one. However, the difference is probably not all that strange, as courts in the Netherlands can refuse to apply legislation on account of it violating international higher law if not the Constitution. The possibility to make use of constitutional interpretation as an instrument of judicial review in the Netherlands is somewhat overshadowed by the judiciary's powers to refuse any application to legislation that infringes upon the country's treaty obligations. This scenario is not possible in the United Kingdom, hence the focus on interpreting legislation in conformity with the HRA where possible.

259 In effect, in the Netherlands the powers of the legislature and the courts are more strongly separated when it comes to applying national higher law to legislation, than to applying higher law sourced from international law to legislation. Depending on the source of higher law the doctrine of separation becomes blurred or not. The landmark *Harmonisation Act* case of 1989 affirmed this not only in respect of the Constitution, but also regarding other sources of national higher law.[630] This judgment has been referred to already and will be discussed again in Chapter 7 on the consequences of review.[631] Suffice it to note for present purposes that in this matter an act of parliament that limited state grants for higher education was contested, as the act limited such grants with retrospective effect. Although the Supreme Court was allowed to apply treaty law to the act of

---

[628]*Van den Bergh* judgment, *supra* note 473, at 33.

[629]Hoge Raad, 19 February 1858, *W.* 1936; Hoge Raad, 28 February 1868, *W.* 2995; Hoge Raad, 5 May 1959, *NJ* 1959, 361; Hoge Raad, 28 January 1994, *NJ* 1994, 687; Van Houten, *supra* note 107, at 46–51; F.T. Groenewegen, *Wetsinterpretatie en rechtsvorming* (The Hague: Boom, 2006), at 160. On the promise that this type of interpretation holds, *see* R. de Lange, "Constitutionele toetsing van wetgeving in Nederland", *Regelmaat* 142 (2006), at 148–150.

[630]*Harmonisation Act* judgment, *supra* note 105. Cf. Belifante and De Reede, *supra* note 101, at 197–198.

[631]For other references, *see* §§ 47–49 and § 311.

parliament in question, the Court concluded that the act did not contradict any binding international law and therefore had to be applied by the judiciary and executive.[632] The norms of international higher law clearly provided no solace to the applicants, while section 120 of the Constitution meant that the Court had to apply the act even though it might have been incompatible with the Constitution.

260   The applicants tried to outflank the constitutional bar by arguing that the Constitution only contained a bar on applying constitutional provisions to legislation and that from this one could conclude that other sources of national higher law were fair game for the courts to use in judging the legitimacy of the act in question.[633] By this they meant the principle of legal certainty which is recognised as an unwritten, yet fundamental, legal principle and which is in addition protected by section 49 of the Charter of the Kingdom of the Netherlands. The argument seemed ideal, as the Charter of the Kingdom is silent on whether it may be reviewed by the courts or not, unlike the Constitution. The Supreme Court, in considering this line of argumentation, reasoned that although limited to the Constitution, the bar on judicial review in section 120, had to be applied to the Charter and unwritten fundamental principles of law as well.[634] This was because section 120 expressed the wider state of play in the Netherlands' constitutional order, namely that of not enforcing higher norms of national law in the face of acts of parliament. The Court held that apart from enforcing the country's treaty obligations it could only ever refuse to apply the literal meaning of an enactment if such a meaning would otherwise lead to harsh consequences which parliament had not foreseen and intended, a scenario which was not apparent from the facts.[635] At most, the Court was willing to exercise a form of weak review by indicating that the principle of legal certainty had been violated although it could not do anything to remedy the breach, something which will be discussed further in the next chapter.[636] This means that a court may only ever refuse to apply an act of parliament for want of legitimacy based on binding international norms.

---

[632]*Harmonisation Act* judgment, *supra* note 105, at paras. 5.2, 5.3.

[633]Ibid., at paras. 3.3, 3.4, 4.1.

[634]Ibid., at paras. 3.8, 4.6.

[635]Ibid., at par. 3.4; Hoge Raad, 12 April 1978, *NJ* 1979, 533; Hoge Raad, 15 July 1988, *RvdW* 1988, 133. This refers to what are known as the *contra legem* cases where an act of parliament is not applied because its strict application would be at odds with the legislature's intention. At first glance, this may seem like a form of legitimacy review, as it can lead to the wording of an act being ignored, but it is actually an interpretive method designed to ascertain and give effect to the legislative will without being distracted by the wording of an enactment.

[636]Ibid., at par. 3.1.

261 As in the discussion of legality review, the bigger picture will only be complete by understanding how the Halsema Proposal will, were it to be successful, influence legitimacy review in the Netherlands. The exception to be added to section 120, foreseen by the Proposal, will only lift the bar on binding review in respect of provisions that are deemed to guarantee directly enforceable rights.[637] In the Proposal, most provisions of the bill of rights in chapter one of the Constitution qualify for the exception. Almost all, because not all provisions on socio-economic rights are deemed to confer directly applicable rights, such as section 22(1), which provides that "[t]he authorities shall take steps to promote the health of the population". In addition to the provisions of the bill of rights, the Proposal earmarks a number of other provisions for judicial review, such as section 121, which prescribes public trials and judgments.[638] In its selection, the Proposal is not particularly adventurous but chooses to mirror the distinction between civil and political rights on the one hand and socio-economic rights on the other, similar to that made on the basis of section 94. Rights protecting socio-economic interests are seen as somehow incomplete, meaning that they cannot be enforced by the courts until they have been given more flesh by ordinary legislation.

262 The adoption of the Halsema Proposal will thus mean that the legitimacy of acts of parliament as measured against the exempted constitutional provisions will become a ground in addition to international law on which to refuse application to acts found wanting. In general this would mean that in order to be legitimate, an interference with a right must pursue a legitimate aim. Some rights in the Constitution specifically indicate the purpose for which rights may be limited, such as the right to freedom of association in section 8 which may only be limited in the interest of public order. The effect is to limit the range of aims which the legislature may pursue in limiting such a right, while other rights leave the legislature more discretion in choosing an aim on account of which to limit a right by stating no permissible aims, such as the right to personal integrity in section 11. This still leaves the important question as to how far an aim may be pursued in limiting a right, which brings the debate to the doctrine of proportionality. However, this doctrine has been somewhat contentious in constitutional theory and law in the Netherlands for quite sometime. This is because nowhere does the Constitution state that a right may only be limited to the extent that it is necessary or reasonable in a democratic society, thereby implying proportionality review.[639]

---

[637]*Parliamentary Proceedings II*, 2002–2003, 28, 331, no. 9, at 18–19.

[638]Secs. 54(1), (2)(a)-(b), 56, 99, 113(3), 114, 121, and 129(1).

[639]In what is probably the only exception, s. 15(4) of the Constitution reads: "A person who has been lawfully deprived of his liberty may be restricted in the exercise of fundamental rights in so far as the exercise of such rights is not compatible with the

263   The reason for this omission is that the aim of the Constitution is chiefly to indicate the authority capable of limiting a right, which is usually the legislature, while trusting its judgment as to the extent of the limitation. This again shows the degree to which parliament's electoral legitimacy is favoured in the theoretical scheme of good governance in the Netherlands. This vote of confidence in popular democracy in formulating limitation provisions to rights has not gone unnoticed or without comment. In 1999 the Society for Media and Communication Law recommended that the right to freedom of expression in section 7 of the Constitution be redrafted so as to read that any limit to that right had to be "necessary in a democratic society".[640] However in 2000 the Franken Commission, entrusted with evaluating the worth of the Constitution in the digital age, recommended leaving the limitation methodology intact. On a similar note, the government of the day reasoned that the principle of proportionality was inherent to the Constitution and need not be invited by phrases such as "reasonableness" or "necessity".[641] Likewise, others have argued that the doctrine of proportionality should be applied to the Constitution as an unwritten principle of law if proportionality is not included expressly in the Constitution.[642]

264   However, such views have not satisfied everyone. Echoing the earlier views of L. Prakke, A.W. Hins points out that nothing prohibits the courts from leaving parliament a free hand in limiting rights were a substantive brake not required in so many words.[643] The fear is clearly that for all its efforts the Halsema Proposal may come to expand review only for it to be watered down in practice. Courts' experience of reviewing laws of a lesser status than acts of parliament, such as provincial and local ordinances that are not covered by the bar in section 120, does not provide a definite answer either. This is because such cases of review hardly ever deal with the question whether power was exercised prudently, but deal mostly with the question whether an organ of state had the right to exercise power

---

deprivation of liberty." The words "in so far as" are generally understood to require a proportionality exercise.

[640] Studiecommissie VMC, "Preadvies inzake een nieuwe tekst voor de artikelen 7 en 13 van de Grondwet", 11(11–12) *Mediaforum* (1999) on http://www.mediaforum.nl/ (last accessed on 19 November 2009).

[641] H. Franken, *Rapport: Commissie grondrechten in het digitale tijdperk* (The Hague: Ministry of the Interior, 2000), at 56–58; *Parliamentary Proceedings II*, 2000–2001, 27 460, no. 1, at 6.

[642] Schutgens, *supra* note 249, at 26.

[643] A.W. Hins, "Constitutionele toetsing, proportionaliteit, Verhältnismässigkeit", in Aernout J. Nieuwenhuis, Ben J. Schueler and Carla M. Zoethout (eds.), *Proportionaliteit in het publiekrecht* 61 (Deventer: Kluwer, 2005), at 77–78; Prakke, *supra* note 123, at 23.

at all.[644] In other words, mostly issues relating to jurisdiction and not the content of power.

It is safe to say that evaluating the content of review in the Netherlands results in a mixed picture, with treaties requiring legitimacy review, a feature which would also be expected of the Constitution but of whose desirability not everyone is convinced.

6.4 South Africa: Wide-Ranging Scrutiny

265 Identifying higher law in South Africa is no longer a difficult task. The Constitution is a purpose-designed instrument that creates and sits atop an authoritative hierarchy of legal norms and so symbolises the unity of South African law. The country's Constitution is the benchmark which all action, including legislation, must meet in order to be valid.[645] It clearly differs from earlier constitutions that were adopted against the background of parliamentary sovereignty. Such documents were ordinary acts of parliament and in no way intended to curb the legislative will as expressed by parliament. The Constitution, and its interim predecessor, signified quite a leap in the 1990s from a system that denied higher law to one that embraced it with particular vigour that has the courts playing an important role in ensuring that constitutional imperatives are lived up to in practice. Judging the content of legislation on constitutionality is therefore very much a judicial task in South Africa.

6.4.1 Legality

266 Section 59 of the 1961 Constitution forbade the courts from enquiring into or pronouncing on the validity of acts of parliament. The provision seemingly tried to bring about a strict adherence to the doctrine of parliamentary sovereignty, similar to that in the United Kingdom but then based on a written instrument. However, section 34 of the last apartheid Constitution, which was adopted in 1983, allowed the courts to rule whether an act of parliament came about validly provided its substance was in no way questioned. The purpose in allowing such power was not meant to discard the principle of parliamentary sovereignty though, but instead served to clarify its meaning as the doctrine had come to be understood in South Africa. The emphasis still rested on the courts' duty to give effect to parliament's will without question, but in order to know whether parliament

---

[644]Ilins, ibid., at 66.
[645]S. 2 of the Constitution.

"spoke" courts needed to know that the prescribed parliamentary procedure was followed, thereby verifying such "speech". In a way this testing capacity of the courts can actually be viewed as bolstering parliamentary sovereignty by enabling them to better recognise parliament's "voice" in order to give it full effect.[646] The difference between the 1961 and the 1983 Constitutions centred not so much on the notion of adopting constitutional supremacy, as it did on interpreting parliamentary sovereignty.[647]

267 Judicially enforced constitutional supremacy meant far-reaching change of course, balancing the scales out more evenly than ever before between the jurisdiction of parliament and the courts respectively. Section 172(1) is a vivid illustration of this, as it states that courts adjudicating constitutional matters within their power must declare any law invalid where and to the extent it contradicts the Constitution. A constitutional matter, so the Constitution explains in section 167(7) "includes any issue involving the interpretation, protection or enforcement of the Constitution". Making the entire Constitution judicial territory in this way obviously brings with it that the courts are not only to test whether a law satisfies the substantive standards laid down in the Constitution, but also any operative or formal standards created by the document. This would include the national legislative process detailed in sections 73–82 including constitutional amendments, as well as the provincial legislative process in sections 119–124 and the procedure prescribed for adopting provincial constitutions in sections 142 and 144–145. Testing for legality is not only possible in respect of acts of parliament or provincial laws for example, but can also be conducted of bills.[648] Judicial concern for legality does not stop at checking legislative procedures, as the Constitutional Court made clear in *Dawood; Shalabi; Thomas v. Minister of Home Affairs* where it required that "rules must be stated in a clear and accessible manner".[649] Whereas the Court implied these requirements from the Constitution, the general limitation provision in section 36(1) makes it clear that a law, in order to limit any

---

[646]Moreover, apart from a single exception relating to the equality of the two official languages in s. 89, the 1983 Constitution could be amended by simple majority, s. 99. This reaffirmed the idea that parliament's will had to decide the day while being obstructed as little as possible.

[647]*See* generally Dion Basson and Henning Viljoen, *South African Constitutional Law* (Cape Town: Juta, 1988), at 169–200.

[648]Consider, for example, the president or premier's constitutional power to refer a bill whose constitutionality they doubt to the Constitutional Court before agreeing to assent to it, provided that the bill was first sent back to the relevant legislature for fresh consideration. Secs. 79, 121 of the Constitution. On the abstract review of bills in South Africa, *see* also §§ 202–204.

[649]*Dawood; Shalabi; Thomas v. Minister of Home Affairs*, 2000 (8) BCLR 837 (CC), 2000 (3) SA 936 (CC), at par. 47; the separate opinion of Mokgoro J. in *President of the RSA v. Hugo*, 1997 (6) BCLR 708 (CC), 1997 (4) SA 1 (CC), at paras. 99, 102.

right, must be of general application. Courts are therefore to control not only the legislative process but also the accessibility, clarity and general applicability of all law.

268 To date the best example of legality review is probably the decision of the Constitutional Court in *Doctors for Life International v. Speaker of the National Assembly*.[650] The case dealt with a number of important constitutional issues as well as sensitive social issues including abortion and sterilisation. In essence, the applicant averred that an adopted, but as yet unsigned, bill and three acts of parliament were unconstitutional as the upper house of parliament, the National Council of Provinces, had failed to comply with its constitutional duty to allow for public involvement during the legislative process.[651] This contention was based on section 72(1) of the Constitution which stipulates among other things that:

> The National Council of Provinces must-
> (a) facilitate public involvement in the legislative and other processes of the Council and its committees.

Clearly, the complaint related not to the substance and therefore legitimacy of the legislation, but centred on whether the legislation had been correctly enacted, which made it very much a topic for legality review.[652]

269 It was accepted by the applicant that the lower house of parliament, the National Assembly, complied with its duty to facilitate public involvement, as it had invited written submissions on the bills and had held public hearings on them too.[653] However, the proceedings in the Council came under attack as the body neither invited submissions, nor held public hearings. Instead it decided that public hearings had to be held in each of the nine provinces, reflecting the fact that the Council represents the country's provinces and is also appointed from the provinces. The Constitutional

---

[650]*Doctors for Life International v. Speaker of the National Assembly, supra* note 278; Rassie Malherbe, "Openbare betrokkenheid by die wetgewende proses kry oplaas tande", *J. S. Afr. L.* 594 (2007); Rassie Malherbe, "South Africa: The National Council of Provinces", in Gerhard van der Schyff (ed.), *Constitutionalism in the Netherlands and South Africa: A Comparative Study* 103 (Nijmegen: Wolf Legal Publishers, 2008), at 115–118.

[651]*Doctors for Life International v. Speaker of the National Assembly, supra* note 278, at paras. 4–7.

[652]On public involvement as a constitutional imperative, *see Doctors for Life International v. Speaker of the National Assembly, supra* note 278, at par. 14; *King and Others v. Attorneys Fidelity Fund Board of Control and Another*, 2006 (4) BCLR 462 (SCA), 2006 (1) SA 474 (SCA), at par. 7.

[653]S. 59(1)(a) of the Constitution; *Doctors for Life International v. Speaker of the National Assembly, supra* note 278, at par. 5.

Court accepted this choice given the role the Council fulfils in the constitutional scheme of things, but added that hearings did in fact have to take place in the provinces.[654] Upon closer inspection it became clear that some provinces had not held any hearings for some of the bills, while one province only scheduled for the public to be heard on a particular bill *after* having instructed its delegates to the Council how to vote on the proposal, thereby making the hearing academic at most.[655] This state of affairs was caused by the fact that the Council had imposed narrow deadlines on the provinces for involving the public in the process. Moreover, requests from some provinces to have the deadlines extended to allow for proper hearings to be conducted were denied by the Council.

270   In giving thought to the constitutional setting, the Constitutional Court emphasised the importance of parliament as the primary legislative organ, given the separation of powers, and noted the sensitive nature of reviewing parliamentary proceedings in particular.[656] The Court recognised that parliament enjoyed a wide discretion as to how it organised its proceedings, but was also quick to point out that the Court was the ultimate guardian of the Constitution and its values.[657] This important duty meant that the Court, however difficult the situation, could not shy away from judging issues that would inevitably bring with it important political consequences.[658] In going about its task the Court held that it was called upon to decide whether the course of action adopted by the Council was reasonable in the light of the Constitution.[659] It found the decision of the Council to hold hearings in the various provincial legislatures and not organising such hearings at the national level to be reasonable, but then found the way in which the hearings of some bills was conducted to have been unreasonable.[660]

271   The Council's excessive emphasis on unrealistic deadlines meant that the public was not consulted properly on some of the bills, which violated the constitutional requirement of public involvement in the legislative process. The Court reasoned that public involvement had to be the measure against which timetables needed to be matched, and not the other way

---

[654]*Doctors for Life International v. Speaker of the National Assembly, supra* note 278, at par. 164.

[655]Ibid., at paras. 167–197.

[656]Ibid., at par. 24.

[657]Ibid., at paras. 22, 36, 70, 122–124; *President of the Republic of South Africa and Others v. South African Rugby Football Union and Others*, 1999 (7) BCLR 725 (CC), 1999 (4) SA 147 (CC), at par. 72.

[658]*Doctors for Life International v. Speaker of the National Assembly, supra* note 278, at paras. 22, 199.

[659]Ibid., at par. 146.

[660]Ibid., at paras. 146, 198.

round, unless a real emergency dictated the opposite, something which was not the case.[661] The affected pieces of legislation were consequently found to be unconstitutional and therefore invalid. This decision, which was handed down by Ngcobo J., was supported by seven other judges, while only judges Van der Westhuizen, Yacoob and Skweyiya dissented.[662] Legality review, admittedly a difficult brief, is one which the Constitutional Court will not avoid in upholding the Constitution against the whims of parliamentary majorities that threaten sound constitutionalism. While the National Council of Provinces allowed itself to disregard constitutional requirements in helping the National Assembly to rush through controversial legislation, the Constitutional Court was not willing to turn a blind eye. In the words of the Court:

> [W]hile the doctrine of separation of powers is an important one in our constitutional democracy, it cannot be used to avoid the obligation of a court to prevent the violation of the Constitution. The right and the duty of this Court to protect the Constitution are derived from the Constitution, and this Court cannot shirk from that duty.[663]

6.4.2 Legitimacy

272   If legality review were to be described as a necessary part of judicial review in South Africa, legitimacy review can best be described as the inspiration for judicial review. The apartheid structures, although for the most part formally legal, amounted to denying the majority of South Africans the most basic of rights, such as those to dignity and equality. In addressing the legacy of racial discrimination the new order was clear about the principles upon which it was founded, by providing in section 1 of the Constitution that:

> The Republic of South Africa is one sovereign democratic state founded on the following values:
>
> (a) Human dignity, the achievement of equality and the advancement of human rights and freedoms.
> (b) Non-racialism and non-sexism.
> (c) Supremacy of the constitution and the rule of law.
> (d) Universal adult suffrage, a national common voters roll, regular elections and a multi-party system of democratic government, to ensure accountability, responsiveness and openness.

---

[661] Ibid., at par. 194.
[662] Ibid., at paras. 225, 245, 339.
[663] Ibid., at par. 200.

These values are brought to life by the Bill of Rights, which the courts are called upon to respect in the name of constitutionalism.

273 Or in the formulation of section 7, the "Bill of Rights is the cornerstone of democracy in South Africa" whose rights the state "must respect, promote and fulfil". The courts are thus entrusted with an important duty to ensure that this cornerstone of democracy is respected in practice. This is largely achieved by checking whether interferences with the protected conduct and interests of rights withstand limitation analysis in terms of the general limitation provision in section 36. This provision controls not only the legality of an interference in that it must be based on a "law of general application", but also directs its legitimacy by requiring that each interference must be "reasonable in a democratic society". Reasonableness must be ascertained by weighing the following factors:

    (a) the nature of the right;
    (b) the importance of the purpose of the limitation;
    (c) the nature and the extent of the limitation;
    (d) the relation between the limitation and its purpose; and
    (e) less restrictive means to achieve the purpose.

Section 36 has been interpreted as requiring the courts to conduct a proportionality exercise to determine if an interference goes too far in achieving its aim or whether it satisfies its aim without over-reaching itself.[664] This obviously implies that a legitimate aim must be identified first. This is something which is not expressly catered for in the general limitation provision, but is nonetheless implied from the provision by the courts.[665]

274 South African courts, led by the Constitutional Court, are very particular about these two requirements being satisfied. The right to vote presents a good example of the courts' regard for the legitimacy of an interference. In *Minister of Home Affairs v. National Institute for Crime Prevention and the Re-integration of Offenders* the applicants challenged the Electoral Act of 1998, which had been amended to prohibit convicted prisoners serving sentences without the option of a fine, from voting for the duration of their imprisonment.[666] They argued that the amendment was unconstitutional as it unreasonably deprived them of their right to vote, a position contested

---

[664]*S. v. Makwanyane, supra* note 32, at par. 104.

[665]*Coetzee v. Government of the RSA; Matiso v. Commanding Officer, Port Elizabeth Prison,* 1995 (10) BCLR 1382 (CC), 1995 (4) SA 631 (CC), at par. 11: "At the very least a law or sanction limiting the right to freedom must have a reasonable goal (...)."

[666]*Minister of Home Affairs v. National Institute for Crime Prevention and the Re-integration of Offenders,* 2004 (5) BCLR 445 (CC), 2005 (3) SA 280 (CC), at par. 2.

by the minister of Home Affairs. The Court reiterated the importance of the right to vote by quoting Sachs J. who held in *August and Another v. Electoral Commission and Others* that:

> [T]he universality of the franchise is important not only for nationhood and democracy. The vote of each and every citizen is a badge of dignity and of personhood. Quite literally, it says that everybody counts.[667]

Evidently, a serious right was being limited, and this the Court would not take lightly even though it concerned prisoners.

275 One of the main arguments advanced by the minister was that limiting the right sent a signal to the public that the government was not soft on crime.[668] The Court explained that this stated purpose would have been illegitimate and hence unconstitutional if it meant that the government intended to disenfranchise voters merely for the sake of its image.[669] Yet, on a balance of probabilities the Court came to the conclusion that the government intended that crime must be denounced and that rights also imply duties, whose neglect may justify people's rights being limited.[670] This aim was judged to be legitimate, which meant that a proportionality exercise had to be conducted which the aim failed to pass. More recently in *Richter v. Minister for Home Affairs and Others* the Constitutional Court did not even get to venturing its hand at proportionality analysis.[671] In this matter, the right to vote of South African citizens who were absent from the country on polling day was severely limited by the Electoral Act. As the minister did not advance any legitimate aim for the limitation, the Court did not hesitate to find a violation.[672]

276 Where the Court has had the opportunity to conduct proportionality analysis it thoroughly investigated the logic underpinning laws that interfere with people's rights. One of the best examples to date remains the decision in *S. v. Makwanyane* where the death penalty was found to be unconstitutional.[673] Far from wanting to limit the role of judicial decision-making in constitutional matters, the drafters of the Constitution had left the question of the death penalty undecided by simply stating that everyone had the right to life, thereby forcing the Constitutional Court to cast

---

[667] Ibid., at par. 28; *August and Another v. Electoral Commission and Others*, 1999 (4) BCLR 363 (CC), 1999 (3) SA 1 (CC), at par. 16.

[668] *Minister of Home Affairs v. National Institute for Crime Prevention and the Re-integration of Offenders, supra* note 666, at par. 55.

[669] Ibid., at par. 56.

[670] Ibid., at par. 57.

[671] *Richter v. Minister for Home Affairs and Others*, [2009] ZACC 3, 2009 (3) SA 615 (CC).

[672] Ibid., at paras. 72–73.

[673] *S. v. Makwanyane, supra* note 32.

the final word as to whether this excluded capital punishment.[674] The Attorney General of the Witwatersrand had prepared a careful case as to why the death penalty was arguably constitutional by emphasising its deterrent effect and the need it fulfilled in bringing about retribution for severe crimes.[675] Chaskalson P. considered the arguments and found that they had to be proportional to the aim pursued in order to trump the guarantees to life and dignity as guaranteed by the Bill of Rights.[676]

277 This exercise left the President of the Court to conclude that the rights to life and dignity, which he viewed as the most important guarantees in the Bill, could not be overridden in favour of the death penalty because the identified aims could also be achieved by means of handing down sentences of life imprisonment.[677] In other words, requiring the death penalty would go too far in the pursuit of criminal justice, which would violate the rights of those sentenced to death too much. This judgment was reached against the background of a country wracked by violence and where popular support for the death penalty might very well be overwhelming. This shows the Court's singular commitment to upholding the Constitution as it believes it to be interpreted irrespective of political or public opinion. As Chaskalson P. argued, the question before the Court is not whether the majority of South Africans preferred the sentence or not, but whether the Constitution allowed for it.[678] Otherwise, the judge reasoned there would be no need for legitimacy review as one could simply revert to majoritarianism. These decisions regarding the right to vote and those to life and dignity, which are but a sample of the courts' rich jurisprudence, show that state sanctioned limits to people's rights will not be tolerated easily, even when it concerns those who caused harm to society such as prisoners.

278 But while these examples pertain to core civil and political rights, it may not be forgotten that the bill of rights contained in the Constitution of 1996 can rightly be described as a "full" bill of rights by also guaranteeing a wide range of socio-economic rights. The intention was clearly to give as much flesh as possible to the values aspired to by South Africa and which had to guide its young democracy. Because the Constitution makes no distinction between the justiciability of the rights it guarantees, judicial concern stretches not only to civil and political rights, but to those rights protecting socio-economic interests as well. In drafting the Constitution, views such as those of Dennis Davis doubting whether socio-economic rights had to amount to enforceable rights, did not enjoy much

---

[674]Ibid., at paras. 5, 25.

[675]Ibid., at paras. 112, 116, 125, 136, 141.

[676]Ibid., at par. 104.

[677]Ibid., at paras. 144–146.

[678]Ibid., at paras. 87–89.

currency.[679] Socio-economic rights have also met with a welcome reception by the courts.[680] As a matter of fact, the South African Constitutional Court has internationally come to be seen as a leader in enforcing socio-economic rights that courts in many other jurisdictions might shy away from.[681]

279   One of the best known examples to date remains *Government of the RSA v. Grootboom*.[682] In this case homeless people were evicted from land on which they had squatted.[683] The Constitutional Court decided the evicted people's rights against the background of the right to housing in section 26 of the Bill of Rights. The Court stressed that this right entailed not only negative obligations for the state, but also required the state to act in promoting access to housing for all.[684] The state's actions or omissions were considered no less justiciable because socio-economic rights were concerned, as this would have confined people's rights to paper only. According to the Court the real question centred on how these rights had to be applied by the courts.[685] In this regard, the Court identified common reason as the benchmark to be satisfied by the public housing programme. Upon application of this standard it became clear that the programme fell short of providing for those people in desperate need of shelter.[686] This left the onus on the government to remedy the defects in its programme to grant people the constitutional enjoyment of their rights.

---

[679]Dennis Davis, "The Case Against the Inclusion of Socio-economic Demands in a Bill of Rights Except as Directive Principles", 8 *S. Afr. J. Hum. Rights* 475 (1992).

[680]For example, *Soobramoney v. Minister of Health, KwaZulu-Natal*, 1997 (12) BCLR 1696 (CC), 1998 (1) SA 765 (CC); *Khosa and Others v. Minister of Social Development and Others; Mahlaule and Another v. Minister of Social Development and Others, supra* note 499; *President of the RSA and Another v. Modderklip Boerdery (Pty) Ltd*, 2005 (8) BCLR 786 (CC), 2005 (5) SA 3 (CC).

[681]Cf. Cass R. Sunstein, *Designing Democracy: What Constitutions Do* (Oxford: Oxford University Press, 2001), at 221–237; Rassie Malherbe, "The Development of Social and Economic Rights in South Africa", 60 *Zeitschrift für öffentliches Recht* 111 (2005); Motala and Ramaphosa, *supra* note 148, at 390–408; Pierre de Vos, "Pious Wishes or Directly Enforceable Human Rights? Social and Economic Rights in South Africa's 1996 Constitution", 13 *S. Afr. J. Hum. Rights* 67 (1997); Marius Pieterse, "Coming to Terms with Judicial Enforcement of Socio-economic Rights", 20 *S. Afr. J. Hum. Rights* 383 (2004); Theunis Roux, "Legitimating Transformation: Political Resource Allocation in the South African Constitutional Court", in Siri Gloppen, Roberto Gargarella and Elin Sklaar (eds.), *Democratization and the Judiciary: The Accountability Function of Courts in New Democracies* 92 (London: Frank, 2003).

[682]*Government of the RSA v. Grootboom, supra* note 189.

[683]Ibid., at par. 3.

[684]Ibid., at paras. 34–35.

[685]Ibid., at paras. 20, 94.

[686]Ibid., at paras. 41, 96–99.

280 Yet, the *Grootboom* decision does not mean that the courts are to protect socio-economic interests exactly as they would many civil and political rights, such as that to vote. This point was confirmed in the later decision in *Treatment Action Campaign and Others v. Minister of Health and Others*, where it was explained that:

> Courts are ill-suited to adjudicate upon issues where court orders could have multiple social and economic consequences for the community. The Constitution contemplates rather a restrained and focused role for the courts, namely, to require the state to take measures to meet its constitutional obligations and to subject the reasonableness of these measures to evaluation. Such determinations of reasonableness may in fact have budgetary implications, but are not in themselves directed at rearranging budgets. In this way the judicial, legislative and executive functions achieve appropriate constitutional balance.[687]

In essence, courts must adopt a responsible approach to socio-economic rights by knowing their own limits, which is different from denying or shirking their duty to enforce such rights. Explained differently, all rights are justiciable, even though their review might not be identical under all circumstances given their particular nature.

But essentially, and regardless of the nature of the right concerned, courts in South Africa are enjoined to give teeth to both civil and political and socio-economic rights in meeting the counter-majoritarian demands of the Constitution in both range and depth.

6.5 Concluding Remarks

281 The ideal of a democratic society is not simply a synonym for justification through the device of majority rule. The European Court of Human Rights has reiterated this point on a number of occasions:

> Although individual interests must on occasion be subordinated to those of a group, democracy does not simply mean that the views of a majority must always prevail: a balance must be achieved which ensures the fair and proper treatment of minorities and avoids any abuse of a dominant position.[688]

Through having opted for the judicial review of legislation, all three countries being studied have accepted this statement. While it may not be controversial that self-respecting societies strive to become model democratic societies through a measure of judicial review, differences emerge in just how much of a judicial say may be allowed in constructing such a

---

[687]*Minister of Health and Others v. Treatment Action Campaign and Others (no. 2)*, 2002 (10) BCLR 1033 (CC), 2002 (5) SA 721 (CC), at par. 38.

[688]*Chassagnou v. France* of 25 April 1999, *Reports*, 1999-III, at par. 112; *Leyla Şahin v. Turkey* of 10 November 2005, *Reports of Judgments and Decisions*, 2005-XI, at par. 108.

society, as also became clear from previous chapters. Comparing the content of judicial review in the United Kingdom, the Netherlands and South Africa proves the point vividly by evidencing different approaches in dividing the middle ground between the legislature and the judiciary. This shows that there is not just a single variant of constitutionalism that answers all questions that relate to legality and legitimacy review.

282   Comparing legality review shows that functioning democracies are not agreed on the need to allow the courts to review legislative procedures. In other words, the question of whether the accepted or prescribed way of enacting laws must become part of the judicial domain, in addition to being a legislative matter, cannot be answered with a simple yes or no response. The United Kingdom shows that introducing the judicial review of legislation to a system that is predicated on a strong parliamentary tradition warrants against such review being extended to the workings of parliament. Similarly, the Halsema Proposal stops short of putting the case for lifting the bar on constitutional review in the Netherlands when it comes to reviewing operative provisions in the Constitution and not only provisions that guarantee fundamental rights.

While the United Kingdom and the Netherlands both answer the question of reviewing legislative procedure in the negative, South Africa has resolutely chosen for a positive answer. Its Constitution expects the judiciary to pronounce on the validity of legislation's formal coming about. *Doctors for Life v. Speaker of the National Assembly* presents a near-perfect example, as the Constitutional Court paid great attention to whether sufficient public consultation had taken place during the hearing of a number of bills by the National Council of Provinces.[689] The Court made it known that the separation of powers could not be used to distract its gaze from upholding complete constitutional supremacy in the face of a parliamentary majority's naked political will.

283   A similar vigilance that verges on urgency does not preoccupy the constitutional dispensations of the United Kingdom and the Netherlands. The *Van den Bergh* case shows that courts in the Netherlands will only check whether the legislative actors necessary for an act of parliament to come about did indeed act, without concerning themselves as to how they acted.[690] In doing so, Dutch courts will look at parliamentary proceedings to decide if the necessary steps have taken place, which goes further than what their counterparts in the United Kingdom do; they leave the integrity of parliamentary proceedings entirely to parliament by following the enrolled rule. This clear division between the courts and parliament

---

[689]*See* §§ 268–271, where the decision was discussed.
[690]*See* §§ 245–247.

was explained in lucid terms by Lord Craig of Hopehead in *Jackson v. Her Majesty's Attorney General*:

> As a judge I am very conscious of the proper reluctance of the courts to intervene in issues of the validity of Acts of Parliament. I should be most unwilling to decide this or any other case in a way which would endanger that tradition of mutual respect. I do not, and I have no doubt your Lordships do not, have any wish to expand the role of the judiciary at the expense of any other organ of the State or to seek to frustrate the properly expressed wish of Parliament as contained in legislation. The attribution in certain quarters of such a wish to the judiciary is misconceived and appears to be the product of lack of understanding of the judicial function and the sources of law which the courts are bound to apply.[691]

This exposition of the state of play in the United Kingdom not only sets out the role of the judiciary, but also makes it plain that there is no apparent wish or need to shift the parameters of judicial review to legislative procedures.

284 One could explain this by pointing to the fact that introducing judicial review in the United Kingdom was never intended to upset the institutional balance as it applies to majoritarianism, but to refine it instead. A similar desire behind the Halsema Proposal probably explains why it views the extension of judicial review to matters of legislative procedure as not being imperative. Moreover, in the United Kingdom the Parliament Acts of 1911 and 1949, which make it possible for the House of Commons to legislate without the House of Lords' approval, have been used on very few occasions. This means that Westminster's parliamentary tradition is strong enough to withstand a whole-scale abandoning of checks and balances during the legislative process. Were these checks to be diluted though, it might very well warrant greater judicial oversight in curbing unbridled political power.[692] South Africa shows that where the wisdom and experience of a consolidated democracy are lacking and constitutionalism has to be forged from scratch, the judicial review of legislative procedures is more readily accepted in checking majoritarianism.

285 It would be rash to deduce from comparing the three countries' experiences that well-functioning and consolidated democracy means that legality review will never be adopted. The effect of the European Convention on Human Rights in both the United Kingdom and the Netherlands allows for the courts to investigate the accessibility and foreseeability of legislation. This aspect of legality review is not particularly novel, but actually amounts to recasting in constitutional terms the courts' traditional role of only applying intelligible legislation. This is something which experience

---

[691]*Jackson v. Her Majesty's Attorney General, supra* note 93, at par. 168.

[692]For example, the Government of Ireland Act (1914); Welsh Church Disestablishment Act (1915); Parliament Act (1949); War Crimes Act (1991); European Parliamentary Elections Act (1999); Sexual Offences (Amendment) Act (2000); Hunting Act (2004).

with the common law in the United Kingdom proves, as the requirements attaching to phrases such as "prescribed by law" in the HRA overlap to a large extent with what has developed under common law. This aspect of legality review can therefore be more properly be said to have been brought up to date more than having been introduced. The requirements of accessibility and foreseeability are also very much part of judicial review in the Netherlands through the courts' duty to apply treaties such as the European Convention on Human Rights. The Halsema Proposal aims to add to this by allowing the review of constitutional provisions that regulate the delegation of the power to limit rights.

286 Still, what can be deduced is that the existence of well-established democratic traditions, such as those in the United Kingdom and the Netherlands, militates against such systems opting for the judicial review of legislative procedures. The absence of significant political momentum and real constitutional need caused by an acute democratic deficit in these systems meant that the "default" position, namely that of parliament controlling its own procedures, was maintained by both countries. As a matter of fact, had the judicial review of legislative procedures been introduced in the United Kingdom, serious questions could have been put about the continued viability of parliamentary sovereignty. However, the HRA was calculated to avoid this contest as it only supplements the parliamentary protection of rights, instead of radically reshaping constitutionalism in that country. In contrast, the ideal of recognising a constitutional supremacy which was not at the mercy of political majorities meant that bipolar constitutionalism in the field of reviewing legislative procedures was readily adopted in South Africa. If these experiences of the three countries had to be reduced to a single conclusion, it would probably be that checking legislative procedures does not constitute an essential element of judicial review that must be present were one to speak of judicial review at all. There is no agreement on the universal need for such review, as it seems to be decided on a case-by-case basis by focusing on the absence or presence of reliable majoritarian traditions.

287 Somewhat different, though, is the case of legitimacy review. Whereas legality review is beset by the question whether legislative procedures may be reviewed at all, legitimacy review is marked by a general consensus that such review must consider the extent to which legislation complies with fundamental rights. This is borne out of the countries studied, as the HRA focuses on selected rights from the European Convention on Human Rights, while these and other treaty rights have been enforced by courts in the Netherlands for decades. Also, the core of South Africa's transition to full democracy rested on a justiciable bill of rights being adopted in contrast to previous constitutions. This consensus also extends to conducting proportionality review in testing the legitimacy of an interference, but ends when the range of rights to be reviewed needs to be decided.

288   Turning first to the consensus on proportionality, courts are not content with taking legislatures at their word that a piece of legislation pursues a legitimate aim in an acceptable manner. The HRA is a sterling example, because incorporating certain rights from the European Convention on Human Rights led to proportionality analyses, which proved to require a higher level of scrutiny than was until then commonplace under the rules of *Wednesbury* reasonableness. South African case law and jurisprudence will also be hard to imagine without the doctrine of proportionality, which is deduced by the courts from the general limitation provision in section 36 of the Bill of Rights. Although courts in the Netherlands conduct proportionality exercises in carrying out treaty review, it became clear during its discussion that some commentators doubt whether the Halsema Proposal will be as successful in bringing about proportionality analysis, were it to succeed in amending the bar on constitutional review in section 120 of the Constitution.[693] It is feared that as the formulation of constitutional rights does not make reference to the doctrine of proportionality in some way, for instance by requiring that legislation interfering with people's rights must be "necessary in a democratic society", the constitutional amendment may run the risk of not achieving effective judicial review. This again points to the apprehension felt in some quarters that a general reluctance to change the current arrangement in the Netherlands pertaining to the judicial review of legislation might bedevil any real reform.[694] However, such views might be a little alarmist, as it would be difficult for the courts to avoid proportionality exercises on such a formal ground, and not be accused of bad faith. Such is the normative effect of proportionality review as an essential device of counter-majoritarianism. Not only is such review essential for legitimacy review in countries such as South Africa, where the parliamentary opposition is particularly weak in getting the merits of its arguments taken seriously given the ANC's dominance, but proportionality analyses are also vital for legitimacy review in other systems, in order for one to speak of worthwhile judicial review.[695]

289   While there may be agreement on the need for proportionality review, there is little consensus about the range of rights to be reviewed, as legal systems are very selective of the rights that may be reviewed. Civil and political rights are treated as uncontroversial standards of review in all three systems, and this is probably because these rights stand closest to the

---

[693]For example, Hins, *supra* note 643, at 77–78; Prakke, *supra* note 123, at 23. *See* § 264.

[694]For example, Mevis, *supra* note 301, at 934–935, laments the fact that the Halsema Proposal is "stingy" and only "supplements" current judicial protection, whereas it should have been a "revolution".

[695]Robert A. Schrire, "Parliamentary Opposition After Apartheid: South Africa", 14 *J. Legis. Stud.* 190 (2008), at 206.

workings of democracy and are therefore considered to be indispensable benchmarks for correcting the legislative process if needed; whereas socio-economic rights are less clearly connected with the workings of democracy and so less of a judicial priority.[696] The HRA expresses a preference for the review of civil and political rights by concentrating on the European Convention on Human Rights, while the Halsema Proposal continues the practice of treaty review by classifying socio-economic rights as "unenforceable" by the judiciary.[697] Both instruments therefore focus on typical rights with which to ward off state intrusion from people's sphere of personal freedom. At the same time though, both systems illustrate the porous side of this division between civil and political rights on the one hand and socio-economic rights on the other.[698] This is because the HRA can also be an instrument with which to protect socio-economic interests in addition to purely civil land political matters if the European Court of Human Rights' case law were to be followed throughout. In the Netherlands the usual judicial reluctance to review socio-economic matters was discarded decisively in relation to the right to strike in the European Social Charter, even though the treaty was never really intended to bind domestic courts of law.

290 South African courts conversely have never had any theoretical qualms about what to do with socio-economic rights.[699] The country's Constitution simply recognises rights and does not allow for any distinction to be made on the basis of civil and political versus socio-economic interests in deciding whether to judicially enforce rights or not. Judgments such as that in the *Grootboom* case also prove that the courts do not hesitate to take the government to task about if and how it chooses to fulfil its socio-economic obligations. Although South African courts have shown themselves not to be blind to the difficulties inherent to enforcing socio-economic rights, as the judgment in *Treatment Action Campaign* shows, they have not been deterred from reviewing socio-economic claims, but have risen to the challenge by exploring the possibilities of the judicial function in this field.

291 Given the explicit treatment of socio-economic rights in South Africa, the more cautious approach adopted in the United Kingdom and the Netherlands may very well be attacked as making distinctions between rights that are ultimately capable of being bridged, if such distinctions were not of questionable origin in the first instance. However, the picture may change when the reality of the everyday situation is considered. The

---

[696]I.e. civil and political rights are treated as core instruments of constitutionalism.

[697]*Parliamentary Proceedings II*, 2002–2003, 28, 331, no. 9, at 20.

[698]*See* again §§ 235–236 on the United Kingdom, and §§ 253–255 on the Netherlands.

[699]On socio-economic rights before South African courts, *see* again §§ 278–280.

Netherlands and the United Kingdom are highly developed countries with elaborate social welfare systems and in 2008 enjoyed the sixth and 21st place respectively on the Human Development Index – which is weighted by factors such as life expectancy and literacy.[700] They are essentially societies of little want in comparison to most other countries and South Africa in particular, which came in at position 125 on the index. This enviable state of affairs has to date then also chiefly been the product of the political process as the large-scale introduction of social legislation in the United Kingdom and the Netherlands, starting in the 1950s, came about not so much by judicial imperative as through parliamentary initiative.[701] This could lead to the plausible conclusion that the legislative process is in no particular need to be corrected by the courts in these two countries regarding its socio-economic track record. This would explain their caution in allowing such rights to be reviewed.

292 South Africa, on the other hand, is undoubtedly justified in having a judiciary which is called upon to test legislation and government policy in the socio-economic sphere to the extent it does.[702] It may not be forgotten that South Africa knew a watershed moment, namely that between a society based on a supreme parliament that negated rights and a dispensation based on a justiciable and supreme Constitution that treasures rights. South Africa, given its past experience with the overconcentration of power in the legislative branch, is arguably correct to be wary of placing all its eggs in one basket. Engaging the courts then seems to be a logical response to the country's history. The great social need in South Africa could certainly also be mentioned as another reason why not only the legislative branch of government is to be engaged, but also the judicial branch.[703] Simply put, the social project to be embarked upon is so vast and important that the courts, as co-arbiters, may serve to help parliament and the executive to approach such important matters from the right perspective.

---

[700]United Nations Development Programme, *Human Development Report* (2008) table 1.

[701]For example, the National Health Service in the United Kingdom, the publically funded health care system which is based on the needs of the patients and not on their ability to pay, was introduced by legislation and started operating in 1948. In 1957, the Algemene Ouderdomswet (AOW, General Old Age Pensions Act) was adopted by the Dutch legislature, the effect of which was to create a guaranteed state pension for every resident in the country irrespective of their employment history.

[702]Gerhard van der Schyff, "The Protection of Fundamental Rights in the Netherlands and South Africa Compared: Can the Many Differences be Justified?", *Potchefstroom Electr. L. J.* 1 (2008), at 14–15.

[703]*See* the remarks by the Constitutional Court in *Government of the RSA v. Grootboom*, *supra* note 189, at par. 1.

293 Although the judicial review of socio-economic matters might be good theory and practice in South Africa, it might not always be as warranted in practice as the United Kingdom and the Netherlands illustrate. This is because overt judicial review, such as that chosen by South Africa, might upset the balance between the legislature and the judiciary by more than is called for in these countries. As Cass R. Sunstein explains, South Africa's experience shows that adjudicating socio-economic rights is possible, but that in some nations this might raise more questions than it answers.[704] The test seems to be whether rights need to be adjudicated in order to give groups that are disorganised and overlooked in the reality of ordinary politicas a much needed voice – a situation that is more readily accepted in the case of civil and political rights than socio-economic rights due to the latter's less immediate connection with the democratic process.[705] Courts in South Africa have been doing just that in the sphere of socio-economic rights by concerning themselves with the plight of people living on the fringes of society and to whom the adjudication of socio-economic rights might be more beneficial than a preference for civil and political rights. In so doing South African courts go some way towards discounting the views of Ran Hirschl that the introduction of judicial review would mean very little for the poor, as such review was primarily conceived as a way of protecting white privilege after this became impossible through parliamentary means because of the black majority's enfranchisement.[706]

294 Although this overview of the content of review touches upon a large subject, it does show that consensus is absent on the question whether legality review must include the review of legislative procedures. Countries that have experienced a constitutional trauma, such as South Africa's democratic crisis, might be more inclined to allow this aspect of their legislatures' competence to be made a legal and not simply a political fact. Legitimacy review is far less divisive a topic to agree on than legality review. All three case studies, be they systems with long traditions of parliamentary democracy such as the United Kingdom and the Netherlands, or systems with much younger democratic traditions such as South Africa, recognise that judicial review must mean checks involving the legitimacy of legislative aims and the manner of their pursuit. This uniformity of approach becomes fragmented when the range of rights to be reviewed is considered,

---

[704] Sunstein, *supra* note 681, at 235–237.

[705] Ibid., at 235.

[706] Hirschl, *supra* note 6, at 92–93, 216–218. Also putting the views of Hirschl into perspective, *see* Maurice Adams and Gerhard van der Schyff, "Grondwettigheidstoetsing door de rechter als 'list van de rijke'? Methodologische en andere vragen bij processen van rechtsverandering", 45 *Tijdschrift voor Privaatrecht* 913 (2008), at 958–959; Leslie Friedman Goldstein, "From Democracy to Juristocracy", 38 *L. Soc. Rev.* 611 (2004), at 626.

with the review of civil and political rights being seen as a bare minimum and socio-economic rights as a possible but not necessary object of judicial protection. Irrespective of which avenues a system explores, ultimately for judicial protection to add anything to constitutionalism depends very much on courts taking their duty seriously in ensuring that the parameters of a democratic society are not breached.

Chapter 7
Consequences of Review

7.1 Introduction

295 Georg Vanberg defines constitutional review as "the power of judicial bodies to set aside ordinary legislative or administrative acts if judges conclude that they conflict with the constitution".[707] Although accurate, this definition is too narrow to reflect constitutional law and practice. The reason for this, apart from the fact that constitutions are not the only source of higher law which can guide review, is that according to the definition a court's ruling of conflict with higher law entails that the offending norm is to be set aside. Instead, the consequences of identifying an intrusion upon higher law can be placed along a spectrum of possible outcomes of which setting aside is but one of the available options. The one end of this spectrum can be classified as "strong" review, the other as "weak" review. At the outset, it needs to be remarked that this distinction centres on characterising the consequences of review and not on the intensity of review, such as diluting review by allowing a margin of appreciation. This topic was dealt with in the previous chapter on the content of review.

296 Strong-form review amounts to leaving the legislature no room to respond to a court that strikes down legislation on account of it violating higher law, bar an amendment of such higher law.[708] In other words, the only option if a legislature does not agree with a court's ruling is to change the higher law which led to the judgment, thereby allowing the offending legislation to be readopted in the assurance that higher law now no longer provides an obstacle to the majority's will. Scenarios of strong review can even be imagined where an amendment of higher law might not be possible because provisions may never be amended, such as provisions

---

[707]Georg Vanberg, *The Politics of Constitutional Review in Germany* (Cambridge: Cambridge University Press, 2005), at 1.

[708]Stephen Gardbaum, "The New Commonwealth Model of Constitutionalism", 49 *Am. J. Comp. L.* 707 (2001), at 712–713; Tushnet, *supra* note 284, at 174.

G. van der Schyff, *Judicial Review of Legislation,*
Ius Gentium: Comparative Perspectives on Law and Justice 5,
DOI 10.1007/978-90-481-9002-7_7, © Springer Science+Business Media B.V. 2010

in the German and Czech constitutions to this effect.[709] Still, the point remains, that strong review does not provide the legislature with an everyday mechanism with which to respond to rulings that nullify legislation. The judiciary's word is thus binding and must be accepted by the legislature in unqualified terms. Strong review, of which the United States is a prime example as the Supreme Court's decisions are final, guards against higher law being reduced to parchment barriers, so its supporters argue. The exercise of strong-form review means that the legislature may only pursue the original aims of a nullified law within the confines of the judgment that struck down the legislation. The purpose is clearly to protect the idea of higher law as the supreme expression of the law to be guarded in unqualified terms by the courts against the legislature.

297 On its part, weak-form review refers to systems of judicial review where it is constitutionally foreseen that the judiciary does not enjoy the last word in interpreting and applying higher law, but where it has to share this jurisdiction to varying degrees and through different methods with the legislature.[710] The New Zealand Bill of Rights Act of 1990 is a good example.[711] This Act affirmed or codified a host of fundamental rights while enjoining the courts to prefer a meaning that is consistent with the rights guaranteed in the Act over a meaning that contradicts their protection when interpreting legislation.[712] The achievement of the Act was to introduce a narrative based on human rights into a system that always treated rights more as statements of political morality than legal entitlement. However, the Act expressly denies the courts the power to declare legislation invalid or refuse to apply legislation that violates the rights guaranteed by the Act.[713] In other words, judicial review under the New Zealand Bill of Rights Act is non-binding and therefore weak, which is very similar to judicial review in the United Kingdom under the HRA that will be discussed below.

To qualify as weak review, a court's judgments can also be binding, provided that some or other measure is foreseen which allows the legislature to avert such rulings or respond to them. Section 33 of the Canadian Charter of Rights of 1982 is just such an instrument, as it provides that an act of parliament or provincial law may be passed notwithstanding the Charter of

---

[709]For example, s. 79(3) of the German Constitution (1949); s. 9(2) of the Czech Constitution (1992).

[710]Mark Tushnet, *Weak Courts, Strong Rights. Judicial Review and Social Welfare Rights in Comparative Constitutional Law* (Princeton, NJ: Princeton University Press, 2008), at 18–42.

[711]Cf. Paul Rishworth, Grant Huscroft, Scott Optican and Richard Mahoney, *The New Zealand Bill of Rights* (Melbourne: Oxford University Press, 2003).

[712]Sections 2 and 6 of the New Zealand Bill of Rights Act, 1990.

[713]Ibid., at s. 4.

Rights.[714] The effect of the provision is that such a law becomes immune from judicial scrutiny under the Charter, but this immunity lapses after 5 years, after which the law must be readopted in order to again oust the courts' constitutional jurisdiction.

298 Essentially, the reason for weak-form review is to stimulate an institutional dialogue between the legislature and the judiciary, instead of what is perceived by many as the judicial monologue caused by strong-form review. The idea of establishing a dialogue is grounded in the fact that because of its democratic legitimacy the voice of parliament needs to be factored in designing review and not left by the wayside, as is the case with strong review.[715] In other words, because parliament is democratically accountable, in contrast to the courts, parliament should at best be advised by the courts but not overruled, or empowered to respond if it is overruled. Supporters of weak review usually argue that strong review does not mean constitutional supremacy, but actually amounts to swapping parliamentary sovereignty for judicial supremacy. The purpose of opting for weak review is thus to avoid a situation of judicial supremacy from developing that cannot be questioned by democratically legitimated representatives. Weak review has been favoured by many systems grounded in the doctrine of parliamentary sovereignty as a way to embrace judicial review, without dealing an immediate deathblow to legislative supremacy. Consequently, this form of review is called the Commonwealth model by some, as many former British colonies and territories sought to strike a compromise between the legislature and the judiciary by experimenting with weak forms of review.[716] The model of strong review is sometimes referred to as the American model to indicate systems without a tradition of parliamentary sovereignty and hence less resistance to adopting strong-form review. But as with the fora of review where the description of a system as being decentralised or centralised was preferred over references to the American and European models, this chapter will speak of strong and weak review and not of the American and Commonwealth models.

299 In practice, though, a judgment that reviews the compatibility of a law with higher law can always generate debate and discussion irrespective of the design of a particular system. The United States, while being a prime exponent of strong review, is a good example. The controversial decision handed down by the Supreme Court in *Roe v. Wade* on the constitutionality of abortion in 1972, led to a wide-ranging debate in society as to merits of abortion and also fired state governments and Congress to test the limits

---

[714]Cf. Peter W. Hogg, *Constitutional Law of Canada* (Ontario: Thomson Carswell, 2007), at 839–850.

[715]*See* generally, Hogg and Bushell, *supra* note 239, at 75.

[716]For example, Gardbaum, *supra* note 708.

of the decision.[717] The decision came to be a catalyst for activism instead of simply settling the matter as one would expect from a system based on the strong review of the Constitution. As a matter of fact, such has the importance of the debate been that Christine A. Bateup has commented that subsequent decisions of the Supreme Court have converged towards mainstream public opinion on abortion, which has come to moderate the reach of the Court.[718] In Canada, on other other hand, a strong constitutional convention seems to have developed against the use of the override provision in section 33 of the Charter, which means that the effect of constitutional review is nearly always strong in practice.[719] Nonetheless, the idea of weak review made the judicial control of legislation more palatable in a country such as Canada that had a strong democratic tradition of protecting people's rights, but which still required a "deeper realization of the basic norms of liberal democracy" in the words of Lorraine Eisenstat Weinrib.[720] Simply put, the consequences of review have to fit the purpose for which judicial review was adopted, and which will be investigated in the context of the United Kingdom, the Netherlands and South Africa.

7.2 United Kingdom: Preferring Weak Review

300 Where Canada and New Zealand set the example of how parliamentary sovereignty could be reconciled with the judicial review of legislation, the United Kingdom followed with the HRA. The adoption of weak review had to enable the survival of parliamentary sovereignty as the organising principle of constitutionalism in the United Kingdom, albeit in a new constitutional environment. Embarking on the road of weak review did not mean, however, that the Canadian or New Zealand examples were simply copied. Whereas the Charter of Rights in Canada allows for an act of parliament to be struck down by the courts, the same course of action is not available to courts under the HRA. The HRA only allows for a declaration of incompatibility to be issued in terms of section 4 of the Act. In this, it goes further than the New Zealand Bill of Rights that only provides for legislative enactments to be interpreted in conformity with the rights contained in the bill without something similar to a declaration belonging to a court's arsenal. But what is a declaration of incompatibility exactly?

---

[717]*Roe v. Wade*, 410 US 113 (1973).

[718]Christine A. Bateup, "Expanding the Conversation: American and Canadian Experiences of Constitutional Dialogue in Comparative Perspective", 21 *Temple Int. Comp. L. J.* 1 (2007), at 21.

[719]Lorraine Eisenstat Weinrib, "Canada's Constitutional Revolution: From Legislative to Constitutional State", 33 *Israel L. Rev.* 13 (1999), at 34–37.

[720]Ibid., at 27–28.

301   First of all it needs to be understood that declarations of incompatibility are not the only measure by which the HRA can be implemented. This was made clear in *Ghaidan v. Godin-Mendoza* where Lord Steyn stressed that interpreting legislation to fit the requirements of the HRA, in terms of section 3, provided the "prime remedial measure" intended by the Act and that declarations of incompatibility are only ever to be used as a measure of "last resort" by a competent court.[721] This is evident from the Act as it enjoins all courts to interpret legislation against the background of any relevant Convention right, while only allowing the higher courts to issue declarations of incompatibility in terms of section 4(5) of the HRA.[722] From this can be deduced that such declarations are the exception in administering justice and not the rule. It is only when a designated court cannot bring itself to interpret a law in conformity with the HRA that issuing a declaration becomes a possibility, and even then it remains at the discretion of the court to do so or not.[723]

302   A declaration of incompatibility amounts to a court signalling the government that it cannot read and give effect to a Convention right *and* implement a piece of legislation at the same time. Where such a conflict arises a court must implement the act of parliament and not the higher law contained in the Convention right at issue. A declaration of incompatibility is not binding on the parties before a court and has no effect on the validity, continuing operation or enforcement of legislation.[724] Once a court has indicated what it perceives to be a violation of higher law, it is up to the political process to decide further action, if at all. In other words, the HRA allows the judiciary the jurisdiction to apply higher law provided it does not extend to setting aside acts of parliament. As the Home Secretary remarked during the third reading of the bill that ultimately became the HRA:

> [I]t was important to enshrine Parliament's sovereignty in the Bill. We therefore developed the scheme of declarations of incompatibility. We did not propose that the Judicial Committee of the House of Lords should have the power to override Acts of Parliament by stating that, because they were incompatible with the Convention, they were unenforceable and of not effect. We said that the Judicial Committee of the House of Lords would be able to declare whether, in its opinion, an Act of Parliament was incompatible with the Convention, and subsequently refer the matter back to Government which is responsible to Parliament.[725]

---

[721]*Ghaidan v. Godin-Mendoza, supra* note 220, at par. 46.

[722]These courts are, the Supreme Court [formerly the House of Lords]; Judicial Committee of the Privy Council; Courts-Martial Appeal Court; in Scotland, the High Court of Justiciary sitting otherwise than as a trial court or the Court of Session; in England and Wales or Northern Ireland, the High Court or the Court of Appeal.

[723]For example, *R. v. Her Majesty's Attorney General (Appellant) Ex parte Rusbridger (Respondent), supra* note 323, at par. 46.

[724]S. 4(6)(b) of the HRA.

[725]*Hansard*, HC, 21 October 1998, col. 1300.

Judicial review is therefore weak, because although a court can bring something to the attention of the government through a declaration of incompatibility, it remains powerless to undertake independent action in remedying the problem. A court may only ever remove an incompatibility where it is not barred from doing so by an act of parliament, something which means significant powers for the courts in administrative law and possibly also where it concerns delegated legislation, as long as the parent act is not affected in the process.[726]

303 Once a declaration of incompatibility has been made the government can decide to follow what has been called the fast-track procedure in amending or repealing the offending legislation.[727] A minister may, according to section 10(2) of the HRA, amend legislation so as to remove any incompatibility where there are considered to be compelling reasons. This essentially means that legislation may be changed by executive order. This procedure applies to delegated legislation but also to acts of parliament. In amending legislation two procedures are distinguished.[728] The first calls on a minister to table the order before parliament for a period of 60 days accompanied by a statement explaining the incompatibility, as well as why the minister deems it appropriate to proceed under section 10. Representations from within and outside parliament can be made in the 60-day period, although ministers may, they are not compelled to amend their orders accordingly. After this initial period an order must be laid down again, this time with a summary of any recommendations made. The order then only comes into effect after it has been adopted by a resolution in both the House of Commons and the House of Lords within 60 days. Apart from this standard procedure, a minister can also choose to follow the emergency procedure, which resembles the standard route but differs in that the order has already been drawn up when it is tabled.[729] The fast-track procedure is also a possibility where, following a judgment of the European Court of Human Rights, the government decides that a law is incompatible with a Convention right.

304 To put matters in perspective, a declaration of incompatibility is therefore the only remedy available where provisions in acts of parliament are impugned for colliding with Convention rights.[730] An award of

---

[726]S. 4(4)(b) of the HRA.

[727]Wadham et al., *supra* note 57, at 98–100.

[728]Schedule 2 of the HRA.

[729]Such as in *R. (H.) v. Mental Health Review Tribunal*, [2001] EWCA Civ 415.

[730]David Feldman, "Remedies for Violations of Convention Rights Under the Human Rights Act", 6 *Eur. Hum. Rights L. Rev.* 691 (1998), at 698. Interestingly, David Jenkins, "Common Law Declarations of Unconstitutionality", 7 *Int J. Const. L.* 183 (2009), argues that British courts have an inherent ability to issue "common law declarations of unconstitutionality" where legislation offends common law rights in addition to, or apart from Convention rights.

damages might be appropriate in many other instances of collision, such as in the case of delegated legislation and other executive acts that were not calculated to give effect to acts of parliament.[731] Furthermore, as was mentioned above, a court is not obliged to hand down a declaration of incompatibility on discovering a conflict between the HRA and other laws.[732] The House of Lords made this quite clear in *R. v. Her Majesty's Attorney General (Appellant) Ex parte Rusbridger (Respondent)*, where it was explained that such declarations will only be made in cases of actual worth and not simply as a tool to update dusty old statute books, which is the duty of parliament.[733] Courts have consequently been careful not to issue declarations of incompatibility. To date a relatively small number of declarations have been issued, while the government has been very keen to adjust or correct the law in response to them.[734] This willingness to follow the courts' advice probably has to do with the fact that the European Court of Human Rights does not consider such declarations to be effective legal remedies in the spirit of article 13 of the Convention on Human Rights, which means that litigants can take their cases before the Court in Strasbourg. When one adds to this equation the fact that litigants in Strasbourg are then armed with a legal opinion that vindicates them, it becomes increasingly probable that the state will be hard pressed to defend itself against such claims. But whatever the cause of declarations of incompatibility being followed up by government, the then Home Secretary's prediction in debating the HRA has proved well-founded:

> In the overwhelming majority of cases, regardless of which party was in government. I think that Ministers would examine the matter and say, "A declaration of incompatibility has been made and we shall have to accept it. We shall therefore have to remedy the defeat in the law spotted by the Judicial Committee of the House of Lords".[735]

---

[731] Ibid.; s. 8 of the HRA; Leigh and Lustgarten, *supra* note 579, at 527–531.

[732] Cf. Richard Clayton QC, "Remedies for Breach of Human Rights. Does the Human Rights Act Guarantee Effective Remedies?", in Jeffrey Jowell and Jonathan Cooper (eds.), *Delivering Rights: How the Human Rights Act is Working* 147 (Oxford: Hart Publishing 2003), at 159.

[733] *R. v. Her Majesty's Attorney General (Appellant) Ex parte Rusbridger (Respondent)*, *supra* note 323, at par. 46 (*per* Lord Hutton).

[734] For example *R. v. Secretary of State for the Home Department, Ex parte Anderson and Taylor* [2002] UKHL 46, [2002] CrAppR 167 (declaration regarding s. 29 of the Crime (Sentences) Act (1997) followed in secs. 303(b)(I), 332 and schedule 37, point 8 of the Criminal Justice Act (2003); *Bellinger v. Bellinger*, [2003] UKHL 21, [2003] 2 AC 467 (declaration regarding s. 11(c) of the Matrimonial Causes Act (1973) followed in Gender Recognition Act (2004)). *See* also the examples mentioned by Wadham et al., *supra* note 57, at 95–97. For the impact on dialogue, *see* Roger Masterman, "Interpretations, Declarations and Dialogue: Rights Protection under the Human Rights Act and Victorian Charter of Human Rights and Responsibilities", *Pub. L.* 112 (2009), at 116–117. *See* also Kavanagh, *supra* note 86, at 410, who remarks that this shows that the dialogue metaphor has been overstated in relation to declarations of incompatibility.

[735] *Hansard*, HC, 21 October 1998, col. 1300.

305 The main effect of the HRA and the possibility it creates to issue declarations of incompatibility has been to preserve parliamentary sovereignty, while also making it possible for the courts to render some input in evaluating legislation. One can identify both positive and negative aspects depending on the angle from which this constitutional arrangement is viewed. The negative side of any judicial input falls to the litigant in whose case a declaration is made, because although in the opinion of a court they proved their case, this does not result in an immediate remedy for them. Quite understandably, this had led to the mechanism of declarations of incompatibility being described as a "booby prize".[736] A Pyrrhic victory, especially when viewed from the ideal that the judicial function is to be built on effective remedies. As to the positive side of things, declarations of incompatibility are the ideal instrument to enter into a dialogue with the legislature on the interpretation and application of fundamental rights. Under the HRA the courts have a formal voice which they can now choose to use in engaging parliament. According to Richard Clayton, this "democratic dialogue" should serve to embolden courts to heighten their scrutiny as the Act gives both the legislature and the executive "a second bite at the cherry" which in turn avoids any hint of judicial supremacy.[737]

306 While it may be agreed with Janet L. Hiebert that it is still too early to give "firm pronouncement on how the HRA is influencing political behaviour", a few examples of effective dialogue between the courts and political organs are apparent and worth mentioning.[738] The earlier discussed case of *A. and Others v. Secretary of State for the Home Department* presents just such an example.[739] In this matter a declaration of incompatibility was issued for a violation of the right to a fair trial by the Anti-Terrorism, Crime and Security Act of 2001, which provided for the indefinite detention of foreign nationals suspected of terrorism without the benefit of a trial. In response the government decided to adopt the Prevention of Terrorism Act 2005. The 2005 Act replaced indefinite detention without trial with a system of control orders designed to monitor suspects, a move that was seemingly inspired by remarks in the speech of Lord Bingham of Cornhill pointing to alternative ways in which the government could pursue its purpose of combating terrorism other than indefinite detention.[740] However, the 2005 Act has since also come under

---

[736]Clayton, *supra* note 732, at 159.

[737]Richard Clayton QC, "Judicial Deference and 'Democratic Dialogue': The Legitimacy of Judicial Intervention under the Human Rights Act 1998", *Pub. L.* 33 (2004), at 46–47.

[738]Janet L. Hiebert, "Parliamentary Bill of Rights: An Alternative Model?", 69 *Mod. L. Rev.* 7 (2006), at 21.

[739]*A. and Others v. Secretary of State for the Home Department*, *supra* note 230.

[740]Ibid., at par. 35.

judicial attack. Although this time the House of Lords stopped short of issuing another declaration of incompatibility, it did decide on the strength of section 3 of the HRA to read down offending provisions in the 2005 Act so that they would take effect only when it was consistent with fairness for them to do so.[741] This amounted to a second judicial response to the legislature on this topic, but this time one which ameliorated the effect of its legislation.

307 In short, although not forced to react to the declaration of incompatibility in respect of the 2001 Act, political organs in the United Kingdom chose to do so anyhow by adopting the 2005 Act and even heeded comments made from the bench in designing the new law. In its judicial capacity, the House of Lords continued the dialogue by interpreting controversial provisions in the 2005 Act to fit the standards set by the relevant Convention rights. As this short excursion shows, the HRA provides the basis for an inter-institutional dialogue between judges and politicians. What is more, Thomas Poole convincingly shows that *A. and Others v. Secretary of State for the Home Department* also encouraged parliamentarians, especially members of the House of Lords, to subject the government's anti-terrorism policies to closer scrutiny than ever before.[742] Parliament became more independent-minded after the judiciary's criticism and instead of simply following the wishes of the executive, members of parliament started to challenge its policies. The achievement of the HRA in this instance was thus three-fold, it guaranteed parliamentary sovereignty while allowing the courts to render an opinion on controversial legislation, which in turn fired the workings of parliamentary democracy.

7.3 The Netherlands: Non-application of Legislation

308 The traditionally strict separation of powers in the constitutional order of the Netherlands becomes evident when the effect of treaty review is considered. Section 94 of the Constitution, which regulates treaty review, stipulates that statutory regulations "shall not be applicable if such application is in conflict with provisions of treaties or of resolutions by international institutions that are binding on all persons". In other words, a court that establishes an infringement of international higher law may not strike down an offending law, as is common practice in jurisdictions with particularly strong forms of review such as that of the United States of America. Regardless of the gravity of a particular violation, a law will

---

[741]*Secretary of State for the Home Department v. MB (FC)*, [2007] UKHL 46, par. 44 (*per* Lord Bingham of Cornhill); Thomas Poole, "Tilting at Windmills? Truth and Illusion in the 'the Political Constitution'", 70 *Mod. L. Rev.* 250 (2007), at 271.

[742]Poole, ibid., at 273–274.

remain on the statute books but is simply not applied by a court in a particular instance. This is because in the Netherlands such an action would mean claiming too much of the middle ground for the judiciary. At the heart of this division lies the idea that rules of law are to be created by parliament, while the courts are to apply the law to individual cases and desist from laying down generally binding rules from the bench.[743]

309 Tied in with the idea of a civil law jurisdiction that does not follow the doctrine of binding precedent is the notion that courts can refuse to apply a law in particular cases, but not bind themselves or other courts to ruling in similar vein in future. It is then not so much legal certainty as retaining the separation of powers that is a priority, because a judgment only creates a reason for other courts to rule similarly, while not obliging them to do so. Treaty review clearly occasions strong review, as a law is not applied by a court which finds that it violated binding norms of international law. At first glance, the strong nature of such review seems to be diluted by the fact that a court cannot strike down offending legislation or bind other courts to follow its judgment. However, the strong nature of review is somewhat strengthened by the fact that although precedents are not formally binding, a court ruling that refuses application to a law is usually followed by other courts which leads to a *de facto* situation of binding precedent.[744] Even so, the central idea remains that it is ultimately up to parliament to repeal an offending law. Because section 94 of the Constitution refers to "statutory regulations" this applies not only to acts of parliament, but also to delegated legislation such as executive orders.

310 The Halsema Proposal builds on this line of thinking, as it proposes an exception to the bar on constitutional review in section 120 of the Constitution by allowing the courts to refuse application to acts of parliament that violate selected constitutional rights.[745] The Proposal foresees no different structure from that already in place with regard to section 94. Crafting constitutional review in this way can probably be explained as a move calculated to drive home change, while not upsetting the current institutional balance between the legislature and the judiciary regarding the review of legislation. The purpose is to undo, at least for the most part, the ban on review first included in the Constitution in 1848, but then in a manner that fits the legal system's established separation of powers. Until such

---

[743] Stressing a strict separation of powers, *see* Kortmann, *supra* note 627, at 11–12.

[744] R.J.B. Schutgens, "Het rechtsgevolg van onverbindendverklaring: Naar een stelsel van materiële vernietiging", *Themis* 96 (2006) explains that it is all but impossible to find examples of lower courts not following the highest courts in holding that legislation is ineffective. Cf. Hoge Raad, 18 February 2005, *NJ* 2005, 283 (*Aujeszky*) where the Supreme Court even went so far as to state that courts presiding over civil law proceedings must in principle follow the decision of the highest administrative law court.

[745] *Parliamentary Proceedings II*, 2001–2002, 28, 331, nos., 2, 9.

time as the Proposal is accepted the current state affairs remains intact, namely that an act of parliament must be implemented by a court irrespective of its constitutional integrity. The consequence of this provision is thus to immunise acts of parliament from constitutional attack. However, it would be rushing matters to conclude from this short exposition that no constitutional consequences can attach to legislation.

311   The *Harmonisation Act* case opened the door to what is arguably weak review.[746] The facts of the case have been set out in other chapters and will not be repeated here, apart from mentioning that the matter concerned legislation with retrospective effect used to reduce student grants. The Netherlands' treaty obligations did not come to the students' rescue as the Court could not fault the contested legislation in the light of such obligations, nor did national higher law offer them an effective remedy by reason of section 120 of the Constitution. With a strict separation of powers in mind the Court should have stopped there, as it might have done in the past.[747] However, it grasped the opportunity to argue that the legal protection of people's rights had become insufficient over the years.[748] Nonetheless, the Court quickly realised that it was not its prerogative to change the constitutional set-up that prohibits the constitutional review of acts of parliament.[749] However limited its possibilities, the Court's lack of any real power to enforce national higher law did not prevent it from lamenting the plight of the applicants and remarking that the act in question did actually violate the principle of legal certainty, although the Court was powerless to provide a remedy.[750] The effect of this judgment was thus to show that the bar in section 120, according to the Supreme Court, could be used to investigate the legitimacy of an act of parliament in the light of national higher law as long as such review remained weak. Theoretical support for the notion of weak review might even be found in the courts' general duty to interpret legislation in conformity with the Constitution, a topic that was discussed in Chapter 6.[751] This is because one could argue that where such conformity cannot be achieved through interpretation, a court should signal a conflict between the Constitution and an act of parliament, while still applying the act given the effect of

---

[746]*Harmonisation Act* judgment, *supra* note 105, at par. 3.1. Similarly, Heringa *supra* note 107, at 68–69.

[747]For an idea of the absolute nature of the bar on constitutional review was construed traditionally, one only has to consider the *dicta* expressed by the Supreme Court in the *Van den Bergh* judgment, *supra* note 473, at par. 33, that acts of parliament have to be treated as if they were above *any suspicion*.

[748]*Harmonisation Act* judgment, *supra* note 105, at par. 3.4.

[749]Ibid., at par. 3.6.

[750]Ibid., at par. 3.1.

[751]Discussed in § 258.

section 120. In essence, such an exercise would amount to weak judicial review, as a constitutional problem is identified, without an act of parliament being refused application.

312 Interestingly, during the debates leading up to the grand revision of the Constitution in 1983 some politicians raised the idea of introducing weak constitutional review.[752] However, the government of the day responded that *every* form of constitutional review by the judiciary had to be excluded in order to avoid the judiciary becoming entangled in political questions.[753] As was argued in Chapter 3, such a division between law and politics is no longer valid, if ever it was.[754] The point here is, however, that the government was of the opinion that section 120 of the Constitution would prohibit acts of parliament from being reviewed on any constitutional grounds. This opinion was contradicted in the *Harmonisation Act* case. However, this spurt of activism by the bench has not been repeated on the quite the same scale since. The reason for this is probably that many cases can be resolved by recourse to international law, which rules out the need for a court to make non-binding remarks about constitutionality of legislation in the first place. Moreover, as has also become clear, courts in the Netherlands are on balance careful not to be accused of judicial activism or legislating from the bench, which could be another reason to avoid constitutional appraisals.[755]

313 It would be wrong to conclude from the above though that constitutional appraisals cannot amount to anything more than a damp squib. Although parliament was not forced to change the offending legislation after the *Harmonisation Act* decision, it did. In other words, the judicial branch signalled a problem to which the legislative branch responded. In a way, although the aggrieved students did not get their day in court, they got their day in parliament with a little help from the courts. This course of events brings to mind the HRA, which allows senior courts to issue declarations of incompatibility in the hope that the legislature will take heed and remove the incompatibility with the relevant Convention rights. The *Harmonisation Act* case is proof that even in a system where the inviolability of acts of parliament is cherished to a considerable degree, the courts can still act as parliament's constitutional conscience, if not quite yet its custodian.

---

[752]*Parliamentary Proceedings II*, 1974–1975, at 2325, 2431; Van Houten, *supra* note 107, at 57–58, sketches the debate.

[753]*Parliamentary Proceedings II*, 1976–1977, 13 872, no. 7, at 9.

[754]*See* § 95.

[755]For example, Hoge Raad, 16 May 1986, *NJ* 1987, 251, where the Supreme Court stressed that it is not the duty of the courts to assess the value or public import of the interests affected by government decisions at their own discretion, and that they must exercise their powers of review with restraint.

314   Institutional dialogue, or communication at the very least, is also evident in the Netherlands when it comes to treaty review. However, far from always working to the advantage of the litigant, it has sometimes arguably led to acts of parliament being protected to a questionable extent. This state of affairs was summed up quite accurately by the European Court of Human Rights in the matter of *Van Raalte*:

> [I]n a number of judgments [the Dutch Supreme Court] has declined to construe Article 26 of the Covenant [on Civil and Political Rights] in such a way as to deprive national legislation of its effect even if it considered that a given measure constituted illegal discrimination between men and women, holding that, where various options were open to the national authorities to remove such discrimination, the choice should be left to the legislature in view of the social and legal implications attending each possible course of action (…).[756]

Such an attitude of courts avoiding strong review by applying legislation, whilst only communicating their unease to parliament in the hope that it will act, has been met with serious criticism from some quarters.[757] It has been warned that where a court essentially abdicates its responsibility by leaving questions of law to be decided by the legislature or where it denies the applicant an effective remedy, it can lead to such a court violating someone's rights instead of enforcing them.[758]

315   However, courts are increasingly willing to exercise strong review by refusing to apply legislation that offends binding treaty obligations.[759] This willingness to engage the legislature more than in the past is evident not only in cases where *refusing* to apply legislation would be a remedy, but also in cases where simply not applying legislation would *not* solve the matter. For example, in 1999 the Supreme Court was confronted by a case where legislation was at odds with the Netherlands' treaty obligations, but where refusing to give effect to the law would have been of no use to the applicant's plight.[760] The legislation clearly had to be changed and not just simply rendered ineffective to benefit the applicant. The Court decided that "for the time being" it would desist from crafting an effective remedy for the applicant, in order to give parliament the opportunity to table an amendment to the legislation.[761] The legislature was thus given the room to decide for itself how to remedy the situation instead of having a solution imposed

---

[756]*Van Raalte v. The Netherlands* of 21 February 1997, *Publ. Eur Court H.R.*, *Reports*, 1997-I, par. 24; Hoge Raad, 12 October 1984, *NJ* 1985, 230; Hoge Raad, 23 October 1988, *NJ* 1989, 740.

[757]Cf. A.K. Koekkoek, *Rechter en bestuur in constitutioneel perspectief* (Utrecht: Lemma, 2001), at 35–41.

[758]Ibid., at 37 (quoting A.W. Heringa).

[759]Cf. Alkema, *supra* note 623, at 4–14.

[760]Hoge Raad, 12 May 1999, *BNB* 1999, 271.

[761]Ibid., at paras. 3.15–3.16.

on it, something which would only happen if the legislature ignored the court's warning. Essentially, the court exercised weak review, but with the threat of strong review if appropriate action was not forthcoming.

316 As to the possible format of such strong review, the courts would in all likelihood not have ordered the legislature to pass the desired legislation, as at the moment the courts consider such an order a bridge too far.[762] Instead, an award for damages caused as a result of the legislation might have been considered.[763] Not agreeing with the courts' reticence, J.E.M. Polak has even gone so far as to argue that the courts are competent to order the legislature to pass any necessary legislation, as he argues that offending legislation is unlawful and according to private law the party responsible for the unlawfulness has to *act* to mend the breach for which it was responsible.[764] This shows that just as the courts are outgrowing their reluctance to exercise strong review by refusing to apply legislation that offends binding international law, legal arguments may be found to sustain strong review by ordering parliament to legislate in giving effect to international law, provided that the courts allow themselves to be tempted in this direction more than has been the case to date.

317 Again, as with the other aspects of characterising a court's powers of review, the Netherlands proves an interesting jurisdiction to investigate. At first sight the bar in section 120 of the Constitution seems to forbid all forms of review, but as has been shown a court could under some circumstances come to a weak appraisal. The political effect of which the legislature must somehow factor in order not to give the impression that it was fixed on violating people's rights. Of still greater everyday importance is the exercise of strong review in accordance with section 94 of the Constitution.

7.4 South Africa: Exploring Strong Review

318 The shift from parliamentary sovereignty to judicially guaranteed constitutional supremacy in South Africa is particularly noticeable in the consequences of review. The dawn of the new dispensation meant that

---

[762]For example, Hoge Raad, 21 March 2003, *NJ* 2003, 691 (*Waterpakt*); Hoge Raad, 1 October 2004, *NJ* 2004, 679.

[763]Cf. R.J.B. Schutgens, *Onrechtmatige wetgeving* (Deventer: Dilligentia, 2009), on the topic of unlawful legislation.

[764]J.E.M. Polak, "Zit er nog muziek in verbods- en gebodsacties ter zake van wetgeving?", *Overheid en Aansprakelijkheid* 168 (2004), at 171. R.A.J. van Gestel and M.S. Groenhuijsen, "Geen rechterlijk bevel tot wetgeving, of toch?", *Nederlands Juristenblad* 2050 (2006), argue that no serious democratic deficit would arise, if a national court were to order the Dutch parliament to pass legislation in order to fulfil its obligations under EU law.

the judicial function was no longer geared solely to applying the law, but also to overturning the law where it violated higher law as codified in the Constitution. This is made patently clear in section 2, which reads:

This Constitution is the supreme law of the Republic; law or conduct inconsistent with it is invalid, and the obligations imposed by it must be fulfilled.

The courts are assigned a prominent role in identifying invalidity, as section 172(1)(a) enjoins them to set aside any actions that contradict the Constitution to the extent of their inconsistency. In contrast to the HRA where the judiciary has a discretion whether to issue declarations of incompatibility and where the law stands despite of such a declaration, courts in South Africa must declare unconstitutional laws or conduct invalid. The best example of strong review to date is undoubtedly *S. v. Makwanyane*, where the Constitutional Court ruled the death penalty to be unconstitutional and therefore no longer an acceptable form of punishment.[765] Very much an example of strong-form review in other words. Invalidity can only be avoided if a law can be interpreted in a reasonable manner that sees it compliant with the Constitution.[766]

319 Having declared legislation to be invalid, a court may make an order which is "just and equitable".[767] This refers not only to existing remedies, but allows the courts to fashion new remedies in order to meet the needs of a particular situation. Yet courts have been careful not to award damages simply because a constitutional provision was violated independent of any actual loss having occurred.[768] But where financial implications flow from an order of invalidity the courts will not be deterred by the question whether the state had budgeted for such extra expenses or not.[769] Courts are also capable of issuing mandatory and structural interdicts that are subject to special supervision. This course of action may be adopted in respect of legislation but also when it comes to matters of policy.[770] As in

---

[765]*S. v. Makwanyane, supra* note 32, at par. 151: "[W]ith effect from the date of this order, (...) legislation sanctioning capital punishment which [is] in force in any part of the national territory (...) [is] declared to be inconsistent with the Constitution and, accordingly, to be invalid. 2. (...) and with effect from the date of this order: (a) the State is and all its organs are forbidden to execute any person already sentenced to death under any of the provisions thus declared to be invalid; and (b) all such persons will remain in custody under the sentences imposed on them, until such sentences have been set aside in accordance with law and substituted by lawful punishments."

[766]Cf. Rautenbach and Malherbe, *supra* note 22, at 254.

[767]S. 172(1)(b) of the Constitution.

[768]*Fose v. Minister of Safety and Security*, 1997 (7) BCLR 851 (CC), 1997 (3) SA 786 (CC), at paras. 67–70, 83, 92.

[769]*Permanent Secretary of the Department of Education, Eastern Cape v. Ed-U-College (PE) (Section 21) Inc*, 2001 (2) BCLR 188 (CC), 2001 (2) SA 1 (CC), at par. 23.

[770]For example, *Government of the RSA v. Grootboom, supra* note 189, at par. 97.

the United Kingdom, the practice of reading down legislative provisions or reading in words is also common to provide litigants with a remedy in the event of unconstitutionality being identified.[771] Judicial powers are thus quite strong. Not only must unconstitutionality lead to invalidity, but the courts are free to decide on a range of measures in remedying any breach of the Constitution, even where such a remedy may prove quite intrusive of the legislature's or executive's domain.

320 One might be forgiven for thinking that this state of affairs means that the consequences of review may never be diluted. This would be wrong.[772] The appearance of a system based on strong review even to a degree that excludes the possibility of institutional dialogue between the judiciary and other organs, especially the legislature, belies the reality of the situation. Although courts may not refuse to make a declaration of unconstitutionality, the wide discretion left to the judiciary in fashioning appropriate remedies creates the ideal opportunity to engage in a dialogue with the competent authority and not only prescribe its course of action. Courts arguably have this room as long as the applicable constitutional benchmarks are satisfied in passing orders, as the Constitutional Court explained in *National Coalition for Gay and Lesbian Equality v. Minister of Justice*:

> In fashioning a declaration of incompatibility, a court has to keep in balance two important considerations. One is the obligation to provide the "appropriate relief" under section 38 of the Constitution, to which claimants are entitled when "a right in the Bill of Rights has been infringed or threatened". (...) The Court's duty to provide appropriate relief, must be read together with section 172(1)(b) which requires the Court to make an order which is just and equitable. The other consideration a court must keep in mind, is the principle of the separation of powers and, flowing therefrom, the deference it owes to the legislature in devising a remedy for a breach of the Constitution in any particular case. It is not possible to formulate in general terms what such deference must embrace, for this depends on the facts and circumstances of each case.[773]

On the strength of this quote it can be said that courts should be careful not to be judge, jury and executioner, but should know when to pass the baton to the legislature in addressing unconstitutionality.

321 The possibility of formulating a legislative response to a judgment is also confirmed, albeit not in so many words, by section 172(1)(b)(ii) of the Constitution. This provision provides for a declaration of invalidity to be suspended for a period of time in order to allow the competent authority to

---

[771]*National Coalition for Gay and Lesbian Equality v. Minister of Justice*, 2000 (1) BCLR 39 (CC), 2000 (2) SA 1 (CC), at par. 70.

[772]For example, according to s. 172(1)(b)(i) of the Constitution a declaration of invalidity may include an order that limits the retrospective effect of the declaration.

[773]*National Coalition for Gay and Lesbian Equality v. Minister of Justice*, *supra* note 771, at paras. 65–66.

correct the defect. When using this provision the courts refrain from simply forcing their views on bodies such as the legislature, but instead point out the constitutional incompatibility while leaving it to the bodies concerned to remedy the matter in a way that they deem fit. Courts are then not the last link in the decision-making chain, but generate constitutional impulses which are to be acted upon by the legislature. This was illustrated in the *Fourie* decisions that related to same-sex marriage.[774] The applicants challenged the country's marriage laws for only allowing people of opposite sexes to marry, something which they considered to be contrary to the ban on unfair discrimination on the grounds of sexual orientation in section 9(3) of the Bill of Rights.

322 Both the Supreme Court of Appeal and the Constitutional Court agreed that such discrimination was indeed unfair and did not pass constitutional muster.[775] In other words, the discriminatory element in the law of marriage was unconstitutional, which meant that it made this aspect of the law invalid and turned the bench's attention to fashioning an appropriate order. In remedying the defect in the law, the Supreme Court of Appeal elected to develop the common law, so that it allowed people of the same sex to marry, thereby providing a tangible and immediate remedy to the applicants.[776] On appeal, however, the Constitutional Court, as the final instance as far as constitutional jurisdiction is concerned, disagreed with the Supreme Court of Appeal as to the remedy to be fashioned.[777] Instead, the Constitutional Court made use of its constitutional power to suspend the order of invalidity for a period of 1 year in order to give parliament the opportunity to decide how it wanted to ensure compliance with the Constitution. Immediate relief for the applicants was no longer forthcoming, but was delayed for at least a year while parliament decided how the marital regime had to be reformed to allow same-sex unions. For parliament, this change of course meant that it was no longer sidelined by judicial action, but actively involved in deciding how the matter had to be brought to its conclusion.

323 Although limited in its scope and by comparison not nearly as pronounced as in the United Kingdom, the *Fourie* decisions of the Constitutional Court show the possibility of dialogue within the limits of strong-form review in South Africa. In addition, the possibility of toning down the stronger sides of review in South Africa might also present

---

[774]*Fourie v. Minister of Home Affairs* (SCA), *supra* note 25; *Minister of Home Affairs v. Fourie; Lesbian and Gay Equality Project v. Minister of Home Affairs* (CC), *supra* note 25.

[775]Ibid. (SCA), *supra* note 25, at paras. 15–17, 20, 49; ibid. (CC), *supra* note 25, at paras. 12, 32.

[776]Ibid. (SCA), *supra* note 25, at paras. 38–49.

[777]Ibid. (CC), *supra* note 25, at paras. 115–161.

further possibilities for understanding and conducting judicial review in socio-economic matters. Although courts in the country are duty bound to enforce socio-economic rights, something which they readily accept, choosing the exact approach to these rights remains more controversial than in the case of civil and political rights. The reason for this is the essentially contested nature of socio-economic rights. Societies are likely to be in greater disagreement about the scope of protection afforded by such rights and about the required role of government in relation to them.[778] This division between civil and political rights on the one hand and socio-economic rights on the other has been criticised in the previous chapter for being overstated sometimes, but the division is nonetheless a reality to be contended with in practice.[779] This is where institutional dialogue might serve to lessen doubts about the judicial review of such rights, thereby alleviating general unease about their judicial treatment.

324 The decision of *Government of the RSA v. Grootboom* is an example of such constitutional dialogue.[780] In the matter, the Constitutional Court went to great lengths to scrutinise the housing policy of the government against a cautious but sincere reading of the Constitution.[781] Yet, this analysis did not result in the Court forcing a detailed course of action upon the housing authorities, even though it found them to have failed in their constitutional duty in a number of important respects. Instead, the Court issued a declaration of rights based on what the Constitution reasonably required under the circumstances, leaving decisions about the necessary steps to be taken to the appropriate authorities but under the supervision of the Human Rights Commission.[782] Although binding in law, the decision recognised that non-judicial action might be as important as judicial action in giving proper effect to the Constitution. The government was obliged to respond, but at the same time the government was made a partner in the constitutional project and not simply caught on the receiving end of the Court's views.

---

[778]For example, in *Richter v. Minister for Home Affairs and Others*, *supra* note 671, at paras. 53–55, the Court was quite clear and decisive about the importance of civil and political rights such as the right to vote, while it tends to stress caution in the field of socio-economic rights, such as in *Soobramoney v. Minister of Health, KwaZulu-Natal*, *supra* note 680, at paras. 29–30, regarding the right to health care in s. 27 of the Constitution.

[779]*See* §§ 289–291.

[780]*Government of the RSA v. Grootboom*, *supra* note 189.

[781]Cautious because the Constitutional Court held that the right to housing in s. 26 of the Constitution does not entail an immediate right to housing and did not to recognise a minimum core of protection to which the applicants could lay claim, *see Government of the RSA v. Grootboom*, *supra* note 189, at paras. 33, 94–95.

[782]*Government of the RSA v. Grootboom*, *supra* note 189, at paras. 96–99.

325 Although it is an example of how the judiciary can make use of the powers of other government branches in serving justice in someone's case, the judgment has also been criticised as being too accommodating of the government. Rosalind Dixon has argued that the failure of the state to carry out its stated policies of poverty alleviation means that the courts must be more assertive in crafting fitting orders in socio-economic matters.[783] According to her, a form of coercive or injunctive relief is more often than not necessary to address inertia on the part of the state in realising important rights, such as those to housing and health care.[784] Other scholars have confirmed this inertia, which provides food for thought as to whether the consequences of judicial review in South Africa must be diluted at all.[785] Whichever approach is chosen, the fact remains that strong-form review in South Africa may on occasion be influenced by what can only be described as elements of weak-form review. In this resides an enormous responsibility for the courts to correctly judge which approach will best serve the implementation of the Constitution.

7.5 Concluding Remarks

326 The combined experience of the countries discussed confirms that the model of strong-form review, so long associated with the United States, is no longer the only way of thinking about the consequences of judicial review. Accepting the principle of judicial review does not necessarily imply strong-form review as it might have done in the past when the two ideas were nearly synonymous. As more countries adopt judicial review, different constitutional contexts come to bear on ultimately deciding this element of the scope of review. In the United States, the founding fathers of the new country's constitutional dispensation sought to create an order that stood in direct contrast to British constitutionalism of the time.[786] This meant a resounding rejection of parliamentary sovereignty in favour of constitutional supremacy which later came to be enforced by the courts in a particularly strong fashion.

---

[783] Rosalind Dixon, "Creating Dialogue about Socioeconomic Rights: Strong-form Versus Weak-form Judicial Review Revisited", 5 *Int. J. Const. L.* 391 (2007), at 412–413. She mentions plans announced by the Cape municipality in 2001 to provide formal housing to thousands of people living in informal settlements that had still not come to fruition more than four years later, as well as plans in Gauteng to provide water, sewerage and electricity to residents in the informal settlement of Diepsloot, which had come to very little a number of years on (at 414–415).

[784] Ibid., at 413–415.

[785] R.J. de Beer and S. Vettori, "Enforcing Socio-economic Rights", *Potchefstroom Electr. L. J.* 1 (2007), at 3.

[786] Gardbaum, *supra* note 708, at 711.

327 However, it has become evident since the 1960s that not all countries feel the need to herald in such a new age of constitutionalism. While constitutionalism might have become synonymous with the judicial review of legislation in most countries, this common ground ends when the consequences of review come into sight. The question is essentially whether a country modifies its brand of constitutionalism when it introduces judicial review, or whether the introduction of review is part of a wider change of direction. The United Kingdom is a sterling example in this regard. The purpose of introducing the judicial review of legislation by means of the HRA was not to exchange parliamentary sovereignty for an entirely new approach to constitutionalism, but to combine judicial review with the country's constitutional traditions. This meant that archetypal American strong review had to be adapted to archetypal British parliamentary sovereignty. The result was a compromise which divided the middle ground between the legislature and judiciary, as the former decides whether it wants to follow the advice rendered by the latter on the compatibility of legislation with fundamental rights.

328 A clear benefit of choosing weak judicial review in the United Kingdom was to make the idea of judicial review palatable in a system that has for so long valued electoral legitimacy in constitutional matters. It is important to remember this, because parliament had to agree to its own decisions being put to a judicial test, something it was not required to do. The idea of introducing an institutional dialogue between legislator and judge by means of weak review undeniably did much to bridge the divide between those favouring and opposing review. But not only does weak review serve the political function of making judicial review acceptable in the United Kingdom, it also serves to strengthen parliamentary democracy because a number of judicial decisions have led to increased debate in parliament about the desirable standard of rights protection.[787] Weak review, as an incentive for parliament to adopt judicial review, has now become an incentive for parliament to engage its own protection of people's rights more critically. Apart from these practical benefits, weak review also manages to address theoretical arguments about the justifiability of judicial review from a counter-majoritarian point of view. It cannot be denied that a legislature is "debilitated", in the words of Stephen Guardbaum, by courts exercising judicial review over the quality of its legislation.[788] Yet this debilitation and the counter-majoritarian problems raised by it, do not always need to be of the same intensity as the scope of review can be adjusted to allow for weak-form, instead of strong-form review.

---

[787] Such as in the case of *A. and Others v. Secretary of State for the Home Department*, *supra* note 230. See § 307.

[788] Gardbaum, *supra* note 708, at 745–746.

329 The Netherlands and South Africa, on the other hand, are systems that have chosen the strong review of legislation. While the Netherlands did not contend with the doctrine of parliamentary sovereignty in the Westminster mould in overcoming qualms about such review, it traditionally favours a strict separation of powers which can also lead to doubts about courts being given the power to overrule the legislature. However, the absence of British-style binding precedent is probably one of the reasons why strong judicial review was never particularly objected to in relation to treaty review in the Netherlands, as a judgment does not bind future courts, thereby allaying fears of a powerful judiciary that might obstruct the legislature.[789] In practice, though, while not binding on other courts, judgments that refuse to apply legislation are often followed by other courts, thereby increasing the real effect of strong-form review. Alternatively, the strict separation of powers might even fuel strong judicial review and not contradict the principle, as one could argue that if courts are to have powers of review, such powers must be strong in order to avoid the dialogue brought about by weak review and consequently the dilution of the separation of powers. It is then interesting to note the possibility that weak judicial review might be expected of a court given its duty to interpret legislation in conformity with the Dutch Constitution, or bar that the unsuccessful proposals made in the 1970s to introduce weak review of the Constitution next to the strong review conducted of the country's treaty obligations in terms of section 94 of the Constitution.[790]

330 Allowing weak judicial review next to strong review in the same system merits two responses. Firstly, such an exercise might be characterised as an obvious appeasement of the legislative establishment that goes too far. If international rights are worthy of binding judicial review in the Netherlands, so it could be argued, the same should be said of the country's national rights in order not to debase their worth, as the Halsema Proposal also argues.[791] While the political context is undoubtedly important in guiding the shape of judicial review, it ought not to be the deciding factor in itself. The HRA is evidence of where the two goals, the one political and the other constitutional, come together. Weak judicial review was chosen in the United Kingdom not only because there was little political appetite for further reform, but also because the reforms brought about by the HRA nicely fitted the country's traditions of constitutional law.[792] Conversely, it can be argued in favour of such a dual construction that the idea of weak constitutional review might ease the way for a bolder judicial

---

[789]*See* § 309.

[790]*See* § 311.

[791]*Parliamentary Proceedings II*, 2001–2002, 28, 331, no. 9, at 11–12.

[792]Bogdanor, *supra* note 298, at 246, observed about adopting the HRA, that there was "neither the political will nor the consensus to do more".

implementation of the Constitution to be allowed over time. This might
be especially valid in the Netherlands where the tradition of parliament,
and not the courts, protecting the Constitution is still strong and where the
courts are generally careful not to tread on the domain of the legislature.[793]
In these circumstances the weak judicial review of the Constitution might
be a suitable compromise to make the idea of reviewing acts of parliament
not only more acceptable to majoritarian decision-making, but more so to
the courts. As the saying goes, a journey of a thousand miles starts with a
single step.

331   The benefit of compromise was also demonstrated by the
Harmonisation Act case, where the Supreme Court after establishing that
treaty review in terms of section 94 of the Constitution provided no solace
for the applicants, conducted non-binding review of the aggrieved act of
parliament irrespective of the bar in section 120.[794] The worth of non-
binding review next to binding review in the Netherlands is further proved
by the fact that the legislature, although not obliged to do so, responded to
the court's concerns by adjusting the act so that it no longer offended the
principle of legal certainty. A case of institutional dialogue in other words.
From this, the conclusion could be drawn that if the Halsema Proposal were
to fail in its ambition to establish parity of protection between constitutional and treaty rights, a worthwhile measure of balance might still be
achieved through the vehicle of non-binding constitutional review. Still, a
constitutional amendment might very well be called for to regulate non-
binding review, instead of only relying on the somewhat unusual spurt of
judicial activism in the *Harmonisation Act* case, or on neglected theories
of constitutional interpretation.

332 Adding South Africa's experience to the discussion highlights a number of important dimensions of the debate. What is striking about the
introduction of judicial review in South Africa is the immediate shift from
parliamentary sovereignty to strong-form review and not to the compromise of weak-form review as in the United Kingdom. This can probably
be attributed to the inadequacies of the old constitutional dispensation as
a guide for the country's future.[795] Parliamentary sovereignty and all the
trappings associated with it were abandoned without much remorse for a
system of judicially enforced constitutional supremacy, in contrast to the
United Kingdom where the tradition of parliamentary sovereignty remains
the point of departure for thought about the constitution. In this, South
Africa resembles the American experience of rejecting erstwhile founda-
tional principles that steered matters prior to its constitutional moment,

---

[793]For example, Hoge Raad, 16 May 1986, *NJ* 1987, 251. *See* § 312.
[794]*See* §§ 311–313.
[795]On the failures of parliamentary sovereignty in South Africa, *see* §§ 55–64.

a rejection which made the introduction of strong judicial review much easier as it meant fewer compromises being made between the legislature and the judiciary. The story might have been different had the country had a long and sound parliamentary tradition that embodied the protection of liberty more than its deprivation, but in the event parliament's dismal legacy steered its future away from the parliamentary protection of the constitution to strong judicial oversight.

333 Experience in South Africa also disproves the idea that a watertight distinction can be drawn between review as being either strong or weak.[796] Even in a system of strong review such as that of South Africa, measured influences of weak review can arguably be identified in those instances where a court structures its order of unconstitutionality to afford some discretion to the legislature (or executive) in responding to the order.[797] Such a tendency to allow for a legislative response is particularly apparent in the context of socio-economic rights. This shows that the distinction between strong- and weak-form review has consequences not only on an institutional level between the legislature and the judiciary, but also for the range of rights capable of review. Weak judicial review might not only make the very idea of review more acceptable to political organs, but it might also serve to allow courts to review complicated socio-economic matters, strengthened in the knowledge that a judicial decision does not need to be as decisive or prescriptive as might be the case with civil and political rights. Courts are so allowed an opinion in matters where particularly strong review might prove a bridge too far. This might provide fuel for the debate in countries such as the United Kingdom and the Netherlands about whether socio-economic rights are to be reviewed more by the courts than is currently the case. Weak judicial review might not just be a reason to allow the idea of judicial review, but also and in particular the idea of reviewing socio-economic rights.

334 However, South Africa also illustrates the reverse side of the coin in that while the idea of the weak review of socio-economic rights might be good theory, it might not always be good practice. Critics of the *Grootboom* decision, for instance, view the judgment not as meritorious for the discretion left to the government in fulfilling its constitutional duty, but lament this room to manoeuvre as a failure to provide firm orders in the face of unacceptable legislative and executive failures in realising legitimate socio-economic claims.[798] Nonetheless, the possibilities encouraged by weak

---

[796]As Tushnet, *supra* note 710, at 75, opines on the basis of American jurisprudence: "At any particular time, courts might be exercising strong-form review in some areas, weak-form review in others."

[797]*See* §§ 320–324.

[798]For example, Dixon, *supra* note 783, at 413–415.

judicial review in the field of socio-economic rights remain an interesting and underexplored avenue at present, even though particular examples in South Africa might sometimes disappoint.[799] Criticism should consequently be understood correctly, not as doubts about the usefulness of reviewing socio-economic rights in a weaker fashion, but as criticism levelled at the address of government for failing in its constitutional duties. In other words, the less government is trusted, the more the courts should be relied upon, which means that weak judicial review might become attractive again if and when there is more reason to trust organs outside the judiciary.

335 If there is a rule of thumb to be deduced from the experiences of the United Kingdom and the Netherlands on the one hand and that of South Africa on the other, it would have to be that the lower the level of trust in the wisdom and self-restraint of parliament, the greater the possibility becomes that strong judicial review will be favoured over weak review. But this observation has to be put in perspective by the fact that the differentiation of review as being strong or weak is not watertight, as the case of South Africa clearly shows. Similarly, the fact that declarations of incompatibility in the United Kingdom nearly always elicit the hoped for results from the legislature and executive could be interpreted as weak review occasioning strong review in the United Kingdom. Such a development might also occur in the Netherlands were the example set by the *Harmonisation Act* case to become common currency. The theoretical implications of these observations go some way towards exposing the artificial premise of Jeremy Waldron's argument against the judicial review of legislation which is only directed at strong-form review.[800] The divide between strong and weak courts might not always be as wide as one imagines, and legal theory must respect this finding to avoid accusations of it denying reality in order to force an unworkable argument aimed at the judicial review of legislation.[801]

---

[799] *See* Tushnet, *supra* note 710, at 161–264.

[800] Waldron, *supra* note 7, at 1353–1355.

[801] On a similar note, *see* Dyzenhaus, *supra* note 211, at 48.

Chapter 8
Constitutionalism Personified

336 The legislative function has undeniably changed over the years. This transformation has quite clearly been a shift from "codification" to "modification".[802] Legislatures in the nineteenth century were conceived of as bodies that had to codify pre-existing norms based on customary and other sources. The law was something that had to be identified and not so much created. However, this limited view of the purpose of legislatures came to be questioned towards the end of the nineteenth century and especially in the twentieth century. Legislation was now perceived as an instrument with which to modify society. On the one hand, this held great potential for improving the human condition through alleviating poverty and expanding education, while on the other it introduced the spectre of an all-encompassing state that could legislate liberty to oblivion.

337 As the comparison of the United Kingdom, the Netherlands and South Africa in Chapter 3 has shown, by itself democratic control of this increase in legislative potential is no longer good enough, but needs to be augmented somehow. Put differently, parliamentary democracy cannot be treated as a synonym for constitutional governance. While there might be an overlap between the two, there is no neat fit. This is exactly where the promise of judicial review becomes apparent. Judicial review can certainly be viewed as part and parcel of essential constitutionalism in modern societies if the experience of the three countries is anything to go by. Tim Koopmans explains along similar lines that:

> We could perhaps put our findings in terms of political philosophy by stating that modern constitutionalism is founded on two currents, or movements, which each have their own rhythm and direction. One of these currents links the administration to the government and to the parliamentary majority supporting it, and thereby to the feelings of the electorate. The other links judicial decisions to the constitutional system, and is finally based on legal traditions rather than personal

---

[802]T. Koopmans, "Legislature and Judiciary – Present Trends", in T. Koopmans (ed.), *Juridisch stippelwerk* 194 (Deventer: Kluwer, 1991).

G. van der Schyff, *Judicial Review of Legislation*,
Ius Gentium: Comparative Perspectives on Law and Justice 5,
DOI 10.1007/978-90-481-9002-7_8, © Springer Science+Business Media B.V. 2010

opinions. In the first current, choices are made; in the second, limits are to be observed. Of course this reality may be somewhat more complicated.[803]

Koopmans rightly notes that the reality of the situation is more complex. The reason for this complexity seats in the fact that the discrepancy in overlap between parliamentary democracy and constitutional governance differs from system to system. A quick glance at the three countries all but confirms this, as parliamentary democracy is not the same across them, yet all three have come to accept the idea of judicial review.

338 While the judicial review of legislation might be justified in principle, this principle still needs to be given flesh. Although it could be said to be something of a universal ideal, judicial review must be afforded local authorship for it to reflect the society it is intended to serve. What is essentially asked for is unity, or at the least a credible attempt at unity, between theory and reality. What must be guarded against is theory only existing in the detached realm of ideas, while on the other hand simply attaching normative worth to a particular practice for fear of critical reflection. This is when it becomes important to understand the particular nature of a country's democracy, as it is in response to a particular democracy that judicial review takes on its desired form. In carrying out this reflection, democracy is to be used not as a weapon with which to deny the added value of judicial review, but instead as a guide in shaping its scope. Democracy is not a reason for refusing to introduce judicial review, but a motivation in shaping review one way or the other. Comparing the United Kingdom, the Netherlands and South Africa confirms this.

339 The lack of a defining constitutional moment in the United Kingdom meant that the function of judicial review was to be that of controlling democracy while not throwing overboard the constitutional foundations of the state at the same time. This is something which the HRA set out to achieve, as J.W.F. Allison summarises:

> The 1998 Act was skilfully drafted to embrace change and respect continuity, to effect an incorporation of the European Convention on Human Rights (. . .) according to parliamentary sovereignty as traditionally understood.[804]

The design of the HRA attests to this desire to preserve parliamentary sovereignty as the central tenet of constitutional law, as the Act denies courts the formal power to overturn acts of parliament. In deciding on the appropriate fora of review to implement the Act, continuity is again stressed over change as existing courts and legal traditions are relied upon to give

---

[803] Koopmans, *supra* note 6, at 251.
[804] Allison, *supra* note 85, at 241.

effect to the HRA's provisions.[805] This emphasis on continuity is balanced by the fact that the HRA has managed to make the principle of proportionality more acceptable to adjudication than ever before, something which allows the courts to heighten their scrutiny of legislation.[806] Nonetheless, the Act might very well be seen as an expression of faith in the country's parliamentary traditions in not having changed the status quo more. This is especially true given the wide scopes of review enjoyed by courts in jurisdictions such as South Africa.

340 However, this does not take away that the constitutional context is constantly evolving. Even though currently judicial control might be intended to only interpret acts of parliament in conformity with Convention rights and not overturn parliament's sovereign will, this might change in future. The recent expenses scandal with members of parliament seemingly abusing the public purse to finance their lifestyles has led to burning anger among the British public and even saw the speaker stepping down.[807] A recent poll conducted on behalf of the BBC shows that in the wake of the scandal 80% of the respondents blamed the "parliamentary system" for the excess and not only members of parliament for taking advantage of the system.[808] Of those polled, 85% wanted an independent judicial body to scrutinise members' financial affairs. Were such momentum to prove more than a flash in the pan but hint at a constitutional moment in the offing, it could ultimately spell radical change for parliament's constitutional role. Change that might show more favour for the courts' scope of review to be expanded in order to better control the misadventures of parliamentary democracy.

341 This situation is comparable to that of the Netherlands, but only to a degree. The Netherlands differs from the United Kingdom in that the judicial review of acts of parliament has been a feature of the country's legal system for many years, but then review against treaties that is, and not against the Constitution (and other sources of national higher law). The Halsema Proposal tries to even out this difference by expanding the courts' powers of the review to include some rights in the Constitution. Whereas the HRA is novel in its attempt to iron out some of the ill fit between constitutional governance and parliamentary democracy in the United Kingdom,

---

[805] This is why decentralised review was preferred over centralised review, *see* again §§ 130–135 above.

[806] *R. v. Secretary of State for the Home Department, Ex parte Daly*, *supra* note 580, at par. 27. *See* again §§ 238–239.

[807] For example, the *Sunday Times* reported on 24 May 2009 that up to half of the 646 members of parliament might lose their seats at the next general election because of voters' anger at the expenses scandal. *See* also Martin Bell, *A Very British Revolution: The Expenses Scandal and How to Save Our Democracy* (London: Icon Books, 2009).

[808] Ipsos Mori poll of 1001 adults, released in June 2009.

the Halsema Proposal is not so novel in wanting to cover the corresponding difference in the Netherlands precisely because of treaty review. In other words, while theoretically it may be very appealing to allow constitutional review, such a move runs the risk of duplicating much of what is offered under treaty review. A case of theory being measured against reality. This duplication by the Proposal can be explained by the absence of a constitutional moment that drives reform.[809] In other words, constitutional review is made appealing in the Proposal by reference to treaty review in order not to upset the established relationship between the legislature and the judiciary because it is generally felt that no great upset is warranted. This the Proposal attempts by favouring the decentralised review of the Constitution, as well as the same modalities of review and roughly the same rights that apply under treaty review. In this lies both the strength and weakness of the Proposal. Its design is not too adventurous to place it outside of what is reassuringly familiar, but in doing so it also looses any novelty value which is often required for reform to be successful.

342 Were the Proposal to fail – and the chance of that happening is real given the lack of political enthusiasm it encountered during its first reading in the Senate, where it passed by a single vote – it does not have to mean that constitutional review by the judiciary in the Netherlands is a lost cause.[810] What would be called for is a constitutional reform bill that highlights the added worth constitutional review will bring to constitutionalism in the Netherlands apart from emphasising the ease with which constitutional review can function next to treaty review. This, it could be reasoned, might mean bold reform proposals such as the creation of a constitutional court, or giving standing to political bodies to request abstract review, or even allowing for review of the legislative process to contrast with treaty review. However, such an assumption could not be further from the truth. Until there is a credible constitutional moment, or even a low frequency one at that, such reforms might be too ambitious given the facts and needs at play. Instead reform might best come in the guise of an interpretive rule which states that rights guaranteed under international law must be interpreted in the light of constitutional rights where such international guarantees fall short of those provided in the Constitution.[811] This

---

[809]On the lack of a clear constitutional moment in the Netherlands, see § 119.

[810]On the Proposal's slim chance of success, see § 53.

[811]On this alternative, see Gerhard van der Schyff, "Rethinking the Justification for Constitutional Review of Legislation in the Netherlands", in R.A.J. van Gestel and J. van Schooten (eds.), *Europa en de toekomst van de nationale wetgever: Liber amicorum Philip Eijlander* 129 (Nijmegen: Wolf Legal Publishers, 2008), at 140–141; "Over een interpretatierichtsnoer en mythes", *Nederlands Juristenblad* 2632 (2009): "Waarom het wetsvoorstel Halsema tekort schiet: Mythes rondom het verdragsargument", *Nederlands Juristenblad* 2408 (2009). Lending perspective, see Jit Peters and Geerten Boogaard, "De myhes van Van der Schyff over het initiatiefwetsvoorstel-Halsema", *Nederlands*

solution would see legislative power curtailed in those instances where the Constitution might question the extent of protection provided internationally without reappraising the settled institutional balance between the legislature and the judiciary in the process. Constitutional rights, on such an interpretation, are applied indirectly as they become aids in interpreting international rights where necessary and practicable to avoid any deficit in protection from arising.[812] The advantage of such reform is that it only makes use of constitutional rights to remedy a perceived deficit, thereby highlighting the actual worth of such rights, instead of merely placing the Constitution next to binding treaties without coordinating their combined application.

343 The inductive nature of constitutional reform in the United Kingdom and the Netherlands becomes apparent when studying the judicial review of legislation in the two countries. Experience counts for much in deciding how, or if, to proceed. This emphasis on experience over adventure also explains the careful and incremental nature of reform in the two countries. In 1922 William R. Anson remarked about the British constitution that:

> Our constitution is (...) a somewhat rambling structure, and, like a house which many successive owners have altered just so far as suited their immediate wants or the fashion of the time, it bears the marks of many hands, and is convenient rather than symmetrical.[813]

This description still holds for the HRA, an Act which attests to careful reform by trying to move ahead but at the same time respecting constitutional law as it had evolved over centuries. Although only dating from after the Napoleonic occupation and therefore not nearly as seasoned as that of the British dispensation, the constitutional order of the Netherlands is also quick to attach worth to tradition over sweeping change. The stubborn nature of section 120 of the Constitution attests to this, while treaty review in terms of section 94 shows how such a contradiction of section 120 could have developed in the absence of clear coordination and unity of thought on judicial review. Anson's observations might then just as well have been made in relation to the Netherlands.

344 Of quite a different order is the judicial review of legislation in South Africa. Instead of resembling a house of somewhat eclectic architecture with a maze of rooms and hidden nooks and crannies, judicial

---

Juristenblad 2628 (2009); Joseph Fleuren, "Waarom het voorstel-Halsema superieur is", *Nederlands Juristenblad* 2630 (2009).

[812] The would be the reverse of the situation in Belgium, where the Constitutional Court interprets constitutional rights in the light of international rights, e.g. decision no. 167/2005 of 23 November 2005.

[813] William R. Anson, *The Law and Custom of the Constitution* (Oxford: Oxford University Press, 1922), at 1.

review of legislation in South Africa attests more to deductive than inductive reason. It is not the result of a piecemeal process that stretches back
generations and which is influenced by the peculiarities or particular pref-
erences of years gone by, but is very much a modern product especially
designed to transform society and guarantee justice. A product which was
fired as a result of the constitutional moment that South Africa experienced in the 1990s and continues to shape its society and law.[814] When
that moment happened, there was no reliable parliamentary tradition in
relation to which the courts' powers had to be determined, as there was
in the United Kingdom and the Netherlands. The lack of a credible parliamentary tradition meant that judicial review was viewed as insurance
against an unpredictable future. The scope of judicial review is consequently far-reaching as the courts enjoy impressive powers of review. For
instance, the institution of a special constitutional court became necessary to act as a clear counter-weight against possible legislative excess, but
was also warranted by a mistrust of the existing courts to implement the
Constitution without special guidance.[815] Moreover, the design of review,
especially mechanisms of abstract review, was constructed with the aim
to reassure the white minority that its loss of power did not mean that
its interests would be unprotected in a new dispensation.[816] By comparison, these factors were not germane to designing review in the United
Kingdom and the Netherlands where judicial review had to be designed
with past parliamentary success in mind and free from unease about an
unknown future such as in South Africa. The constitutional renewal underpinning the South African Constitution also opened the door to reviewing
socio-economic rights, something which if conducted in a similar fashion
by courts in the United Kingdom and the Netherlands might be a bridge
too far, but in South Africa is considered inherent to the function of judicial review.[817] The country's new dispensation has evidently come to rely
heavily on the judicial review of legislation.

345 A word of caution may be called for. Although a heavy reliance on
judicial review might have been justified under the circumstances of South
Africa's constitutional rebirth, the judicial route is not to be viewed as the
cure for all ills. Just as parliamentary democracy is not a perfect match for
constitutional governance, so too does the potential of judicial review have
its limits. Ideally, a country's democratic structures must try to improve

---

[814]See the arguments in § 117 for a constitutional moment to be identified in South
Africa.

[815]On the reasons for (semi-)centralising judicial review in South Africa, see §§ 153–154,
166–168 above.

[816]On the fears of the white minority, and for views on how these fears were addressed
by designing judicial review, see §§ 72, 117, 217.

[817]See § 293.

their vigilance in upholding the constitution without waiting for a judicial reprimand. The recent report by the lower house of parliament in the Netherlands makes a comparable point, when it highlights the need for parliamentarians to focus their efforts on long-term policy objectives instead of being distracted by passing whims.[818] A focus that is seen as a way to increase the quality of political debate as parliamentarians then use their time to weigh in on important matters instead of diluting their impact by drifting from topic to topic. If vigilance is something to be observed by the legislature, then it is also to be valued by the judiciary. Jonathan Lewis makes the point when he pleads for members of South Africa's Constitutional Court to be more judicially experienced.[819] He points out that whereas in June 2008 each of the 12 erstwhile Lords of Appeal in Ordinary in the United Kingdom had on average 14 years of judicial experience, 6 of their 11 counterparts in the Constitutional Court of South Africa had no judicial experience while the five other judges could only boast 4 years of such experience each. Experience, so it could be argued, that can and must be expected in order for the Court to be able to discharge its important functions properly. Getting the balance right between the legislature and judiciary should therefore be a constant concern.

346 To summarise the findings of this work, the judicial review of legislation is desirable as a device of counter-majoritarianism, which leaves the question of fixing its scope. In this regard, judicial review in South Africa is shaped by a programmatic constitution that seeks the most apt, if sometimes hitherto untried ways, to achieve justice and constitutional stability without having to rely exclusively on parliament to achieve these goals. In contrast, the constitutions of the United Kingdom and the Netherlands are better viewed as reliable reservoirs of constitutional experience accumulated over many years and which are best tapped into with circumspection when designing judicial review. Whenever giving flesh to the principle of judicial review, it would be more than wise for such fundamental constitutional differences between systems to be borne in mind. In this way, an acceptable balance can be struck in apportioning the middle ground between the legislature and the judiciary in order to truly mould constitutionalism from country to country.

347 If the normative implications of these conclusions were to be reduced to a single formula, it might arguably read as follows: The ideal of constitutional governance is to be achieved primarily, but not exclusively, through majoritarian decision-making structures, as checked through the judicial review of legislation, whose scope is to be determined relative to the ability

---

[818]*Parliamentary Proceedings II*, 2008–2009, 31 845, no. 2–3, at 11–13.
[819]Lewis, *supra* note 405, at 464.

of such majoritarian decision-making structures to reasonably achieve constitutional governance. And to end on a methodological note, the function of judicial review is, as we have seen, very much prescribed by its institutional setting, which means that it can only be understood and compared properly by valuing its context sufficiently.

Bibliography

Literature

Ackerman, Bruce, "Revolution on a Human Scale", 108 *Yale L. J.* 2279 (1999)

Ackerman, Bruce, *We the People: Foundations* (Cambridge, MA: Belknap Press, 1991)

Adams, Maurice, *Recht en democratie ter discussie: Essays over democratische rechtsvorming* (Leuven: Universitaire Pers Leuven, 2006)

Adams, Maurice, "Precedent Versus Gravitational Force of Courts Decisions: Between Theory, Law and Facts", in Ewoud Hondius (ed.), *Precedent and the Law*, 149 (Brussels: Bruylant, 2008)

Adams, Maurice and Van der Schyff, Gerhard, "Constitutional Review by the Judiciary in the Netherlands: A Matter of Politics, Democracy or Compensating Strategy?", 66 *Zeitschrift für ausländisches öffentliches Recht und Völkerrecht* 399 (2006)

Adams, Maurice and Van der Schyff, Gerhard, "Grondwettigheidstoetsing door de rechter als 'list van de rijke'? Methodologische en andere vragen bij processen van rechtsverandering", 45 *Tijdschrift voor Privaatrecht* 913 (2008)

Addo, Michael K. and Grief, Nicholas, "Does Article 3 of the European Convention on Human Rights Enshrine Absolute Rights?", 9 *Eur. J. Int. L.* 510 (1998)

Albers, C.L.G.F.H. and Schlössel, R.J.N., "Terrorismebestrijding: Het bestuursrecht aan zet, de rechtsstaat in gevaar?", *Nederlands Juristenblad* 2526 (2006)

Alexy, Robert, *A Theory of Constitutional Rights* (Oxford: Oxford University Press, 2002)

Alkema, Evert A., *Een meerkeuzetoets: De rechter en de internationale rechtsorde* (Zwolle: Tjeenk Willink, 1985)

Alkema, Evert A., "The Effects of the European Convention on Human Rights and Other International Human Rights Instruments on the Netherlands Legal Order", in Rick Lawson and Matthijs de Blois (eds.), *The Dynamics of the Protection of Human Rights in Europe: Essays in Honour of Henry G. Schermers*, vol. III, 1 (Dordrecht: Martinus Nijhoff, 1994)

Alkema, Evert A., "Repliek: Toetsing door een speciaal constitutioneel hof", 32 *NJCM-Bull.* 792 (2007)

Allan, T.R.S., *Law, Liberty, and Justice: The Legal Foundations of British Constitutionalism* (Oxford: Clarendon, 1993)

Allan, T.R.S., "Human Rights and Judicial Review: A Critique of 'Due Deference'", 65 *Camb. L. J.* 671 (1996)

Allison, J.W.F., *The English Historical Constitution: Continuity, Change and European Effects* (Cambridge: Cambridge University Press, 2007)

Andeweg, Rudy B. and Irwin, Galen A., *Governance and Politics of the Netherlands* (Basingstoke: Palgrave Macmillan, 2002)

Anson, William R., *The Law and Custom of the Constitution* (Oxford: Oxford University Press, 1922)

Arai-Takahashi, Yutaka, *The Margin of Appreciation Doctrine in the Jurisprudence of the ECHR* (Antwerp: Intersentia, 2002)

Asmal, Kader, "Constitutional Courts – A Comparative Survey", 24 *Comp. Int. L. J. South. Afr.* 315 (1991)

Barak-Erez, Daphne and Gross, Aeyal M., "Introduction: Do We Need Social Rights? Questions in the Era of Globalisation, Privatisation, and the Diminished Welfare State", in Daphne Barak-Erez and Aeyal M. Gross (eds.), *Exploring Social Rights: Between Theory and Practice* 1 (Oxford: Hart Publishing, 2007)

Barendrecht, J.M., "Het constitutionele toetsingsrecht van de rechter", 122 *Handelingen Nederlandse Juristen-Vereniging* 85 (1992)

Basson, Dion and Viljoen, Henning, *South African Constitutional Law* (Cape Town: Juta, 1988)

Bateup, Christine A., "Expanding the Conversation: American and Canadian Experiences of Constitutional Dialogue in Comparative Perspective", 21 *Temple Int. Comp. L. J.* 1 (2007)

Belifante, A.D. and De Reede, J.L., *Beginselen van het Nederlandse staatsrecht* (Deventer: Kluwer, 16th ed., 2009)

Bell, John, "Reflections on Continental European Supreme Courts", in Guy Canivet and Mads Andenas (eds.), *Independence, Accountability, and the Judiciary* 253 (London: British Institute of International and Comparative Law, 2006)

Bell, John, *Judiciaries Within Europe: A Comparative Perspective* (Cambridge: Cambridge University Press, 2006)

Bell, Martin, *A Very British Revolution: The Expenses Scandal and How to Save Our Democracy* (London: Icon Books, 2009)

Bellekom, Th.L., Heringa, A.W., Van der Velde, J. and Verhey, L.F.M., *Compendium van het staatsrecht* (Deventer: Kluwer, 10th ed., 2007)

Bense, M.M., "Aandacht voor recente grondwetswijzigingen", *Regelmaat* 89 (2002)

Berat, Lynn, "The Constitutional Court of South Africa and Jurisdictional Questions: In the Interests of Justice?", 3 *Int. J. Const. L.* 39 (2005)

Besselink, Leonard F.M., "Constitutionele toetsing in internationaal perspectief", 52 *Ars Aequi* 89 (2003)

Besselink, Leonard F.M., *Constitutional Law of the Netherlands: An Introduction with Texts, Cases and Materials* (Nijmegen: Ars Aequi Libri, 2004)

Besselink, Leonard F.M., "Constitutional Referenda in the Netherlands: A Debate in the Margin", 11 *Electr. J. Comp. L.* 1 (2007)

Besson, Samantha, "The Many European Constitutions and the Future of European Constitutional Theory", in Philippe Mastronardi and Dennis Taubert (eds.), *Staats- und Verfassungstheorie im Spannungsfeld der Disziplinen* 160 (Stuttgart: Franz Steiner Verlag, 2004)

Bickel, Alexander M., *The Least Dangerous Branch: The Supreme Court at the Bar of Politics* (Indianapolis: Bobbs-Merrill, 1962)

Bingham, Lord, "The Rule of Law", 66 *Camb. L. J.* 67 (2007)

Bingham, T.H., "The European Convention on Human Rights: Time to Incorporate", 109 *L. Quart. Rev.* 390 (1993)

Birks (ed.), Peter, *English Private Law* (Oxford: Oxford University Press, 2000)

Blankenburg, Erhard, "Dutch Legal Culture", in Jeroen Chorus, Piet-Hein Gerver and Ewoud Hondius (eds.), *Introduction to Dutch Law* 13 (Alphen aan den Rijn: Kluwer Law International, 4th ed., 2006)

Blankenburg, Erhard, "'Warum brauchen wir kein Verfassungsgericht?': Die nieder-
ländische Diskussion im Licht der deutschen Erfahrung", in Anita Böcker et al.,
Migratierecht en rechtssociologie, gebundeld in Kees' studies (Nijmegen: Wolf Legal
Publishers, 2008)

Böckenförde, Ernst-Wolfgang, *State, Society, Liberty: Studies in Political Theory and
Constitutional Law* (New York, NY: Berg, 1991)

Bogdanor, Vernon, "Our New Constitution", 120 *L. Quart. Rev.* 242 (2004)

Botha, Christo, *Wetsuitleg* (Kenwyn: Juta, 3rd ed., 1998)

Botha, Christo, *Statutory Interpretation* (Cape Town: Juta, 4th ed., 2005)

Bouckaert, Peter N., "The Negotiated Revolution: South Africa's Transition to Multiracial
Democracy", 33 *Stanford J. Int. L.* 375 (1997)

Bovend'Eert, Paul P.T., "De wetgevende macht van het parlement", in J.Th.J. van den
Berg, L.F.M. Verhey and J.L.W. Broeksteeg (eds.), *Het parlement* 91 (Nijmegen: Wolf
Legal Publishers, 2007)

Bradley, Anthony W., "The Sovereignty of Parliament – Form or Substance?", in Jeffrey
Jowell and Dawn Oliver (eds.), *The Changing Constitution* 26 (Oxford: Oxford
University Press, 5th ed., 2004)

Bradley, Anthony W. and Ewing, K.D., *Constitutional and Administrative Law*
(Edinburgh: Pearson, 13th ed., 2003)

Breillat, D., Kortmann, C.A.J.M. and Fleuren, J.W.A., *Van de constitutie afwijkende
verdragen* (Deventer: Kluwer, 2002)

Brems, Eva, "Belgium: The Vlaams Blok Political Party Convicted Indirectly of Racism",
4 *Int. J. Const. L.* 702 (2006)

Brems, Eva, "Indirect Protection of Social Rights by the European Court of Human
Rights", in Daphne Barak-Erez and Aeyal M. Gross (eds.), *Exploring Social Rights:
Between Theory and Practice* 135 (Oxford: Hart Publishing, 2007)

Brenninkmeijer, A.F.M., "Judicial Organization", in Jeroen Chorus, Piet-Hein Gerver and
Ewoud Hondius (eds.), *Introduction to Dutch Law* 53 (Alphen aan den Rijn: Kluwer
Law International, 4th ed., 2006)

Brewer-Carías, Alan R., *Judicial Review in Comparative Law* (Cambridge: Cambridge
University Press, 1989)

Burkens, M.C., Kummeling, H.R.B.M., Vermeulen, B.P. and Widdershoven, R.J.G.M.,
Beginselen van de democratische rechtsstaat (Alphen aan den Rijn: Kluwer, 6th ed.,
2006)

Burkens, M.C.B., *Beperking van grondrechten* (Deventer: Kluwer, 1971)

Butler, Andrew S., "The Constitutional Court Certification Judgments: The 1996
Constitution Bills, Their Amending Provisions, and the Constitutional Principles",
114 *S. Afr. L. J.* 703 (1997)

Cals, J.L.M.Th. and Donner, A.M., *Tweede Rapport van de Staatscommissie van advies
inzake de Grondwet en de Kieswet* (The Hague: Government Publication, 1969)

Cappelletti, Mauro, *The Judicial Process in Comparative Perspective* (Oxford:
Clarendon Press, 1989)

Cappelletti, Mauro, "Judicial Review of the Constitutionality of State Action: Its
Expansion and Legitimacy", *J. S. Afr. L.* 256 (1992)

Chanock, Martin, *Unconsummated Union: Britain, Rhodesia, and South Africa
1900–1945* (Manchester: Manchester University Press, 1977)

Chanock, Martin, "A Post-Calvinist Catechism or a Post-Communist Manifesto?
Intersecting Narratives in the South African Bill of Rights Debate", in Philip Alston
(ed.), *Promoting Human Rights Through Bills of Rights: Comparative Perspectives*
392 (Oxford: Oxford University Press, 1999)

Chaskalson, Arthur, "From Wickedness to Equality: The Moral Transformation of South
African Law", 1 *Int. J. Const. L.* 590 (2003)

Clayton QC, Richard, "Remedies for Breach of Human Rights. Does the Human Rights Act Guarantee Effective Remedies?", in Jeffrey Jowell and Jonathan Cooper (eds.), *Delivering Rights: How the Human Rights Act is Working* 147 (Oxford: Hart Publishing 2003)

Clayton QC, Richard, "Judicial Deference and 'Democratic Dialogue': The Legitimacy of Judicial Intervention under the Human Rights Act 1998", *Pub. L.* 33 (2004)

Cliteur, P.B., *Constitutionele toetsing* ('s-Gravenhage: Teldersstichting, 1991)

Cockrell, Alfred, "The South African Bill of Rights and the 'Duck/Rabbit'", 60 *Mod. L. Rev.* 513 (1997)

Corder, Hugh, *Judges at Work: The Role and Attitudes of the South African Appellate Judiciary, 1910–50* (Cape Town: Juta, 1984)

Corder, Hugh, "South Africa's Transitional Constitution", *Pub. L.* 291 (1996)

Corder, Hugh, "Judicial Authority in a Changing South Africa", in Guy Canivet and Mads Andenas (eds.), *Independence, Accountability, and the Judiciary* 187 (London: British Institute of International and Comparative Law, 2006)

Corder, Hugh, "Judicial Activism of a Special Type: South Africa's Top Courts Since 1994", in Brice Dickson (ed.), *Judicial Activism in Common Law Supreme Courts* 323 (Oxford: Oxford University Press, 2007)

Crijns, F.C.L.M., *Het Europese perspectief van het Nederlandse staatsrecht* (Zwolle: W.E.J. Tjeenk Willink, 2nd ed., 1989)

Currie, Iain and De Waal, Johan (eds.), *The New Constitutional and Administrative Law*, vol. I (Lansdowne: Juta, 2001)

Currie, Iain and De Waal, Johan, *The Bill of Rights Handbook* (Lansdowne: Juta, 5th ed., 2005)

Davis, Dennis, "The Case Against the Inclusion of Socio-economic Demands in a Bill of Rights Except as Directive Principles", 8 *S. Afr. J. Hum. Rights* 475 (1992)

De Beer, R.J. and Vettori, S., "Enforcing Socio-economic Rights", *Potchefstroom Electr. L. J.* 1 (2007)

De Klerk, Willem, "The Process of Political Negotiation: 1990–1993", in Bertus de Villiers (ed.), *Birth of a Constitution* 4 (Kenwyn: Juta, 1994)

De Lange, R., "Constitutionele toetsing van wetgeving in Nederland", *Regelmaat* 142 (2006)

De Ville, J.R., *Judicial Review of Administrative Action in South Africa* (Durban: LexisNexis Butterworths, 2005)

De Vos, Pierre, "Pious Wishes or Directly Enforceable Human Rights? Social and Economic Rights in South Africa's 1996 Constitution", 13 *S. Afr. J. Hum. Rights* 67 (1997)

De Werd, Marc and De Winter, Reiner, "Judicial Activism in the Netherlands: Who Cares?", in Rob Bakker, Aalt Willem Heringa and Frits Stroink (eds.), *Judicial Control: Comparative Essays on Judicial Review* 101 (Antwerp: Maklu, 1995)

Denver, David, *Elections and Voters in Britain* (Basingstoke: Palgrave Macmillan, 2003)

Devenish, George, "The Interim Constitution in the Making", 60 *Tydskrif vir Hedendaagse Romeins-Hollandse Reg* 612 (1997)

Devlin, Lord, "Judges and Lawmakers", 39 *Mod. L. Rev.* 1 (1976)

Dicey, A.V., *Introduction to the Study of the Law of the Constitution* (London: Macmillan, 10th ed., 1959)

Dixon, Rosalind, "Creating Dialogue about Socioeconomic Rights: Strong-form Versus Weak-form Judicial Review Revisited", 5 *Int. J. Const. L.* 391 (2007)

Doyle, John and Wells, Belinda, "How Far Can the Common Law Go Towards Protecting Rights?", in Philip Alston (ed.), *Promoting Human Rights Through Bills of Rights: Comparative Perspectives* 17 (Oxford: Oxford University Press, 1999)

Du Plessis, Lourens and Corder, Hugh, *Understanding South Africa's Transitional Bill of Rights* (Kenwyn: Juta, 1994)

Du Plessis, Max, "Between Apology and Utopia: The Constitutional Court and Public Opinion", 18 *S. Afr. J. Hum. Rights* 1 (2002)

Dugard, John, *Human Rights and the South African Legal Order* (Princeton, NJ: Princeton University Press, 1978)

Dworkin, Ronald, *A Bill of Rights for Britain* (London: Chatto & Windus, 1990)

Dworkin, Ronald, "The Forum of Principle", 56 *N.Y. Univ. L. Rev.* 469 (1981)

Dworkin, Ronald, *Taking Rights Seriously* (London: Duckworth, 1978)

Dworkin, Ronald, *A Matter of Principle* (Cambridge, MA: Harvard University Press, 1985)

Dworkin, Ronald, *Freedom's Law: A Moral Reading of the American Constitution* (Cambridge, MA: Harvard University Press, 1996)

Dyzenhaus, David, "Are Legislatures Good at Morality? Or Better at it Than the Courts?", 7 *Int. J. Const. L.* 46 (2009)

Eisenstat Weinrib, Lorraine, "Canada's Constitutional Revolution: From Legislative to Constitutional State", 33 *Israel L. Rev.* 13 (1999)

Ekins, Richard, "Acts of Parliament and Parliament Acts", 123 *L. Quart. Rev.* 91 (2007)

Elias, A.M., *Het Nationaal Sijndicaat 1802–1805* (Bussum: Fibula-Van Dishoeck, 1975)

Elliott, Mark, "The Human Rights Act 1998 and the Standard of Substantive Review", 60 *Camb. L. J.* 301 (2001)

Elliott, Mark, "United Kingdom: Parliamentary Sovereignty under Pressure", 2 *Int. J. Const. L.* 545 (2004)

Ely, John Hart, *Democracy and Distrust: A Theory of Judicial Review* (Cambridge, MA: Harvard University Press, 1980)

Elzinga, D.J., De Lange, R. and Hoogers, H.G., *Handboek van het Nederlandse staatsrecht* (Deventer: Kluwer, 15th ed., 2006)

Ewing, K.D. and Gearty, C.A., *Freedom under Thatcher: Civil Liberties in Modern Britain* (Oxford: Clarendon Press, 1990)

Fallon, Richard H., "The Core of an Uneasy Case for Judicial Review", 121 *Harv. L. Rev.* 1693 (2008)

Feldman, Barry, "The Birth of an Academic Obsession: The History of the Countermajoritarian Difficulty, Part Five", 112 *Yale L. J.* 153 (2002)

Feldman, David, "Remedies for Violations of Convention Rights Under the Human Rights Act", 6 *Eur. Hum. Rights L. Rev.* 691 (1998)

Feldman, David, "Parliamentary Scrutiny of Legislation", *Pub. L.* 323 (2002)

Feldman, David (ed.), *English Public Law* (Oxford: Oxford University Press, 2004)

Feldman, David, "Institutional Roles and Meanings of 'Compatibility' Under the Human Rights Act 1998", in Helen Fenwick, Gavin Phillipson and Roger Masterman (eds.), *Judicial Reasoning under the Human Rights Act* 87 (Cambridge: Cambridge University Press, 2007)

Fenwick, Helen, *Civil Liberties and Human Rights* (London: Cavendish Publishing, 3rd ed., 2007)

Ferreres Comella, Victor, "The European Model of Constitutional Review of Legislation: Toward Decentralization?", 2 *Int. J. Const. L.* 461 (2004)

Fish, Stanley, *Is There a Text in this Class? The Authority of Interpretive Communities* (Cambridge, MA: Harvard University Press, 1980)

Fleuren, Joseph, "Waarom het voorstel-Halsema superieur is", *Nederlands Juristenblad* 2630 (2009)

Foley, Michael, *The Politics of the British Constitution* (Manchester: Manchester University Press, 1999)

Forsyth, C.F., *In Danger of Their Talents: A Study of the Appellate Division of the Supreme Court of South Africa from 1950–80* (Cape Town: Juta, 1985)

Franken, H., *Rapport: Commissie grondrechten in het digitale tijdperk* (The Hague: Ministry of Home Affairs, 2000)

Friedman Goldstein, Leslie, "From Democracy to Juristocracy", 38 *L. Soc. Rev.* 611 (2004)

Friedman, Lawrence M., *The Legal System: A Social Science Perspective* (New York, NY: Russell Sage Foundation, 1977)

Gardbaum, Stephen, "The New Commonwealth Model of Constitutionalism", 49 *Am. J. Comp. L.* 707 (2001)

Garlicki, Lech, "Constitutional Courts Versus Supreme Courts", 5 *Int. J. Const. L.* 44 (2007)

Gearty, Conor, "Reconciling Parliamentary Democracy and Human Rights", 118 *L. Quart. Rev.* 248 (2002)

Gearty, Conor, *Principles of Human Rights Adjudication* (Oxford: Oxford University Press, 2005)

Gewirth, Alan, "Are There Any Absolute Rights?", in Jeremy Waldron (ed.), *Theories of Rights* 93 (Oxford: Oxford University Press, 1984)

Ginsburg, Tom, *Judicial Review in New Democracies: Constitutional Courts in Asian Cases* (Cambridge: Cambridge University Press, 2003)

Goldstone, Richard J., "The South African Bill of Rights", 32 *Texas Int. L. J.* 1451 (1997)

Goldsworthy, Jeffrey, *The Sovereignty of Parliament: History and Philosophy* (Oxford: Clarendon Press, 1999)

Gomez Heredero, Ana, *Social Security as a Human Right: The Protection Afforded by the European Convention on Human Rights* (Strasbourg: Council of Europe, 2007)

Gordon, Richard and Ward, Tim, *Judicial Review and the Human Rights Act* (London: Cavendish Publishing, 2000)

Greer, Steven, "What's Wrong with the European Convention on Human Rights?", 30 *Hum. Rights Quart.* 680 (2008)

Griswold, Erwin N., "The 'Coloured Vote Case' in South Africa", 65 *Harv. L. Rev.* 1361 (1952)

Griswold, Erwin N., "The Demise of the High Court of Parliament in South Africa", 66 *Harv. L. Rev.* 864 (1953)

Groenewegen, F.T., *Wetsinterpretatie en rechtsvorming* (The Hague: Boom, 2006)

Hahlo, H.R. and Kahn, E., *The South African Legal System and Its Background* (Cape Town: Juta, 1968)

Happé, Richard and Gribnau, Hans, "The Netherlands – National Report: Constitutional Limits to Taxation in a Democratic State: The Dutch Experience", 15 *Mich. State J. Int. L.* 417 (2007)

Hart, H.L.A., *The Concept of Law* (Oxford: Oxford University Press, 1961)

Hazell, Robert, "Pre-legislative Scrutiny", *Pub. L.* 477 (2004)

Heringa, Aalt Willem, "Constitutionele schijnbewegingen", in A.W. Heringa and N. Verheij (eds.), *Publiekrechtelijke bewegingen* 67 (Deventer: Kluwer, 1990)

Heringa, Aalt Willem, "Rechterlijke toetsing in Nederland", 17 *NJCM-Bull.* 235 (1992)

Heringa, Aalt Willem and Kiiver, Phillip, *Constitutions Compared: An Introduction to Comparative Constitutional Law* (Antwerp: Intersentia, 2007)

Hertogh, Marc and Halliday, Simon (eds.), *Judicial Review and Bureaucratic Impact: International and Interdisciplinary Perspectives* (Cambridge: Cambridge University Press, 2004)

Hiebert, Janet L., "Parliamentary Bill of Rights: An Alternative Model?", 69 *Mod. L. Rev.* 7 (2006)

Hins, A.W., "Constitutionele toetsing, proportionaliteit, Verhältnismässigkeit", in Aernout J. Nieuwenhuis, Ben J. Schueler and Carla M. Zoethout (eds.), *Proportionaliteit in het publiekrecht* 61 (Deventer: Kluwer, 2005)

Hirsch Ballin, E.M.H., "De harmonisatiewet: Onschendbaarheid van de wet en van het rechtszekerheidsbeginsel", 38 *Ars Aequi* 578 (1989)

Hirsch Ballin, E.M.H., "Constitutionele toetsing van wetten als bijdrage aan de recht-sontwikkeling", in Willem Konijnenbelt (ed.), *Rechter en wetgever* 47 (The Hague: Council of State, 2001)

Hirsch Ballin, E.M.H., "Een levende Grondwet", *Regelmaat* 161 (2005)

Hirschl, Ran, "The Political Origins of Judicial Empowerment Through Constitutionalization: Lessons From Four Constitutional Revolutions", *L. Soc. Inquiry* 91 (2000)

Hirschl, Ran, *Towards Juristocracy: The Origins and Consequences of the New Constitutionalism* (Cambridge, MA: Harvard University Press, 2004)

Hoekstra, R.J., *Hart voor de publieke zaak: Aanbevelingen van de Nationale Conventie voor de 21e eeuw* (The Hague: National Convention, 2006)

Hoffman, David and Rowe, John, *Human Rights in the UK: An Introduction to the Human Rights Act 1998* (Harlow: Pearson Longman, 2nd ed., 2006)

Hogg, Peter W., *Constitutional Law of Canada* (Ontario: Thomson Carswell, 2007)

Hogg, Peter W. and Bushell, Allison A.,"The Charter Dialogue Between Courts and Legislatures", 35 *Osgoode Hall L. J.* 75 (1997)

Holmes, S., "Precommitment and the Paradox of Democracy", in Jon Elster and Rune Slagstad (eds.), *Constitutionalism and Democracy* 231 (Cambridge: Cambridge University Press, 1988)

Hood Phillips, O., Jackson, Paul and Leopold, Patricia, *Constitutional and Administrative Law* (London: Sweet & Maxwell, 8th ed., 2001)

Hoorweg, H.J., "Delegatie", in P.W.C. Akkermans and C.J. Bax, *Interpretatie in het staatsrecht* (Rotterdam: Erasmus University, 1985)

Horspool, Margot and Humphreys, Matthew, *European Union Law* (Oxford: Oxford University Press, 4th ed., 2006)

Hutchinson, Allan C., "A 'Hard Core' Case Against Judicial Review", 121 *Har. L. Rev. Forum* 57 (2008)

Ijzermans, Maria, "Dutch Ways of Doing Justice", in Sanne Taekema (ed.), *Understanding Dutch Law* 59 (The Hague: Boom Juridische Uitgevers, 2004)

Irvine of Lairg, Lord, "Judges and Decision-makers: The Theory and Practice of Wednesbury Review", *Pub. Law* 59 (1996)

Jenkins, David, "Common Law Declarations of Unconstitutionality", 7 *Int. J. Const. L.* 183 (2009)

Joint Committee on Human Rights (UK), "The Committee's Future Working Practices", 23rd Report (2005–2006), August 2006

Joint Committee on Human Rights (UK), "The Work of the Committee in 2007 and the State of Human Rights in the United Kingdom", 6th Report (2007–2008), February 2008

Jowell, Jeffrey, "Judicial Deference: Servility, Civility or Institutional Deference", *Pub. L.* 592 (2003)

Jurgens, E.C.M., "Wetgever heeft laatste woord over uitleg van Grondwet", *Regelmaat* 68 (1995)

Kahn-Freund, O., "On Uses and Misuses of Comparative Law", 37 *Mod. L. Rev.* 1 (1974)

Kavanagh, Aileen, "Deference or Defiance? The Limits of the Judicial Role in Constitutional Adjudication", in Grant Huscroft (ed.), *Expounding the Constitution: Essays in Constitutional Theory* 184 (Cambridge: Cambridge University Press, 2008)

Kavanagh, Aileen, *Constitutional Review under the UK Human Rights Act* (Cambridge: Cambridge University Press, 2009)

Kavanagh, Aileen, "Judging the Judges under the Human Rights Act: Deference, Disillusionment and the 'War on Terror' ", *Pub. L.* 287 (2009)

Kearnes, Paul, "United Kingdom Judges and Human Rights Cases", in Esin Örücü (ed.), *Judicial Comparativism in Human Rights Cases* 63 (London: British Institute of International and Comparative Law, 2003)

Keene, Sir David, "Principles of Deference under the Human Rights Act", in Helen
    Fenwick, Gavin Phillipson and Roger Masterman (eds.), *Judicial Reasoning under
    the Human Rights Act* 206 (Cambridge: Cambridge University Press, 2007)
Kelley, Paul Joseph, *Locke's Second Treatise of Government: A Reader's Guide* (London:
    Continuum, 2007)
Kelsen, Hans, "La garantie juridictionnelle de la Constitution", 44 *Revue de Droit Public*
    197 (1928)
Kende, Mark S., *Constitutional Rights in Two Worlds: South Africa and the United States*
    (Cambridge: Cambridge University Press, 2009)
Kleijn, G.P. and Kroes, M., *Mensenrechten in de Nederlandse rechtspraktijk* (Zwolle:
    W.E.J. Tjeenk Willink, 1986)
Klug, Heinz, "Participating in the Design: Constitution-making in South Africa", 3 *Rev.
    Const. Stud.* 18 (1996)
Klug, Heinz, "Historical Background", in Matthew Chaskalson, Janet Kentridge, Jonathan
    Klaaren, Gilbert Marcus, Derek Spitz and Stuart Woolman (eds.), *Constitutional Law
    of South Africa* 2/10 (Kenwyn: Juta, Revision Service 5, 1999)
Koekkoek, A.K., *Rechter en bestuur in constitutioneel perspectief* (Utrecht: Lemma,
    2001)
Koopmans, Tim, "Legislature and Judiciary – Present Trends", in T. Koopmans (ed.),
    Juridisch stippelwerk 194 (Deventer: Kluwer, 1991)
Koopmans, Tim, *Courts and Political Institutions: A Comparative View* (Cambridge:
    Cambridge University Press, 2003)
Kortmann, C.A.J.M., "Advies van prof. mr. C.A.J.M. Kortmann", 17 *NJCM-Bull.* 305
    (1990)
Kortmann, C.A.J.M., "Is een wetsvoorstel onschendbaar?", 48 *Ars Aequi* 473 (1999)
Kortmann, C.A.J.M., "Nogmaals: Is een wetsvoorstel onschendbaar?", 49 *Ars Aequi* 107
    (2000)
Kortmann, C.A.J.M., *Constitutioneel recht* (Deventer: Kluwer, 5th ed., 2005)
Kortmann, C.A.J.M., *Staatsrecht en raison d'Etat* (Deventer: Kluwer, 2009)
Kortmann, Constantijn A.J.M., Bovend'Eert, and Paul P.T., *Dutch Constitutional Law*
    (The Hague: Kluwer, 2000)
Kranenburg, R., *Het Nederlands staatsrecht* (Haarlem: H.D. Tjeenk Willink, 8th ed.,
    1958)
Learned Hand, *The Bill of Rights: The Oliver Wendell Holmes Lectures* (Cambridge, MA:
    Harvard University Press, 1958)
Leenknegt, Gert-Jan, "Hoe lang is de arm van artikel 120 Gr.w.?", *Regelmaat* 65 (1995)
Leenknegt, Gert-Jan, "The Protection of Fundamental Rights in a Digital Age", in Ewoud
    Hondius and C. Joustra (eds.), *Netherlands Report to the Sixteenth International
    Congress of Comparative Law* 325 (Antwerp: Intersentia, 2002)
Leenknegt, Gert-Jan and Van der Schyff, Gerhard, "Reforming the Electoral System of
    the Dutch Lower House of Parliament: An Unsuccessful Story", 8 *German L. J.* 1133
    (2007)
Leenknegt, Gert-Jan, Kubben, Raymond and Jacobs, Beatrix, *Opstand en eenwording:
    Een institutionele geschiedenis van het Nederlandse openbaar bestuur* (Nijmegen:
    Wolf Legal Publishers, 2006)
Leigh, Ian and Lustgarten, Laurence, "Making Rights Real: The Courts, Remedies, and
    the Human Rights Act", 58 *Camb. L. J.* 509 (1999)
Lester of Herne Hill, Lord and Pannick, David, *Human Rights Law and Practice*
    (London: Butterworths, 1999, first supplement 2000)
Lever, Annabelle, "Is Judicial Review Undemocratic?", *Pub. L.* 290 (2007)
Lewis, Carole, "Reaching the Pinnacle: Principles, Policies and People for a Single Apex
    Court in South Africa", 21 *S. Afr. J. Hum. Rights* 509 (2005)

Lewis, Jonathan, "The Constitutional Court of South Africa: An Evaluation", 125 *L. Quart. Rev.* 440 (2009)

Leysen, R. and Smets, J., *Toetsing van de wet aan de Grondwet in België* (Zwolle: W.E.J. Tjeenk Willink, 1991)

Loveland, Ian, *Constitutional Law, Administrative Law and Human Rights* (Oxford: Oxford University Press, 4th ed., 2006)

Lyon, Ann, *Constitutional History of the United Kingdom* (London: Cavendish Publishing, 2003)

MacCormick, D. Neil and Summers, Robert S., "Further General Reflections and Conclusions", in D. Neil MacCormick and Robert S. Summers (eds.), *Interpreting Precedents: A Comparative Study* 531 (Aldershot: Ashgate, 1997)

Magalhaes, Pedro, *The Limits to Judicialization: Legislative Politics and Constitutional Review in Iberian Democracies* (Doctoral dissertation, Ohio State University, 2002)

Malherbe, E.F.J., "Provinsiale grondwette: 'n Barometer van provinsiale outonomie?", *J. S. Afr. L.* 344 (1998)

Malherbe, Rassie, "Die drankwetsontwerp: Vooraf kontrole en grondwetlike gesagsverdeling verder omlyn", 63 *Tydskrif vir Hedendaagse Romeins-Hollandse Reg* 321 (2000)

Malherbe, Rassie, "The South African Constitution", 55 *Zeitschrift für öffentliches Recht* 61 (2000)

Malherbe, Rassie, "The Role of the Constitutional Court in the Development of Provincial Autonomy", *SA Pub. L.* 255 (2001)

Malherbe, Rassie, "The Development of Social and Economic Rights in South Africa", 60 *Zeitschrift für öffentliches Recht* 111 (2005)

Malherbe, Rassie, "Centralisation of Power in Education: Have Provinces Become National Agents?", *J. S. Afr. L.* 237 (2006)

Malherbe, Rassie, "Openbare betrokkenheid by die wetgewende proses kry oplaas tande", *J. S. Afr. L.* 594 (2007)

Malherbe, Rassie, "South Africa: The National Council of Provinces", in Gerhard van der Schyff (ed.), *Constitutionalism in the Netherlands and South Africa: A Comparative Study* 103 (Nijmegen: Wolf Legal Publishers, 2008)

Mandel, Michael, *The Charter of Rights and the Legitimization of Politics* (Toronto: Thompson Educational Publishing, 1994)

Mandel, Michael, "A Brief History of the New Constitutionalism, or 'How We Changed Everything So that Everything Would Remain the Same'", 32 *Israel L. Rev.* 251 (1998)

Marks, Susan, "The European Convention on Human Rights and Its 'Democratic Society'", 66 *Br. Yearb. Int. L.* 209 (1995)

Masterman, Roger, "Interpretations, Declarations and Dialogue: Rights Protection under the Human Rights Act and Victorian Charter of Human Rights and Responsibilities", *Pub. L.* 112 (2009)

Matthews, Anthony S., *Law, Order and Liberty in South Africa* (Berkeley, CA: University of California Press, 1971)

Maunz, Theodor and Zippelius, Reinhold, *Deutsches Staatsrecht* (München: Beck, 28th ed., 1991)

McWhinney, Edward, *Supreme Courts and Judicial Law-making: Constitutional Tribunals and Constitutional Review* (Dordrecht: Martinus Nijhoff, 1986)

Mevis, P.A.M., "Constitutioneel toetsingsrecht: Zuinigheid in plaats van revolutie", 32 *Delinkt en Delinkwent* 933 (2002)

Michelman, Frank, *Brennan and the Supreme Court* (Princeton, NJ: Princeton University Press, 1999)

Miles, Joanna, "Standing Under the Human Rights Act 1998: Theories of Rights Enforcement & The Nature of Public Law Adjudication", 59 *Camb. L. J.* 133 (2000)

Mill, John Stuart, *On Liberty and the Subjection of Women* (New York, NY: Henry Holt, 1879)

Monteath Thompson, Leonard, *The Unification of South Africa: 1902–1910* (Oxford: Clarendon Press, 2nd ed., 1961)

Motala, Ziyad and Ramaphosa, Cyril, *Constitutional Law: Analysis and Cases* (Oxford: Oxford University Press, 2002)

Mountfield, Helen, "The Concept of a Lawful Interference with Fundamental Rights", in Jeffrey Jowell and Jonathan Cooper (eds.), *Understanding Human Rights Principles* 5 (Oxford: Hart Publishing, 2001)

Mowbray, Alastair, *The Development of Positive Obligations Under the European Convention on Human Rights by the European Court of Human Rights* (Oxford: Hart Publishing, 2004)

Müller, Jörg Paul, "Fundamental Rights in Democracy", 4 *Hum. Rights L. J.* 131 (1983)

Mureinik, Etienne, "A Bridge to Where? Introducing the Interim Bill of Rights", 10 *S. Afr. J. Hum. Rights* 31 (1994)

Nicol, Danny and Marriott, Jane, "The Human Rights Act, Representative Standing and the Victim Culture", *Eur. Hum. Rights L. Rev.* 730 (1998)

Nieuwenhuis, A.J., "Van proportionaliteit tot appreciatiemarge: De noodzakelijkheid-stoets in de jurisprudentie van het EHRM", in Aernout J. Nieuwenhuis, Ben J. Schueler and Carla M. Zoethout (eds.), *Proportionaliteit in het publiekrecht* 37 (Deventer: Kluwer, 2005)

O'Neill, Aidan, "Judging Democracy: The Devolutionary Settlement and the Scottish Constitution", in Andrew Le Sueur (ed.), *Building the UK's New Supreme Court: National and Comparative Perspectives* 23 (Oxford: Oxford University Press, 2007)

Oud, P.J. and Bosmans, J., *Staatkundige vormgeving in Nederland 1840–1940*, vol. 1 (Assen: Van Gorcum, 10th ed., 1990)

Palmer, Ellie, *Judicial Review, Socio-economic Rights and the Human Rights Act* (Oxford: Hart Publishing, 2007)

Parpworth, Neil, *Constitutional & Administrative Law* (Oxford: Oxford University Press, 5th ed., 2008)

Peeters, Patrick, "Expanding Constitutional Review by the Belgian 'Court of Arbitration'", 11 *Eur. Pub. L.* 475 (2005)

Peters, Jit and Boogaard, Geerten, "De myhes van Van der Schyff over het initiatiefwetsvoorstel-Halsema", *Nederlands Juristenblad* 2628 (2009)

Pieterse, Marius, "Coming to Terms with Judicial Enforcement of Socio-economic Rights", 20 *S. Afr. J. Hum. Rights* 383 (2004)

Polak, J.E.M., "Zit er nog muziek in verbods- en gebodsacties ter zake van wetgeving?", *Overheid en Aansprakelijkheid* 168 (2004)

Poole, Thomas, "Tilting at Windmills? Truth and Illusion in the 'the Political Constitution'", 70 *Mod. L. Rev.* 250 (2007)

Popelier, P., "Constitutionele toetsing van wetgeving in België", *Regelmaat* 116 (2006)

Posner, Erica A. and Vermeule, Adrian, "Legislative Entrenchment: A Reappraisal", 111 *Yale L. J.* 1665 (2002)

Pound, Roscoe, *The Formative Era of American Law* (Boston: Little Brown, 1938)

Prakke, L., *Toetsing in het publiekrecht* (Assen: Van Gorcum, 1972)

Prakke, L., "Bedenkingen tegen het toetsingsrecht", 122 *Handelingen Nederlandse Juristen-Vereniging* 1 (1992)

Prakke, L., Koopmans, T., and Barendrecht, J.M., *Handelingen Nederlandse Juristen-Vereniging: Toetsing* (Zwolle: W.E.J. Tjeenk Willink, 1992)

Pünder, Hermann, "Democratic Legitimation of Delegated Legislation – A Comparative View on the American, British and German Law", 58 *Int. Comp. L. Quart.* 355 (2009)

Rautenbach, I.M. and Malherbe, E.F.J., *Constitutional Law* (Durban: Butterworths, 5th ed., 2009)

Reestman, J.II., *Constitutionele toetsing in Frankrijk: De Conseil constitutionnel en de grondwettigheid van wetten en verdragen* (Nijmegen: Ars Aequi Libri, 1996)

Rehorst, Peter, "Constitutional Jurisdiction in the Context of State Powers: Types, Contents and Effects of the Decisions on the Constitutionality of Legal Regulations", 9 *Hum. Rights L. J.* 11 (1988)

Reid, Karen, *A Practitioner's Guide to the European Convention on Human Rights* (London: Sweet & Maxwell, 1998)

Reitz, John C., "Political Economy and Abstract Review in Germany, France and the United States", in Sally J. Kenney, William M. Reisinger and John C. Reitz (eds.), *Constitutional Dialogues in Comparative Perspective* 62 (Basingstoke: Macmillan, 1999)

Rishworth, Paul, Huscroft, Grant, Optican, Scott and Mahoney, Richard, *The New Zealand Bill of Rights* (Melbourne: Oxford University Press, 2003)

Rosenfeld, Michel, "Constitutional Adjudication in Europe and the United States: Paradoxes and Contrasts", 2 *Int. J. Const. L.* 633 (2004)

Roux, Theunis, "Legitimating Transformation: Political Resource Allocation in the South African Constitutional Court", in Siri Gloppen, Roberto Gargarella and Elin Sklaar (eds.), *Democratization and the Judiciary: The Accountability Function of Courts in New Democracies* 92 (London: Frank, 2003)

Rycroft, Theo, "The Rationality of the Conservative Party's Proposal for a British Bill of Rights", 1 *UCL Hum. Rights Rev.* 51 (2008)

Sachs, Albie, *Protecting Human Rights in a New South Africa* (Cape Town: Oxford University Press, 1990)

Sadurski, Wojciech, "Judicial Review and the Protection of Constitutional Rights", 22 *Oxford J. Legal Stud.* 275 (2002)

Sadurski, Wojciech, *Rights Before Courts: A Study of Constitutional Courts in Postcommunist States of Central and Eastern Europe* (Dordrecht: Springer, 2005)

Sadurski, Wojciech, "Rights and Moral Reasoning: An Unstated Case Assumption – A Comment on Jeremy Waldron's 'Judges as Moral Reasoners'", 7 *Int. J. Const. L.* 25 (2009)

Sajó, András, *Limiting Government: An Introduction to Constitutionalism* (Budapest: Central European University Press, 1999)

Sajó, András and Uitz, Renáta (eds.), *The Constitution in Private Relations: Expanding Constitutionalism* (Utrecht: Eleven International Publishing, 2005)

Sap, Jan Willem, "De aanbeveling van de Nationale Conventie om een constitutionele hof in te stellen", 32 *NJCM-Bull.* 590 (2007)

Sarkin, Jeremy, "The Political Role of the South African Constitutional Court", 114 *S. Afr. L. J.* 134 (1997)

Sarkin, Jeremy, "The Drafting of South Africa's Final Constitution from a Human Rights Perspective", 47 *Am. J. Comp. L.* 67 (1999)

Schermers, Henry G., "Some Recent Cases Delaying the Direct Effect of International Treaties in Dutch law", 10 *Mich. J. Int. L.* 266 (1989)

Schmitt, Carl, *Verfassungsrechtliche Aufsätze aus den Jahren 1924–1954* (Berlin: Duncker & Humblot, 1958)

Schoepen, G.K. and Teuben, K., "Rechterlijke samenwerking", in E.R. Muller and C.P.M. Cleiren (eds.), *Rechterlijke macht* 403 (Deventer: Kluwer, 2006)

Schrire, Robert A., "Parliamentary Opposition After Apartheid: South Africa", 14 *J. Legis. Stud.* 190 (2008)

Schutgens, R.J.B., "Het rechtsgevolg van onverbindendverklaring: Naar een stelsel van materiële vernietiging", *Themis* 96 (2006)

Schutgens, R.J.B., "Het voorstel-Halsema en de toelaatbaarheid van de wet", *Regelmaat* 12 (2007)

Schutgens, R.J.B., *Onrechtmatige wetgeving* (Deventer: Dilligentia, 2009)

Schutte, C.B., "De verwarring van rechtsstaat en rechtersstaat. Kanttekeningen bij constitutionele rechtspraak volgens het voorstel-Halsema", *Regelmaat* 93 (2004)

Sedley, Sir Stephen, "The Rocks or the Open Sea: Where Is the Human Rights Act Heading?", 32 *J. L. Soc.* 3 (2005)

Shapiro, Martin, *Freedom of Speech: The Supreme Court and Judicial Review* (Englewood Cliffs, NJ: Prentice Hall, 1966)

Shapiro, Martin, "The European Court of Justice", in Paul Craig and Gráinne de Búrca (eds.), *The Evolution of EU Law* 321 (Oxford: Oxford University Press, 1999)

Shapiro, Martin J. and Stone, Alec, "The New Constitutional Politics of Europe", 26 *Comp. Pol. Stud.* 397 (1994)

Singh, Rabinder, *The Future of Human Rights in the United Kingdom* (Oxford: Hart, 1997)

Sottiaux, Stefan and Van der Schyff, Gerhard, "Methods of International Human Rights Adjudication: Towards a More Structured Decision-making Process for the European Court of Human Rights", 31 *Hastings Int. Comp. L. Rev.* 115 (2008)

Steenkamp, A.J., "The South African Constitution of 1993 and the Bill of Rights: An Evaluation in Light of International Human Rights Norms", 17 *Hum. Rights Quart.* 101 (1995)

Stellinga, J.R., *De Grondwet systematisch gerangschikt* (Zwolle: Tjeenk Willink, 1950)

Steyn, Johan, "The Case for a Supreme Court", 118 *L. Quart. Rev.* 382 (2002)

Steyn, Lord, "2000–2005: Laying the Foundations of Human Rights Law in the United Kingdom", 4 *Eur. Hum. Rights L. Rev.* 349 (2005)

Steytler, Nico, "Concurrency and Co-operative Government: The Law and Practice in South Africa", 16 *SA Pub. L.* 241 (2001)

Stone Sweet, Alec, *Governing with Judges: Constitutional Politics in Europe* (Oxford: Oxford University Press, 2000)

Stone Sweet, Alec and Shapiro, Martin, *On Law, Politics and Judicialization* (Oxford: Oxford University Press, 2002)

Studiecommissie VMC, "Preadvies inzake een nieuwe tekst voor de artikelen 7 en 13 van de Grondwet", 11(11–12) *Mediaforum* (1999) on http://www.mediaforum.nl/

Sunstein, Cass R., *Designing Democracy: What Constitutions Do* (Oxford: Oxford University Press, 2001)

Taekema, Sanne, "Introducing Dutch Law", in Sanne Taekema (ed.), *Understanding Dutch Law* 17 (The Hague: Boom Juridische Uitgevers, 2004)

Tate, C. Neal and Vallinder, Torbjörn (eds.), *The Global Expansion of Judicial Power* (New York, NY: New York University Press, 1995)

Teitel, Ruti, "Transitional Jurisprudence: The Role of Law in Political Transformation", 106 *Yale L. J.* 2009 (1997)

Troper, Michel, "The Logic of Justification of Judicial Review", 1 *Int. J. Const. L.* 99 (2003)

Tushnet, Mark, "Judicial Review of Legislation", in Peter Cane and Mark Tushnet (eds.), *The Oxford Handbook of Legal Studies* 164 (Oxford: Oxford University Press, 2003)

Tushnet, Mark, *Weak Courts, Strong Rights. Judicial Review and Social Welfare Rights in Comparative Constitutional Law* (Princeton, NJ: Princeton University Press, 2008)

Van der Hoeven, J., "Toetsen aan de Grondwet. Hoe en door wie?", *Nederlands Juristenblad* 784 (1991)

Van der Pot, C.W., *Handboek van het Nederlandse staatsrecht* (Zwolle: W.E.J. Tjeenk Willink, 6th ed., 1957)

Van der Schyff, Gerhard, *Limitation of Rights: A Study of the European Convention and the South African Bill of Rights* (Nijmegen: Wolf Legal Publishers, 2005)

Van der Schyff, Gerhard, "Referenda in South African Law", 13 *Tilburg Foreign L. Rev.* 125 (2006)

Van der Schyff, Gerhard, "Rethinking the Justification for Constitutional Review of Legislation in the Netherlands", in R.A.J. van Gestel and J. van Schooten (eds.), *Europa en de toekomst van de nationale wetgever: Liber amicorum Philip Eijlander* 129 (Nijmegen: Wolf Legal Publishers, 2008)

Van der Schyff, Gerhard, "The Protection of Fundamental Rights in the Netherlands and South Africa Compared: Can the Many Differences be Justified?", *Potchefstroom Electronic L. J.* 1 (2008)

Van der Schyff, Gerhard "Waarom het wetsvoorstel Halsema tekort schiet: Mythes rondom het verdragsargument", *Nederlands Juristenblad* 2408 (2009)

Van der Schyff, Gerhard, "Over een interpretatierichtsnoer en mythes", *Nederlands Juristenblad* 2632 (2009)

Van der Schyff, Gerhard, "Het nieuwe Britse Supreme Court belicht", 1 *Tijdschrift voor Constitutioneel Recht* 69 (2010)

Van der Schyff, Gerhard, "Constitutional Review by the Judiciary in the Netherlands: A Bridge Too Far?", 11 *German L. J.* 275 (2010)

Van der Ven, Johannes A., Dreyer, Jaco S. and Pieterse, Hendrik J.C., *Is There a God of Human Rights? The Complex Relationship between Human Rights and Religion: A South African Case* (Leiden: BRILL, 2004)

Van der Westhuizen, Johann, "The Protection of Human Rights and a Constitutional Court for South Africa: Some Questions and Ideas, with Reference to the German Experience", 24 *De Jure* 1 (1991)

Van Gestel, R.A.J. and Groenhuijsen, M.S., "Geen rechterlijk bevel tot wetgeving, of toch?", *Nederlands Juristenblad* 2050 (2006)

Van Houten, M.L.P., *Meer zicht op wetgeving* (Zwolle: Tjeenk Willink, 1997)

Vanberg, Georg, *The Politics of Constitutional Review in Germany* (Cambridge: Cambridge University Press, 2005)

Velaers, Jan, "De samenloop van grondrechten in het Belgische rechtsbestel", in A.J. Nieuwenhuis et al. (eds.), *Samenloop van grondrechten in verschillende rechtsstelsels, multiculturaliteit in het strafrecht & schuldsanering en collectieve schuldenregeling* (The Hague: Boom Juridische Uitgevers, 2008)

Venter, Francois, "Requirements for a New Constitutional Text: The Imperatives of the Constitutional Principles", 112 *S. Afr. L. J.* 32 (1995)

Venter, Francois, "Aspects of the South African Constitution of 1996: An African Democratic and Social Federal *Rechtsstaat*", 57 *Zeitschrift für ausländisches öffentliches Recht und Völkerrecht* 51 (1997)

Verhey, L.F.M., *Horizontale werking van grondrechten, in het bijzonder van het recht op privacy* (Zwolle: W.E.J. Tjeenk Willink, 1992)

Wadham, John, Mountfield, Helen, Edmundson, Anna and Gallagher, Caoilfhionn, *Blackstone's Guide to the Human Rights Act* (Oxford: Oxford University Press, 4th ed., 2007)

Waldron, Jeremy, *Law and Disagreement* (Oxford: Oxford University Press, 1999)

Waldron, Jeremy, "The Core of the Case Against Judicial Review", 115 *Yale L. J.* 1346 (2006)

Waldron, Jeremy, "Judges as Moral Reasoners", 7 *Int. J. Const. L.* 2 (2009)

Walker, Neil, "The Legacy of Europe's Constitutional Moment", 11 *Constellations* 368 (2004)

Waluchow, W.J., *A Common Law Theory of Judicial Review: The Living Tree* (Cambridge: Cambridge University Press, 2007)

Warwick, Peter, *Black People and the South African War 1899–1902* (Cambridge: Cambridge University Press, 1983)

Weinrib, Lorraine E., "Constitutional Conceptions and Constitutional Comparativism", in Vicki C. Jackson and Mark Tushnet (eds.), *Defining the Field of Comparative Constitutional Law* 3 (Westport: Praeger, 2002)

Wengler, Wilhelm, *Die Unanwendbarkeit der Europäischen Sozialcharta im Staat* (Bad Homburg: Gehlen, 1969)

Wiarda, G.J., *Drie typen van rechtsvinding* (Zwolle: W.E.J. Tjeenk Willink, 3rd ed., 1988)

Wicks, Elizabeth, *The Evolution of a Constitution: Eight Key Moments in British Constitutional History* (Oxford: Hart Publishing, 2006)

Winterton, George, "The British Grundnorm: Parliamentary Supremacy Re-examined", 92 *L. Quart. Rev.* 591 (1976)

Witteveen, Willem J., *Evenwicht der machten* (Zwolle: Tjeenk Willink, 1991)

Witteveen, Willem J., "Inhabiting Legality", in Sanne Taekema (ed.), *Understanding Dutch Law* 75 (The Hague: Boom Juridische Uitgevers, 2004)

Witteveen, Willem J., "Nomoi: Hamilton, Koopmans en Ackerman over constitutionele toetsing", *Regelmaat* 177 (2006)

Woolman, Stuart, "Provincial Constitutions", in Stuart Woolman and Theunis Roux (eds.), *Constitutional Law of South Africa* 21i (Cape Town: Juta, 2nd ed., 2006)

Wright, Tony, *Citizens and Subjects. An Essay on British Politics* (London: Routledge, 1994)

Young, James, "The Politics of the Human Rights Act", 26 *J. L. Soc.* 27 (1999)

Yourow, Howard Charles, *The Margin of Appreciation Doctrine in the Dynamics of the European Human Rights Jurisprudence* (The Hague: Kluwer, 1996)

Zander, Michael, *The Law-making Process* (Cambridge: Cambridge University Press, 6th ed., 2004)

Zoethout, Carla M., "The End of Constitutionalism? Challenges to the Ideal of Limiting Governmental Power", in P.W.C. Akkermans, D.J. Elzinga and E. Pietermaat-Kros (eds.), *Constitutionalism in the Netherlands* 9 (Groningen: Groningen University Press, 1995)

Zoethout, Carla M., Sap, Jan Willem, Kuiper, Roel and Ramadan, Omar, *Een grondwet voor de 21ste eeuw: Voorstudie van de werkgroep Grondwet van de Nationale Conventie* (The Hague: National Convention, 2006)

Zweigert, K., and Kötz, H., *An Introduction to Comparative Law* (Oxford: Clarendon Press, 3rd ed., 1998)

Case Law

Belgium

Court of Cassation's judgment of 27 May 1971, *Pas.*, 1971, I, 886 (*Le Ski*)

Canada

The Queen v. Oakes, (1986) 26 DLR (4th) 200 (SCC)

Council of Europe

Broniowski v. Poland of 22 June 2004, *Reports of Judgments and Decisions*, 2004-V
Castells v. Spain of 23 April 1992, *Publ. Eur Court of H.R.*, Series A, no. 236
Chahal v. The United Kingdom of 15 November 1996, *Reports*, 1996-V
Chassagnou v. France of 25 April 1999, *Reports*, 1999-III

Cyprus v. Turkey of 10 May 2001, *Reports of Judgments and Decisions*, 2001-IV

Dudgeon v. The United Kingdom of 22 October 1981, *Publ. Eur. Court H.R.*, Series A, no. 45

ECmHR, no. 4403/70 (joined with other applications), *East African Asians v. The United Kingdom* of 10 October 1970

Goodwin v. The United Kingdom of 27 March 1996, *Reports*, 1996-II

Klass v. Germany of 6 September 1978, *Publ. Eur. Court H.R.*, Series A, no. 28

Leyla Şahin v. Turkey of 10 November 2005, *Reports of Judgments and Decisions*, 2005-XI

McGonnell v. The United Kingdom of 8 February 2000, *Reports of Judgments and Decisions*, 2000-II

Norris v. Ireland of 26 October 1988, *Publ. Eur. Court H.R.*, Series A, no. 142

Procola v. Luxemburg of 29 September 1995, *Publ. Eur. Court H.R.*, Series A, no. 326

Relating to Certain Aspects of the Laws on the Use of Languages in Education in Belgium v. Belgium of 23 July 1968, *Publ. Eur. Court H.R.*, Series A, no. 6

Selmouni v. France of 28 July 1999, *Reports and Judgments and Decisions*, 1999-V

Silver v. The United Kingdom of 25 March 1983, *Publ. Eur. Court H.R.*, Series A, no. 61

Sunday Times v. The United Kingdom of 26 April 1979, *Publ. Eur. Court of H.R.*, Series A, no. 30

Sunday Times v. The United Kingdom of 26 April 1979, *Publ. Eur. Court H.R.*, Series A, no. 30

Van Raalte v. The Netherlands of 21 February 1997, *Publ. Eur Court H.R.*, *Reports*, 1997-I

South Africa

August and Another v. Electoral Commission and Others, 1999 (4) BCLR 363 (CC), 1999 (3) SA 1 (CC)

Bruce v. Fleecytex Johannesburg CC, 1998 (4) BCLR 415 (CC), 1998 (2) SA 1143 (CC)

Certification of the Amended Text of the Constitution of the Republic of South Africa, 1996, 1997 (1) BCLR 1 (CC), 1997 (2) SA 97 (CC)

Certification of the Constitution of the Republic of South Africa, 1996, 1996 (10) BCLR 1253 (CC), 1996 (4) SA 744 (CC)

Christian Education South Africa v. Minister of Education, 2000 (10) BCLR 1051 (CC), 2000 (4) SA 757 (CC)

Coetzee v. Government of the RSA; Matiso v. Commanding Officer, Port Elizabeth Prison, 1995 (10) BCLR 1382 (CC), 1995 (4) SA 631 (CC)

Dawood; Shalabi; Thomas v. Minister of Home Affairs, 2000 (8) BCLR 837 (CC), 2000 (3) SA 936 (CC)

Doctors for Life International v. Speaker of the National Assembly, 2006 (12) BCLR 1399 (CC), 2006 (6) SA 416 (CC)

Ex parte President of the Republic of South Africa In re: Constitutionality of the Liquor Bill, 2000 (1) BCLR 1 (CC), 2000 (1) SA 732 (CC)

Fereirra v. Levin; Vryenhoek v. Powell, 1996 (1) BCLR 1 (CC), 1996 (1) SA 984 (CC)

Fose v. Minister of Safety and Security, 1997 (7) BCLR 851 (CC), 1997 (3) SA 786 (CC)

Fourie v. Minister of Home Affairs, 2005 (3) BCLR 241 (SCA)

Freeman v. Colonial Secretary, 1889 NLR 73

Government of the RSA v. Grootboom, 2000 (11) BCLR 1169 (CC), 2001 (1) SA 46 (CC)

Harris v. Minister of the Interior, 1952 (2) SA 428 (A)

In re: Certification of the Amended Text of the Constitution of the Western Cape, 1997, 1997 (12) BCLR 1653, 1998 (1) SA 655 (CC)

In re: Certification of the Constitution of the Province of KwaZulu-Natal 1996, 1996 (11) BCLR 1419 (CC), 1996 (4) SA 1098 (CC)

In re: Certification of the Constitution of the Western Cape, 1997, 1997 (9) BCLR 1167 (CC), 1997 (4) SA 795 (CC)

In re: Constitutionality of the Mpumalanga Petitions Bill, 2001 (11) BCLR 1126 (CC), 2002 (1) SA 447 (CC)

In re: KwaZulu-Natal Amakhosi and Iziphankanyiswa Amendment Bill of 1995; In re: Payment of Salaries, Allowances and Other Privileges to the Ingoyama Bill of 1995, 1996 (7) BCLR 903 (CC), 1996 (4) SA 653 (CC)

In re: The National Education Policy Bill No. 83 of 1995, 1996 (4) BCLR 518 (CC), 1996 (3) SA 289 (CC)

In re: The School Education Bill of 1995 (Gauteng), 1996 (4) BCLR 537 (CC), 1996 (3) SA 165 (CC)

JT Publishing (Pty) Ltd v. Minister of Safety and Security, 1996 (12) BCLR 1599 (CC), 1997 (3) SA 514 (CC)

K. v. Minister of Safety and Security, 2005 (3) SA 179 (SCA)

Khosa and Others v. Minister of Social Development and Others; Mahlaule and Others v. Minister of Social Development and Others, 2004 (6) BCLR 569 (CC), 2004 (6) SA 505 (CC)

King and Others v. Attorneys Fidelity Fund Board of Control and Another, 2006 (4) BCLR 462 (SCA), 2006 (1) SA 474 (SCA)

Minister of Health and Others v. Treatment Action Campaign and Others (no. 2), 2002 (10) BCLR 1033 (CC), 2002 (5) SA 721 (CC)

Minister of Home Affairs v. Fourie; Lesbian and Gay Equality Project v. Minister of Home Affairs, 2006 (3) BCLR 355 (CC), 2006 (1) SA 524 (CC)

Minister of Home Affairs v. Fourie; Lesbian and Gay Equality Project v. Minister of Home Affairs (CC)

Minister of Home Affairs v. National Institute for Crime Prevention and the Re-integration of Offenders, 2004 (5) BCLR 445 (CC), 2005 (3) SA 280 (CC)

Minister of the Interior v. Harris, 1952 (4) SA 769 (AD)

New National Party of SA v. Government of the RSA, 1999 (5) BCLR 489 (CC), 1999 (3) SA 191 (CC)

Nxasana v. Minister of Justice, 1976 (3) SA 745 (D)

Permanent Secretary of the Department of Education, Eastern Cape v. Ed-U-College (PE) (Section 21) Inc, 2001 (2) BCLR 188 (CC), 2001 (2) SA 1 (CC)

Pharmaceutical Manufacturers of SA; in re Ex parte Application of the President of the RSA, 2000 (3) BCLR 241 (CC), 2000 (1) SA 674 (CC)

Phoebus Apollo Aviation CC v. Minister of Safety and Security, 2003 (1) BCLR 14 (CC), 2003 (2) SA 34 (CC)

President of the Republic of South Africa and Others v. South African Rugby Football Union and Others, 1999 (7) BCLR 725 (CC), 1999 (4) SA 147 (CC)

President of the RSA and Another v. Modderklip Boerdery (Pty) Ltd, 2005 (8) BCLR 786 (CC), 2005 (5) SA 3 (CC)

President of the RSA v. Hugo, 1997 (6) BCLR 708 (CC), 1997 (4) SA 1 (CC)

Richter v. Minister for Home Affairs and Others, [2009] ZACC 3, 2009 (3) SA 615 (CC)

S. v. Lawrence; S. v. Negal; S. v. Solberg, 1997 (10) BCLR 1348 (CC), 1997 (4) SA 1176 (SA)

S. v. Makwanyane, 1995 (6) BCLR 665 (CC), 1995 (3) SA 391 (CC)

Shabalala v. Attorney General of the Transvaal, 1995 (12) BCLR 1593 (CC), 1996 (1) SA 725 (CC)

Soobramoney v. Minister of Health, KwaZulu-Natal, 1997 (12) BCLR 1696 (CC), 1998 (1) SA 765 (CC)

Zantsi v. Council of State, Ciskei, 1995 (10) BCLR 1424 (CC), 1995 (4) SA 615 (CC)

The Netherlands

Gerechtshof te 's-Gravenhage, 27 September 1990, *AB* 1991, 85
Hoge Raad, 19 February 1858, *W.* 1936
Hoge Raad, 28 February 1868, *W.* 2995
Hoge Raad, 25 November 1912, *W.* 9419
Hoge Raad, 27 January 1961, *NJ* 1963, 248 (*Van den Bergh*)
Hoge Raad 6 March 1959, *NJ* 1962, 2 (*Nyugat*)
Hoge Raad, 5 May 1959, *NJ* 1959, 361
Hoge Raad, 3 March 1972, *NJ* 1972, 339
Hoge Raad, 12 April 1978, *NJ* 1979, 533
Hoge Raad, 28 November 1978, *NJ* 1979, 93
Hoge Raad, 18 January 1980, *NJ* 1980, 463
Hoge Raad, 2 February 1982, *NJ* 1982, 424
Hoge Raad, 4 June 1982, *NJ* 1983, 32
Hoge Raad, 30 May 1986, *NJ* 688
Hoge Raad, 15 July 1988, *RvdW* 1988, 133
Hoge Raad, 14 April 1989, *AB* 1989, 207 (*Harmonisation Act*)
Hoge Raad, 12 October 1984, *NJ* 1985, 230
Hoge Raad, 21 March 1986, *NJ* 1986, 585
Hoge Raad, 23 October 1988, *NJ* 1989, 740
Hoge Raad, 10 November 1989, *NJ* 1990, 628
Hoge Raad, 28 January 1994, *NJ* 1994, 687
Hoge Raad, 10 May 1996, *NJ* 1996, 578
Hoge Raad, 12 May 1999, *BNB* 1999, 271
Hoge Raad, 19 November 1999, *NJ* 2000, 160
Hoge Raad, 14 April 2000, *NJ* 2000, 713
Hoge Raad, 21 March 2003, *NJ* 2003, 691 (*Waterpakt*)
Hoge Raad, 3 September 2004, *RvdW* 2004, 102
Hoge Raad, 1 October 2004, *NJ* 2004
Hoge Raad, 18 February 2005, *NJ* 2005, 283 (*Aujeszky*)
Ondernemingskamer Hof Amsterdam, 18 February 1999
Ondernemingskamer Hof Amsterdam, 22 July 1999
Rechtbank's Gravenhage, 18 January 1995
Rechtbank's Gravenhage, 18 April 2007 (*Society of Local Councils*)

United Kingdom

A. and Others v. Secretary of State for the Home Department (no. 2), [2005] UKHL 71, [2006] 2 AC 221
A. and Others v. Secretary of State for the Home Department, [2004] UKHL 56, [2005] 2 WLR 87, [2005] 2 AC 68
A. v. B. plc and another, [2002] ECWA Civ 337, [2003] QB 195
Bellinger v. Bellinger, [2003] UKHL 21, [2003] 2 AC 467
Bernard and Another v. Enfield LBC, [2002] EWHC 2282, [2003] 2 HRLR 4
Bribery Commissioner v. Ranasinghe, [1965] AC 172, PC
Derbyshire County Council v. Times Newspapers, [1992] QB 770
Douglas v. Hello! Ltd, [2001] QB 967
Edinburgh and Dalkeith Railway Co v. Wauchope, (1842) 8 Cl and F 710
Entick v. Carrington, (1765) 19 Howell's State Trials 1029
Ghaidan v. Godin-Mendoza, [2004] UKHL 30, [2004] 2 AC 557
Gillick v. West Norfolk and Wisbech Area Health Authority, [1986] AC 112

Indyka v. Indyka [1976] 2 All ER 689 (HL)

Jackson v. Her Majesty's Attorney General, [2005] UKHL, 56

Madzimbamuto v. Lardner Burke, [1969] 1 AC 645, PC

Pickin v. British Railways Board, [1974] AC 765

R. (Burke) v. The General Medical Council, [2005] EWCA Civ 1003

R. (H.) v. Mental Health Review Tribunal, [2001] EWCA Civ 415

R. (on the application of Pro-Life Alliance) v. BBC, [2003] UKHL 23, [2003] 2 WLR 1403

R. (Q and Others) v. Secretary of State for the Home Department, [2003] EWCA Civ 364, [2003] 3 WLR 365

R. v. A., [2001] UKHL 25, [2001] 3 All ER 1

R. v. Director of Public Prosecutions, Ex parte Kebilene, [1999] UKHL 43, [200] AC 326, HL

R. v. Khan, [1996] 3 WLR 162

R. v. Lord Chancellor, Ex parte Witham, [1997] 2 All ER 779

R. v. Ministry of Defence, Ex parte Smith, [1996] QB 517, CA

R. v. Secretary of State for the Home Department, Ex parte Anderson and Taylor [2002] UKHL 46, [2002] 1 CrAppR 167

R. v. Secretary of State for the Home Department, Ex parte Brind, [1991] UKHL 26, [1991] 1 AC 696

R. v. Shayler, [2002] UKHL 11

Secretary of State for the Home Department v. MB (FC), [2007] UKHL 46

Taylor v. Lancashire County Council and Secretary of State for the Environment, Food and Rural Affairs, [2005] EWCA Civ 284, (2005) HRLR 17

Thoburn v. Sunderland City Council, [2002] EWHC, 195, [2003] QB 151

United States of America

Bush v. Gore, 531 US 98 (2000)

Marbury v. Madison, 1 Cranch 137 (1803)

Roe v. Wade, 410 US 113 (1973)

United States v. Lovett, 328 US 303 (1946)

West Virginia State Board of Education v. Barnette, 319 US 624 (1943)

Index